TRANS-AFFIRMATIVE PARENTING

Trans-Affirmative Parenting

Raising Kids Across the Gender Spectrum

Elizabeth Rahilly

NEW YORK UNIVERSITY PRESS
New York

NEW YORK UNIVERSITY PRESS
New York
www.nyupress.org

References to Internet websites (URLs) were accurate at the time of writing. Neither the author nor New York University Press is responsible for URLs that may have expired or changed since the manuscript was prepared.

Library of Congress Cataloging-in-Publication Data
Names: Rahilly, Elizabeth P., author.
Title: Trans-affirmative parenting : raising kids across the gender spectrum / Elizabeth Rahilly.
Description: New York : New York University Press, [2020] | Includes bibliographical references and index.
Identifiers: LCCN 2019041959 | ISBN 9781479820559 (cloth) | ISBN 9781479817153 (paperback) | ISBN 9781479833603 (ebook) | ISBN 9781479812806 (ebook)
Subjects: LCSH: Parents of transgender children. | Transgender children. | Gender-nonconforming children. | Gender identity in children.
Classification: LCC HQ759.9147 .R34 2020 | DDC 306.76/8083—dc23
LC record available at https://lccn.loc.gov/2019041959

New York University Press books are printed on acid-free paper, and their binding materials are chosen for strength and durability. We strive to use environmentally responsible suppliers and materials to the greatest extent possible in publishing our books.

Manufactured in the United States of America

10 9 8 7 6 5 4 3 2 1

Also available as an ebook

*To all the parents and children
blazing new trails.*

And to my mother Anne.

CONTENTS

Introduction

This is a historical moment, it really is, and I don't know how it's going to come out, but it is a very historical process. You know I'm seventy-two . . . I lived through the women's movement. . . . When we talked about gender in those days, we were talking about the differences between men and women . . . it was all social, I was around for that . . . and then you're here with this, which takes on another whole aspect of gender.
—Leigh, founder of support group for parents of gender-nonconforming children

It is a quiet, early morning in January 2015, and I pull into the empty parking lot of a high school, which is still on holiday break. A few minutes later, Jayne and Glenn arrive too, a white, upper-middle-class, heterosexual-identified married couple in their thirties.[1] After months of e-mailing back and forth, and with a babysitter on duty back at their house, they were finally able to break away from the daily demands of work and family and meet with me. This will be my last formal interview with parents, marking a capstone to a project that started six years prior, with many other families much farther away. Jayne and Glenn have three young children, two of whom will be the focus of our conversation today: Jared, the eldest, a nine-year-old transgender boy, and Amy, the middle child, a six-year-old transgender girl. After exiting our cars and exchanging a few nervous pleasantries, we make our way into the school's library. It is quiet, vacant, and calm, and a perfect place to hear about their parenting journey.

Over the course of our interview, Jayne and Glenn tell me about their vastly different experiences raising Jared and Amy. Jared is on the autism spectrum, and while he is the eldest, they did not recognize or identify him as gender-nonconforming until years after they began observing

Amy's nonconformity, as early as eighteen months of age. As they articulated throughout our conservation, hers seemed so much more noticeable. Indeed, Amy's name appears roughly twice as many times as Jared's in our transcript. Jared, assigned female at birth, was their "smart little scientist girl" and all about "dinosaurs and autopsy movies."[2] In contrast, Amy, assigned male at birth, was all about the feminine: "It was not just the pinks and purples, it was the sparkliest, the glitteriest, the most diamonds and fake jewels on clothes or bracelets [she could find]," Jayne said. As of age three, Amy was happily making use of the toys, dresses, nightgowns, and accessories that Jared had discarded, including a princess costume box their grandmother had given to Jared. Amy also started issuing memorable comments about her sense of self and her body: "I'm a girl," "I'm a girl with a penis," and "God made a mistake."

Like many of the parents I interviewed, Jayne and Glenn were at first tickled by the openness of interests their children were displaying. As Jayne said, "In the beginning, I think we were pretty open-minded about it, like, *This is great, both kids are exploring. . . . Amy's going to be nurturing and play with dolls. . . . Jared likes trucks and construction, how cool is that? We're so open-minded, good for us!*"[3] But over time, they both "started to worry" about Amy's behaviors, especially as extended family members seemed to disapprove. As Glenn said, "I started noticing . . . *my boy isn't boyish enough* . . . Jared was never on my radar like that." Per the reactions of Jayne's mother, for example, they eventually gave the princess box away, over which Amy cried and was extremely distraught. Like many of my interview moments with parents, this one was emotional, both for the storytellers and for me as the listener. I sympathized with the guilt that Jayne and Glenn felt about these kinds of restrictions, which seemed so foolish in hindsight.

During these early years, Jayne attempted strategic, and exhausting, gendered compromises with Amy—"gender hedging," as I have observed it among other parents.[4] This included, for example, finding clothes that could pass for "boys'" attire but had some feminine "flair" on them, such as "a black sweatshirt with a little pink on it." As Glenn said, Amy was living in a "hybrid" gendered mode. In the meantime, Jayne and Glenn were consumed with Jared's behavioral health issues: "We're like in major Asperger's diagnosis land with her,[5] so we weren't thinking about gender . . . we were just trying to figure out how the heck to get this kid to function without tantruming in a public school. It was all about OT [occupational therapy], PT [physical therapy], therapeutic horse-back riding, all those autistic accommodations and interventions." They chalked Jared's preference for not-so-feminine "comfortable" clothes up to his related sensory sensitivities, too, including plain leggings and tees. In fact, managing Jared's behavioral issues eventually motivated Jayne to let Amy wear dresses to school; it was one less hurdle in the morning routine.

At four years of age, Amy was experiencing bullying and questioning by her peers at school. While Jayne and Glenn did not think at all in terms of sexuality or sexual orientation, others in their midst did, including a close older family friend, a therapist, who thought Amy might be gay when she grows up. Eventually, their pediatrician referred them to a specialist at a gender clinic several hours away. At the start of the visit, the specialist asked Amy for her preferred pronouns ("she") and, over the course of several hours, gently attuned Jayne and Glenn to the prospects of transgender and gender-nonconforming children. Shortly after this visit, and with the doctor's guidance, Jayne and Glenn experimented with letting Amy dress and express as a girl "full-time" over the weekend. While Glenn was resistant to the idea that this was anything other than a "phase" that they could steer Amy out of, he decided to go "all in" to prove everyone wrong. But this "experiment" only clarified Amy's earnest self-expressions as a girl. As the doctor told them, "You're kind of along for the ride right now, and letting your child lead." In contrast to the "authoritarian style" of her upbringing, Jayne described this as a real "parenting paradigm shift": "I always thought that I could shape [them], whether it's their gender or their autism (*laughs*) . . . and here I have these two kids that exploded that notion for me." Over time, embracing Amy as a girl just felt right, much more than resisting or hedging around her self-expressions.

Jayne admitted that she felt relieved to start using female pronouns with a feminine-presenting child; the pronoun "he" was starting to feel increasingly awkward and tense out in public. Jayne also confessed that she preferred the term "gender-nonconforming" to "transgender" because it sounded less permanent or real to her—like there was room for change—and because it sounded more like a "medical diagnosis" that she could use with others. For Jayne, as for many parents, referring to a biomedical diagnosis or "condition" helped to assuage a sense of undue judgment from others, in terms of her potential influence on her child's gender. On these terms, Amy was born with this; her parents and her home life did not cause or "create" her gender nonconformity. While they came to reject the notion that gender nonconformity is any kind of "birth defect"—more a birth "difference"—Jayne and Glenn do recall using this as an explanatory framework with family and friends. Ultimately, they enrolled Amy in a new school so that she could start fresh as a girl, with only necessary staff knowing about her identity. As of our interview, Jayne and Glenn had fully embraced the term "transgender," too.

While Amy preferred to be private about being transgender, Jared felt much more open about his gender nonconformity among peers, which grew more pronounced following the medical management of his Asperger's. When we first started e-mailing, months prior to the interview, Jayne and Glenn had been identifying Jared as gender-fluid or gender-neutral—"somewhere in the middle"—and not as transgender. During this time, Jared was switching readily between male and female identifications and expressions, sometimes multiple times per day, with related wardrobe, name, and pronoun changes. As Jayne described it, Jared was "gender wild." Admittedly, Jared's fluidity felt taxing to both school staff and parents, who struggled to keep up, but Jayne and Glenn were grateful for the new school director, who was fully committed to gender inclusion. Jayne and Glenn joked, too, that Jared's fluidity didn't really faze them, since in earlier years Jared had insisted on being a "donkey" or "dog" as well. Jared's case was always more of a "mess" and "chaotic" for them, Jayne explained, and it was hard to tease apart what was a matter of his gender and what was a matter of his neurodivergence—perhaps they were related. She joked affectionately, "I've learned to accept the mess." Only recently had Jared started identifying full-time as a boy, and as of our interview, Jayne and Glenn were still trying to get used it. Their transition with Jared was not any easier for them because they already had one transgender child, they advised, but perhaps just faster.

Throughout our interview, I learned how intensely involved Jayne was, in particular, in raising their three children full-time and in managing all aspects of their childhoods, including the gender nonconformity and the autism. As Glenn said, "In all of this, Jayne has been the pioneer, the front-runner, and I sort of grudgingly follow, kicking and screaming behind her." Jayne also took on an advocacy role in the school community, hosting workshops and trainings for staff and students about both transgender identity and autism. In addition, Jayne and Glenn started a support group in the area for other families with trans kids—a more local alternative to another one several hours away. As part of this, they helped to create a masterful online database of trans-aware resources and professionals for local parents like them. In short, their active parental advocacy labor, with clinicians, schools, and other parents and families, was apparent throughout their experiences. Months after our interview, I happened to run into Jayne at a conference on trans identity and community. Excitedly, she told me that since launching their support group's web page, their e-mail had been "blowing up" with interested parents.

Trans-Affirmative Parenting

Jayne and Glenn's story echoes themes I encountered throughout my research on parents who raise gender-nonconforming and transgender children, themes that shape the substantive focus of this book: parents' shifting understandings of sex, gender, and sexuality, refracted through "male" and "female" expectations; parents' use of biomedical and disability frameworks; parents' fraught negotiations with binary and nonbinary gender possibilities; and parents' intensive advocacy labor on behalf of their children. Drawing on in-depth interviews with more than fifty parents in the United States, as well as two parents in Canada, this book captures a burgeoning social phenomenon of trans-affirmative parenting. My analysis contributes to, and in some ways complicates, a rapidly growing conversation in the social sciences and beyond.

The parents I interviewed certainly do not represent the first parents to confront childhood gender nonconformity,[6] but they did feel like no one in their lifetimes has done what they are doing: identifying and raising a young child as the "other sex," from early childhood on. The volume of work unfolding on families like this, just within the last few years, is a testament to how radically new, and radically expanding, the terrain is. Several sociologists have offered foundational insights into these new trans-affirmative families, whose works serve as key interlocutors in this

book. In *The Trans Generation*, Ann Travers examines how binary bureaucracies and spaces unduly dis-able and disadvantage transgender
kids, especially in school settings—from class rosters and other school
documents to bathrooms, locker rooms, and sports teams. Travers
calls for policies that make these settings more inclusive for trans students, especially those students at the most marginalized intersections
of race, class, ability, and nationality. In *Trans Kids*, Tey Meadow documents several fundamental aspects of the trans-affirmative parenting
phenomenon across key institutional arenas, including the medical
clinic, the state, and the law, as well as the major advocacy organizations and their differing rhetorical strategies. Meadow also examines
parents' strategies for understanding their transgender children, including refashioning traditional conceptual frameworks from biology,
psychiatry, and spirituality to embrace and normalize gender variance.
Ultimately, rather than signaling the "erosion" of gender, Meadow argues that gender is becoming that much more significant to social life,
both personally and institutionally—including diverse, nonnormative
forms of gender.[7]

This book explores a new constellation of insights and nuance in parents' experiences. At the heart of the stories I examine are parents' shifting understandings of their children's gender and how they come to help
their children make sense of their identities and their bodies. However,
throughout these processes, I show that parents' meaning-making and
decision-making often challenge LGBT advocacy discourses, as well as
queer political and theoretical tenets, in unexpected ways. I demonstrate
these dynamics in three main conceptual areas: first, gender and sexuality; second, the gender binary; and third, the body and biomedicine.

First, I examine parents' deliberations between *gender identity* and
sexual orientation as the relevant axis of understanding their children's
nonconformity. There are deep-rooted associations between childhood gender nonconformity and adult homosexuality, just as Jayne and
Glenn's family friend indicated above. As such, how these parents come
to embrace their children as "truly transgender," and not as "just gay," is a
key sociological question. Reigning LGBT rights discourses frame "gender" and "sexuality" as fundamentally separate parts of the self, and the
parents I interviewed certainly reiterated these distinctions. However,
parents' comments also signaled something more porous and open to

reinterpretation between these two realms, where some nonconformities once understood as "just gay" might well be relevant to "truly trans" understandings after all. This is the deliberative and *productive* labor, I argue, that is helping to bring broadening *(trans)gendered* possibilities into being—for their kids and for others.[8] This labor also troubles the idea of finite, distinct realms of self in the service of *child-rooted* developments and understandings throughout the life course.

The second area concerns parents' negotiations with *binary* and *nonbinary* possibilities for their children's gender. Despite mounting sociopolitical emphasis on nonbinary, gender-fluid, and/or genderqueer possibilities, gender-expansive child-rearing often looks very binary and gender-stereotypical, per the children's own assertions and expressions. In fact, for many of these parents, nonbinary possibilities proved as much a *crutch* in trying to avoid "truly trans" transitions for their children as any authentic identities of the kids', especially for the transgender girls. To be sure, LGBTQ platforms have never denied binary and gender-normative transitions; as I will discuss, some would argue they unduly exalt them. But nonbinary identities are gaining traction and visibility, especially among youth and many parents grew compelled to think "beyond the binary" in their journeys—often excitedly so—with which their children simply did not align.[9] I learned that parents reckoned with these prospects in markedly politicized and intellectual ways. They engaged in queer deconstructionist debates about the gender binary, and often felt the need to defend themselves against such deconstruction. At the same time, several stories in this area expose the difficulties in realizing nonbinary possibilities for the children who might desire them.

In the third area, I examine parents' *biomedical* understandings of transgender embodiment, where analogies to "birth defects" and/or "disability" frequently came up in interviews. As parents embrace their transgender children, they turn to the realm of biology and medicine as another key grid of understanding—and as a means of protecting their children's privacy. Parents' biomedical frameworks often answered to their children's own embodied sensibilities (e.g., *"Why did God make a mistake?"*), but these frameworks also reiterated and reaffirmed traditional cisgender body logics as much as they marked a refashioning of biological accounts.

Taking these three areas together—gender and sexuality, the gender binary, and the body—I show that parents' practices and perspectives are as much a product of intensive, expert-driven, *child-centered* parenting as they are an outgrowth of LGBTQ paradigms, and the two aren't always aligned. All told, these parents' trans-affirmative journeys reveal important new processes for understanding gender, sexuality, the binary, and related social change.

The journeys parents relayed to me were not simple, linear, or clear-cut. The majority of children represented in this book were identified as transgender (thirty-four of forty-three children). However, some children developed in more cisgender directions following an original round of interviews, which I explore in several follow-up vignettes. These children were never formally identified or transitioned as transgender by their parents. Moreover, a few children were identified by parents as gender-nonconforming, including as "agender" or "two-spirit," but *not* necessarily as "transgender"—just as Jared was for several months. All of these dynamics are part of the story, and the change, this book tells: parents' moving and sometimes murky distinctions along an imagined "spectrum" of possibilities—a spectrum with *(trans)gender, (homo)sexual, binary,* and *nonbinary* connotations.[10] Ultimately, I aim to highlight the profoundly liberating, as well as the potentially limiting, dimensions of this new brand of trans-affirmative parenting, for this generation and beyond.

Terminology

In this book, "gender-nonconforming" serves as an umbrella term for all the children represented in the study, whose expressions and self-identifications departed significantly from the expectations of their assigned birth sex.[11] "Transgender," or "trans," in contrast, refers more specifically to a child who has a firmly "cross-gender" or binary identity and whose parents have affirmed them as such (i.e., children assigned male at birth who identify and live as girls, and children assigned female at birth who identify and live as boys). This is how I encountered this term being used among the parents and professionals I interviewed, and it reflected popular usages of the term at the time as well.[12] Notably, this usage contrasts with the term's queer-based formulations in the 1980s and 1990s—that is, as a broad catchall category for gender nonconformity, with purposefully less specific or binary connotations, especially relative to the gender-normative standards of the medico-psychiatric establishment and for those who did not pursue medical interventions.[13] More recently, however, the increasing visibility and mobilization around "nonbinary" identity may be shifting "transgender" back toward these more fluid and/or queer connotations.

In interviews, parents' use of the term "transgender" was similar to "transsexual" understandings and connotations, though many now reject that term, including these parents, especially when referring to their children. I note this because the children want to be recognized firmly as the "other" sex category, male/boy or female/girl, in ways that are decidedly more binary than the broader "gender-nonconforming" and that often entailed some gesture to body modification in the future.[14] At the time of the interviews, the majority of the children had not yet pursued any medical or hormonal interventions, and would not yet, per their stage of biological maturity.[15] Moreover, according to parents' accounts, the children held more nuanced relationships to their bodies than "wrong body" or "body dysphoria" narratives would suggest (for several at the time, the body aspect was a nonissue), which I address in chapter 4. But per parents' reports, many did indicate to them an interest in having different anatomy down the line (e.g., "I don't want to grow boobs when I grow up"). These kinds of embodied possibilities and interests from children were a critical, although not necessary, distinguishing factor for parents from the broader "gender-nonconforming" label.

Of course, these are by no means firm definitions or distinctions. "Transgender" does not have to mean a binary identity *or* body modification, and "gender-nonconforming" does not have to preclude either. Someone can pursue a range of anatomical changes and transitions without identifying as one particular category or identity.[16] Moreover, the operating terminology I use in this book does not necessarily reflect the preferred parlance of today, which is constantly in flux and varies from person to person, generation to generation. More recently, "gender creative," "gender expansive," and "gender independent" have surfaced as preferred terms, with and without hyphenation. However, to reflect the parents and professionals I spoke with, I use "transgender" to refer specifically to children who were assigned one sex at birth and identify as the "opposite" category. On a broader basis, I use "gender identity" to refer to a child's self-expression as a "boy," "girl," or something less binary altogether (e.g., "two-spirit").

"Gender-nonconforming" had more varying valences and connotations than "transgender," which I examine in chapters 2 and 3. Sometimes it carried *(homo)sexual* and "gay" implications (chapter 2), other times it was more explicitly related to notions of *gender*, but in *nonbinary* capacities (chapter 3). The latter include a range of possibilities that cannot be characterized simply as "boy" or "girl," including, for example, "two-spirit," "agender," or "gender-fluid." While parents rarely explicitly used the term "nonbinary" at the time of the interviews, these were the instances of gender nonconformity where parents confronted and considered nonbinary possibilities for their children. "Gender-nonconforming" also pertains to several cases in which the children had developed in more cisgender directions as of follow-up interviews, but not necessarily as "gender-normative." For example, a child here may identify with their assigned birth sex (male), use male pronouns, and present as a normative boy most of the time, but may occasionally play dress-up at home or don more feminine clothing items (e.g., bright pink jeans). They may also dislike stereotypically masculine interests (sports) and prefer conventionally feminine activities instead (shopping and fashion, dance, theater, etc.). I discuss these follow-up cases in chapter 3 as well. Despite this range of gendered possibilities, however, the majority of children were binary- and transgender-identified at the time of the interviews (more than 80 percent).

In all of these instances, I do not mean to assert objective definitions for these labels and the children to whom they refer. Nor can I tap into the children's "real" gendered interiorities myself, unfettered and unfiltered—at every occasion, I am relying on *parents'* reports of their children. This was a reigning methodological tension of the study, which some might consider "inherently problematic."[17] Indeed, the exclusion of children's voices throughout academic literature, including in the realm of childhood studies, is a problem, which several scholars have sought to address. Travers's book *The Trans Generation*, for example, and sociologist Mary Robertson's book *Growing Up Queer* are works that prioritize kids' vantage points. To be sure, children's accounts are a critical part of this research terrain.

But this "limitation," I would argue—the *parents'* perspectives, practices, and decisions—is intimately related to the range of identities that are made possible for these children in the first place and thus is inherent to the sociology of the phenomenon. In addition, I felt that my status as a cisgender, gender-normative researcher was overly risky vis-à-vis young gender-nonconforming children. I did not want to make them feel "abnormal," interrogated, and scrutinized.[18] The majority of parents echoed this stance preemptively, too, and preferred that their children were absent for the interview (though several parents, I understand, advised their children of my project and asked for their permission to proceed). My ethical concerns in this regard trumped any interests in seeking interviews with the kids, and I never requested permission from the Institutional Review Board (IRB) to include the children in my study.[19]

The last term I introduce, "social transition," further reflects this study's emphasis on the parents, not the children. In this book, "transition" or "social transition" refers to parents fully affirming their children's (trans)gender identity, including permitting related name, clothing, pronoun, and hairstyle preferences of the child, as well as enrolling them in school and other activities as such. Parents often go to friends, extended family, and other adults in the child's life to request recognition of this new identification. In this way, "transition" really emphasizes the *parents'* thoughts and actions, including how they come to recognize their child, and not any real gendered transformations on the part of the children (especially not in any physical or embodied aspects).

The Parents

The overall sample in this book represents an amalgam of different groups of parents, recruitment venues, and snapshots in time between 2009 and 2015, both within these families' lives and within the broader historical context of the last ten to twenty years. Broadly, there were two rounds of recruitment and interviewing for the project, resulting in two main parental groups or "cohorts." First, I interviewed an original group of parents in 2009–11, representing thirteen childhood cases. I conducted follow-up interviews with these parents several years later (2012–13), which I refer to as the "follow-up" group throughout this book. Then, I interviewed a much larger group of parents during 2013–15, which entailed thirty new childhood cases. All told, the stories showcased in this book concern the forty-three cases from the cumulative sample (2012–15), inclusive of fifty-five parents (plus one eighteen-year-old sibling). Children ranged in age from five to eighteen years at the time of the interviews; the average age of the child was eight.

I recruited these parents, in part, from two annual conferences held by a major advocacy organization, which were designed to educate, support, and affirm parents and gender-nonconforming children. I also reached parents via online parent blogs and, indirectly, via online listservs and local parent support groups of parents I already knew. As a nonparent, I did not have direct access to support groups or online forums—a boundary I strictly observed—and parents posted blurbs on my behalf instead. Given my recruitment avenues, this book is limited to a very specific, "purposive" subpopulation of parents, who were immersed in a particularly affirmative set of discourses, practices, and advocacy communities.[20] As such, these families do not represent all parents who have gender-nonconforming children, who exhibit variable degrees of support and affirmation. There are other kids, for example, outside this book, who must leave their families to live as their most authentic selves, a very different scenario from the stories showcased here.[21]

Geographically, more than half of the families (twenty-three) resided in California, while the rest came from various locations throughout the United States and Canada. Regionality is an important factor in LGBTQ studies.[22] Some of the parents felt they lived in more "conservative" parts of the United States, but many of the families came from areas that could be characterized as "liberal," especially those from California, which has been a forerunner in LGBTQ-inclusive legislation. This also certainly impacted the kinds of stories I collected and the degree of trans-affirmative parenting represented in the book.

Racially, the majority of parents were white-identified (just over 80 percent of participants). Nine of the parents were persons of color: four were biracial (including one white/African American, two white/Latinx, and one white/Middle Eastern), and five parents were Latinx.[23] However, this does not reflect the ethnoracial profiles of the children: several white parents, for example, adopted children of color (American Indian, Asian American, and Latinx), and several of the children are biracial, but only the white parent participated in interviews. The majority of households (thirty-six) were classified as middle-class to upper-middle-class. More specific demographic details are provided in appendix I.

Altogether, considering income, occupation, and education, the sample is predominantly white and middle-class to upper-middle-class. The focus of my analysis is parents' shifting understandings of gender, sexuality, the binary, and the body. Though I draw on critical race perspectives in the context of medical care in chapter 4, more extensive racial analyses and comparisons of the interview data would require a more diverse research sample. Nevertheless, parents' raced and classed positions certainly influenced the ways they were able to intensively advocate for their kids, which I discuss later.

Storytelling against Time

Researching these families posed a host of methodological, political, and ethical considerations, on which I elaborate in appendix II and which are key to understanding the sample and the study. First, the two groups of parents represent two different cohorts and samples, both temporally and in terms of the networks from which they were recruited. This presented both limitations and insights. While there were only two to four years between the two rounds of interviewing (2009–11, 2012–15), the advocacy infrastructure for transgender children has evolved rapidly over the years, meaning that interviewing people just a few years apart can mean encountering them in radically different sociohistorical contexts. The parents who started researching childhood gender nonconformity on behalf of their kids prior to 2009—which my first cohort and interviews reflect—were operating within a moment that seemed far less aware of transgender children than is the case now. This is very different from parents in the second group, who waded into the issue after 2009. Indeed, the major advocacy organizations I connected with for the project only launched in or around 2007, and within a few short years of that, their following burgeoned by the hundreds, either at the annual conferences or on the listservs. Moreover, the first major televised special, which arguably put transgender children "on the map," occurred in 2007 on *20/20* with Jazz Jennings and her family. Since that time, landmark cases, policies, and celebrities have dotted an increasingly trans-aware sociopolitical landscape across the United States and Canada.

Tellingly, one of the first parents I interviewed in 2009, Theresa, said that she could not find a single practitioner or support group in her area who was familiar with childhood gender nonconformity when she first reached out. In fact, her therapist advised her to start one up herself. Her city, a large metropolis, is now home to a thriving support group network and hosts one of the most robust clinics for trans youth in the United States, inaugurated in 2009. Like several parents in my sample, Theresa had to do a lot of start-up educational work, both for herself and for others—doctors, therapists, schools, and hospitals—that many parents now find alive and kicking in their hometowns. Additionally, one of the advocates I interviewed said that since 2013, their listserv's growth rate actually "leveled off," not because fewer parents are raising transgender kids, in her view, but because of the "information overload" everywhere else: "Three, four, five years ago, we were basically the only game in town; now there's a lot of local resources that schools will [use] to do a training . . . and there's also more doctors [and] more therapists around the country who are working with the kids." In short, the second group of parents, whom I started interviewing in 2013, were immersed in a very different sociohistorical context, wherein the prospect of a transgender child was far more crystallized in both popular and institutional consciousness. As one parent wrote to me in an e-mail, regarding the anonymity of my research subjects, "Sometimes I feel like everyone can find me . . . and sometimes I think our numbers are growing so large that I will just be another parent."

Related to these factors, most parents from the second cohort came from an online listserv more heavily associated with specifically transgender-identified children. While the listserv's organization would never exclude parents of children who are not necessarily transgender— and they certainly had such subscribers—by and large, the forum was populated by parents of transgender, socially transitioning or transitioned children. As one of the educators told me when accounting for the organization's constituency, "transgender" is explicitly in its title. This contrasts with the first group of parents I recruited, who were drawn not from this forum but via a different organization's annual conference, which many perceived as catering to issues of gender and gender nonconformity more broadly.[24] In addition, the author of the parenting blog I used was actually a parent not of a transgender child but of a gender-nonconforming boy.

However, it would be remiss to distinguish these venues too firmly, as these characterizations did not always hold up. In fact, both times I attended the conference, parents of transgender children seemed to be in the majority and were a visible presence. (I also encountered several interviewees who gave diametrically opposing impressions of these organizations.) And most parents from the original group came to identify their children as transgender, just a bit later in time, especially for children assigned male. Nevertheless, these different forums and networks, and the time frames during which I recruited them, yielded different groups of families, some more trans-specific than others. The first cohort represented something more broadly gender-nonconforming than the second, which I explore in chapter 3.

Apart from these historical "cohort" dynamics, my analysis is complicated by the "history" of any one family and any one child's life course developments, which is necessarily a terrain of movement, growth, and change. The interviews this book relies on present diverse but singular snapshots in time within the daily unfolding of family life, sometimes captured once, sometimes captured twice. It is thus hard to burrow into data that are specific to one particular moment but that stand within a much larger, moving trajectory, which my reporting could never keep up with in real time. This dynamic is most visible in the follow-up cases from the first cohort, wherein the parents were articulating different markers, pronouns, identifiers, and overall perspectives between interviews, just a few years apart. Capturing just such changes is further complicated by wanting to honor the children's affirmed gender identities. In several places in this book, I quote parents who were using the wrong pronouns and identifiers at the time relative to a child's later affirmed identity. Outside of direct analysis of the parents, I would never want to risk misgendering a child, but I decided to preserve the quotes verbatim in the service of capturing the *parents'* journeys.

Emblematic of these dynamics, I often encountered among parents the notion that this is "*their* transition," not their child's, that "everyone's on their own journey" and takes their own time. As such, while a child's gender identity may or may not be in flux—and may be known and expressed from the beginning—the notion that the *parents* were part of an evolving, fluid process was integral to the analysis. Overall, while this background of constant change and dynamism can be challenging for in-depth qualitative research, it is also deeply connected to the sociology of the study: the practices, discourses, and processes through which social change, and gender change, come to pass, both within one family and in the culture at large.

The Outsider With(out)

In her essay "Learning from the Outsider Within," sociologist and feminist theorist Patricia Hill Collins discusses the unique intellectual insights of women of color scholars. As Collins explains, women of color carry specific cultural knowledge as marginalized "outsiders" within the white, male-dominated spaces of academia, a standpoint that has advanced Black feminist thought, among other spheres of knowledge. My own research experiences, however, could best be characterized as the "outsider without": I am not transgender, and I present gender-normatively for my sex category most of the time. Equally important, I am not a parent, let alone a parent of a transgender child. My outsider status was further compounded by my role as a sociologist, including the theoretical paradigms I use in that capacity—such as the "social construction" of sex, gender, and sexuality. This theoretical perspective emphasizes the *cultural* and *historical* influences on human social experience and identity, not innate biology or genetic dispositions.[25] A sociologist is not the typical role, or position, from which most parents seek support and guidance; parents sooner look to mental health specialists, doctors, and professional LGBT educators and advocates outside the academe.

Parents' fundamental interests in my project were to help spread greater understanding about transgender children and to make the world a safer place for them to live. On that point, we were perennially aligned. However, social-scientific paradigms have had a fraught relationship with LGBT identities and activism. While not necessarily mutually exclusive, many feel that "social-constructionist" perspectives deny essentialist, "born-this-way" accounts for identity, which have been the rallying cry of the modern-day LGBT rights movement. Some scholars argue that social constructionism falsely insinuates something "caused" or "created" personal identities, while biological accounts about an innate, unabiding sense of self ring more true.[26] I do not believe these paradigms are contradictory, but my sociological interests in the trans-affirmative parenting phenomenon—including what new understandings about sex, gender, and sexuality might emerge—did not always feel immediately in sync with my participants. This was intimately related to my positionality in the project and the "outsider" status I often felt viscerally in the field, which I address further in appendix II.

There is, however, one "insider" dimension I believe I shared with my actual interviewees: like the majority of them, I am cisgender, gender-normative, and from a white, middle-class, college-educated background. While never discussed outright, our common sociodemographic signifiers likely aided in building rapport, even when I had no personal claims to parenting or to trans experience. I often felt that being cisgender and gender-normative gave me an "in" with my cisgender, gender-normative subjects, who were newly encountering and processing these issues on behalf of their children, at times anxiously so, about which they dialogued with me in interviews.

Historical and Cultural Contexts

In *The History of Sexuality*, social theorist Michel Foucault famously argued that the "homosexual" was "invented" by the psychiatric sciences in the nineteenth and twentieth centuries. While homosexual acts and desires have long existed, Foucault explained, the notion of a distinct type of same-sex-oriented *person* did not. Instead, this was a product of modern social-scientific discourses, knowledge, and systems of classification.[27] In Foucauldian terms, my research project shadowed the emergence of, and "invention" of, the "transgender child," a category largely inconceivable to parents prior to the twenty-first century.[28] Like all parents, the parents I studied are situated in a very specific historical moment, one in which parent support groups and social networks for transgender children have grown exponentially across the United States and Canada, new medical options for childhood transitions have emerged, new possibilities for self-identity exist, and new terminology is ever evolving. The whole world of gender and sexuality, it seems, is being challenged afresh—and gender-nonconforming youth are at the center of these shifts.[29]

But beyond the sociocultural advent of the transgender child are broader historical developments that are key to understanding the contemporary families in this book. These developments include (1) intensive, child-centered parenting, including the raced and classed aspects of this; (2) second-wave feminism, which left an imprint on contemporary parents in its wake; (3) the history of psychiatric research on gender-nonconforming children; and (4) the LGBTQ rights movement. Collectively, these four broad areas offer key sociohistorical context for my research participants and shed light on the culturally specific modes of parenting I observed.

Parenting, Race, and Class

As a researcher of gender and sexuality, I did not set out to study parenting and childhood socialization. However, it became hard to ignore the parent-child relationship, on its own terms, when listening to parents' stories. The experiences I collected transpired against a larger cultural backdrop in the twenty-first century of a particularly intensive, child-centered approach to parenting, one that is marked by unprecedented amounts of time, energy, and money.[30] Indeed, as I will argue, parents' trans-affirmative efforts were fueled as much by this modern brand of parenting, if not more, as by broadening LGBTQ awareness. These parenting dynamics intersect with socioeconomic factors as well. While my analysis in the chapters ahead does not foreground race or class—rather, I focus on parents' shifting understandings of gender, sexuality, and the binary—parents' sociodemographic positions certainly aided the kind of resource-rich, expert-guided, child-centered mode of parenting they practiced, which I discuss here.

As historians have shown, our very conceptions of "childhood," and what "the child" is, are culturally and historically contingent, and change across time and place.[31] For example, prior to the Industrial Revolution in the United States, many children worked as valuable laborers and producers in their own right, first of the farmland and the household, and later of the industrializing economy. This changed over the course of the nineteenth and twentieth centuries with the help of child labor laws and expanding school systems. The rise of the gendered division of household labor contributed as well, especially among the white middle class. New cultural ideologies, in tandem, marked the child as "precious," as someone to be nurtured and protected at home under their mother's care while fathers earned money outside the home.[32] Of course, these cultural ideals relied on real structural inequalities, in which the low-wage labor of working-class families, immigrant families, and/or families and children of color permitted such idealized arrangements among middle-class nuclear households.[33] But this history demonstrates that "childhood" and "the child" are intimately tied to cultural, historical, and economic contexts.

Today, children are considered an all-important labor unto themselves, an individualized project to be "sculpted, stimulated, instructed, and groomed" by their parents.[34] Parents do this through a smorgasbord of resource- and time-intensive activities, from soccer practice and dance rehearsal to mommy dates and daddy dates to college prep and private tutoring, all coupled with the help of biomedicine, psychology, and psychiatry. As journalist Jennifer Senior put it, "Kids . . . went from being our staffs to our bosses."[35] This intensive mode of child-rearing is not only reinforced by consumer capitalism, with a marketplace of goods, services, and experts that drive it, but is morally imposed and surveilled by a collective social other, in which "good" and "bad," "right" and "wrong" parenting is constantly assessed and scrutinized—in popular discourse and media, across parenting blogs and advice pages, and within parenting groups.[36] Amid this wider culture of intensive, moralized child-rearing—and in the wake of both a feminist parenting legacy and the LGBTQ rights movement, as I chart later in the chapter—the gender-nonconforming child presents a particularly apt project for specialized attention, scrutiny, and care. Indeed, as I learned, the care of a gender-nonconforming child can entail a host of services and expenses, including mental health therapists, medical doctors, and related fees; annual conferences and summer camps; consultations with various advocacy organizations, as well as the time and the means to look into all these options in the first place.

Because child-rearing labor so often falls to women, sociologist Sharon Hays has labeled this modern mode of parenting "intensive mothering," a highly gendered phenomenon: "The contemporary model of socially appropriate mothering . . . [is] a gendered model that advises mothers to expend a tremendous amount of time, energy, and money in raising their children."[37] Hays describes this kind of mothering as child-centered, expert-guided, emotionally absorbing, labor-intensive, and financially expensive.[38] Sociologist Annette Lareau argues that such intensive parenting is a *classed* phenomenon as well. Compared with low-income families, with less capital at their disposal, Lareau found that middle-class parents actively, intensively managed their children's growth. They invested in expensive extracurricular activities and resources for their children, and they engaged earnestly with their children's thoughts and comments during mundane conversations. As Lareau said, "Children of middle-class parents have a sense that they are special, that their opinions matter, and that adults should, as a matter of routine, adjust situations to meet children's wishes."[39]

Lareau argues that this parenting mode, or "concerted cultivation," as she coined it, ultimately advantages middle-class children in other institutions—like schools—which privilege this demographic's particular brand of self-advocacy and interacting. Similar kinds of intensive parenting were observed more recently by sociologist Margaret Hagerman, but in ways that are racialized, not just classed. In *White Kids*, the upper-middle-class white parents Hagerman studied took pains to pick the "right" kinds of neighborhoods, schools, and daily activities that would most benefit their children, seizing on the social capital they had to do so.[40] Hagerman argues that these parental decisions ultimately perpetuate racist hierarchies and advantages, which privilege their white children, even if unintentionally.

Research suggests, however, that this ethos of intensive child-rearing cuts across social classes, with all parents today spending more time and energy on and with their kids than earlier generations, even as the majority still don't think they spend enough time with them.[41] Moreover, many scholars resist the idea that less economically advantaged parents are somehow less child-centered, or structured, in their approach—let alone in ways that would implicate trans-affirmative parenting. As students of the CUNY Graduate School assert, in an article titled "Bodies and Violence," focusing on "upper-class families [obscures] the history, traditions and ongoing existence of gender variance among working-class people and people of color."[42]

Nevertheless, while most parents today are compelled to expend this kind of time and energy on their children, not all of them have the literal capital to invest in their children in these ways, or the cultural capital to move institutional others accordingly, as Hagerman, Lareau, and others have shown. In addition, decades of Black feminist theorizing have emphasized the inextricable relationships among race, class, and other dimensions of social identity.[43] One's relative position within broader social hierarchies—or, as Patricia Hill Collins calls it, the "matrix of domination"—will impact one's experiences with other dimensions of difference and marginalization, including LGBTQ identity.[44] Even if two children are both transgender, their divergent socioeconomic backgrounds may well impact how they experience their gender in other social contexts, as well as the kinds of resources and support their parents are able to secure.[45] In "Retelling Racialized Violence," for example, legal scholar Sarah Lamble documents how Pauline Mitchell, a low-income Navajo woman, was routinely dismissed by school authorities when defending her two-spirit child's gender-nonconforming expressions.[46]

In short, all kinds of parents practice intensive parenting and trans-affirmative parenting, but the relative socioeconomic privilege among many of my participants certainly assisted the ways in which they could engage on behalf of their kids. These parents met with school authorities to lay out specific accommodations, rewrite district policy, push for new teacher trainings, or even pursue litigation. They also urged doctors to take on trans-affirmative care for their children when doctors were otherwise resistant or unfamiliar. They intensively advocated for their children's gender nonconformity, all in ways that could be more risky, or simply financially out of reach, for low-income parents, parents of color, and/or undocumented or immigrant families. Notwithstanding the critical caveats and perspectives noted here, I draw on "concerted cultivation" and "intensive parenting" as key conceptual models for understanding contemporary parenting. These models greatly resonated with my observations among the parents I studied, including how they intently observed their children's self-expressions and sought out the resources, specialists, and support networks that would best assist.

Beyond discussions of intensive parenting, most scholars of childhood development give parents a primary role in children's socialization.[47] Indeed, the import of *parents'* roles in their children's development is the focus of this book: the parents are the ones buying clothing, permitting toys, scheduling haircuts, conducting online searches, registering for conferences, meeting with school administrators, consulting health practitioners, writing letters to other parents, deciding to switch pronouns, and ultimately embracing transgender labels and understandings of their children. That said, both psychologists and sociologists have increasingly emphasized the work of *children* themselves, rejecting traditional models that frame children as passive learners of adult society and understanding them instead as active agents in the socialization process.[48] As sociologist Barrie Thorne wrote, children are "complex actors, strategists, performers, users of language, creators of culture,"[49] whose "interactions are not preparation for life, they are life itself."[50] Similarly, sociologist Spencer Cahill said, "Children are not passively molded by the environment but interpretively organize and respond to the environment along lines laid down by their native language."[51]

In this vein, childhood development scholars have dubbed parent-child socialization in more dynamic terms, such as "reciprocal influence," "bidirectional," and "interdependent." Childhood sociologist William Corsaro, for example, proposes an "interpretive reproduction" framework, which moves beyond simple, linear theories of children's socialization and instead envisions a multivalent dynamic between parents, children, and their changing social environments. According to Corsaro: "Children are not simply internalizing society and culture but are actively contributing to cultural production and change."[52] In this way, childhood socialization is not a mere means to an end, but legitimate sociological terrain on its own terms.

While this book centers on *parents'* developing perceptions and practices, the foregoing perspectives on the agentic child, who acts within and against a wider sociocultural milieu, strongly resonate with the trans-affirmative phenomenon I encountered in the field. Parents acted as much *in response to* their children's expressions and articulations as in accordance with their own assumptions, norms, and values—including the LGBTQ-inclusive ones they were learning along the way. Indeed, "follow the child's lead" resounded as the modus operandi within the parental forums I observed. At almost every possible juncture, it was their child's articulations of who they were, what they preferred, how they would come to be identified, who would know about it, and what medical treatments they wanted, if any, that governed parents' decisions. One could say it was the parents who were being socialized to their children's gender as much as the other way around. Moreover, parents felt bound to focus on the "present," and their children's current assertions, regardless of what their child's development may bring in the future. As one mother said via e-mail, "You raise the child standing before you." All told, *child-directed, child-centered* parenting, spurred by active, agentic children, is a pertinent theoretical framework for the trans-affirmative practices I recorded and the social mechanisms that enabled them.

Feminist Precursors

Intensive, child-centered parenting is not the only historical development in child-rearing that has impacted the families I studied. Attentive to the complexities of gendered inequalities, many second-wave feminist scholars and activists called for child-rearing practices that resisted the stereotyping of male and female children, often referred to as "gender-neutral" or "feminist" parenting.[53] Growing through the 1970s and 1980s, this brand of parenting included modeling egalitarian divisions of household labor, as well as permitting gender-inclusive toys, interests, and activities for young children. Feminist psychologist Sandra Bem, for example, one of the pioneers of such "gender-aschematic" parenting, as she termed it, often modified the characters in her children's storybooks to undo gendered patterns (e.g., drawing breasts and long hair on a truck driver or a beard on an elementary schoolteacher).[54] She also let her son wear barrettes and other stereotypically feminine items to school.[55]

However, Bem advised that she always tried to reduce the difference between boys and girls to anatomy when speaking to her children, ultimately reiterating a *cisgender* relationship between sex and gender: "A boy, we said again and again, is someone with a penis and testicles; a girl is someone with a vagina, a clitoris, and a uterus."[56] On these terms, then, gender-neutral parenting failed to rupture the quintessential link between sex and gender, even as parents tried to minimize the relevance of that link, effectively erasing childhood transgender possibilities. In fact, excerpts from other practitioners of this genre at the time seem stunningly transphobic and homophobic.[57] In short, in its original formulations, gender-neutral parenting encouraged boys and girls to pursue whatever interests they wanted, regardless of stereotypes—but they were ever and always cisgender boys and girls, respectively, and ideally heterosexual.

More recent feminist sociologists have exposed the "stalled revolution" of these parenting ideals, which they largely attribute to lingering, negative associations between childhood gender nonconformity and adult homosexuality. Sociologist Karin Martin, for example, reviewed a variety of parenting guides published through the end of the twentieth century and found that gender-neutral parenting was still not wholeheartedly endorsed due to fears over encouraging homosexuality.[58] Martin concluded that "the gendered socialization of children seems only to have mildly waned since the height of the second wave. . . . There may well be rich research territory in the area of gender socialization that has been abandoned by many feminist researchers."[59] Similarly, sociologist Emily Kane found that even the most gender-progressive parents will succumb to the "gender trap," or social expectations that limit parents' best intentions against traditional gender norms.[60] This was especially true in the cases of male children and "icons of femininity," such as frilly skirts and dresses and Barbie dolls—parents drew the line at these.[61] Indeed, few, if any, of the parents in Kane's research seemed cognizant of the prospect of a transgender child. As one particularly gender-inclusive mother said, "'Eli, you'll never be a girl, but if you want that Barbie pool you can have it.'"[62] Evidently, as conventionally conceived and practiced, gender-neutral parenting has remained ignorant of, or perhaps resistant to, transgender possibilities. For all its limitations, however, this legacy has enabled a baseline level of openness to children's gender-atypical preferences among contemporary parents, which I discuss in chapter 1.

The Transgender Child

Children's normative gender identity development has consumed decades of research and theorizing in the fields of psychology and social psychology.[63] Sociologists, too, have studied the ways in which young children actively incorporate, and sometimes challenge, normative gender expectations.[64] The governing questions of much of this research are, what are the processes through which children become normatively differentiated boys and girls, in accordance with the expectations of their assigned birth sex, and how are aberrations from those norms addressed or regulated among otherwise culturally compliant children? In these ways, perhaps refreshingly so, much of the traditional research on children's gender development aimed to explain gender-*conforming* outcomes, not the nonnormative ones.

Gender-nonconforming children, however, have consumed a different vein of psychological research, namely that of "gender identity disorders" in the *Diagnostic and Statistical Manual of Mental Disorders* (*DSM*).[65] As sociologist Karl Bryant has documented, longitudinal studies of gender-nonconforming children, or of "feminine boys," as they were often called at the time, took hold in the 1960s, following the development of adult transsexual medicine in the United States.[66] Though these children were originally surveilled for insights into the potential origins of adult transsexuality, the resulting data suggested a strong statistical correlation between childhood gender nonconformity and adult *homosexuality*. That is, most of these children allegedly did *not* grow up to identify as transgender, but as gay.[67]

Of course, these outcomes ("gay" and "trans") are not necessarily mutually exclusive or divergent—one can go on to identify as *both* gay and trans, for example—but they have figured as such in parents' and practitioners' deliberations, which I examine more extensively in chapter 2. These statistical outcomes raised red flags about the "gender identity disorder in childhood" diagnosis that came out of this body of research, which was hotly contested by clinicians, academics, and gay rights activists. Many scholars argued, for example, that the diagnosis served as a "backdoor" preventative tool against homosexuality,[68] especially since some of the early studies on children entailed reparative interventions.[69] The childhood diagnosis was also formalized around the same time that adult homosexuality was *removed* from the *DSM* because it was no longer considered a disorder. In the eyes of the critics, if childhood gender conformity is correlated with adult homosexuality, what is the motivation behind its diagnostic category? Why is it up for scrutiny? Notwithstanding, the statistical relationship between childhood gender nonconformity and adult homosexuality continued through the latter half of the twentieth century, albeit with decreasing majorities.[70] This includes studies on children assigned female as well, in both the United States and Europe.[71]

Eventually, parents and practitioners moved to depathologize childhood gender nonconformity, often explicitly in terms of pro-gay advocacy. Leigh, one of the founders of a major support group for families of gender-nonconforming children in the 1990s, was a key informant for my project. She explained to me that her group's purpose was to normalize gender nonconformity, and ultimately "gay" outcomes, for parents, especially for children assigned male, but that the group was largely oblivious to transgender possibilities. For Leigh, as for many parents and therapists at the time, childhood gender nonconformity was almost always a matter of "proto-homosexuality" or not, dialectics I review in chapter 2.

Decades since, a particularly trans-aware, trans-affirmative paradigm has gained traction among mental health professionals.[72] Under this approach, parents are encouraged to embrace their children's gender-nonconforming expressions as natural and healthy, not to repress or pathologize them.[73] As part of this, practitioners promote serious consideration for early childhood social transitions, if and when a child expresses a desire for this. They are also skeptical of the "just gay" narrative from prior longitudinal studies, as the statistics from other studies have increasingly swayed toward more transgender outcomes.[74] In addition, new research in cognitive psychology has used traditional cognitive assessments on trans-identified children, and the results indicate that their responses mirror their cisgender counterparts.[75] This effectively "proves" to psychologists that these children are not "confused" or "faking" their gender identities, that their identities are no less cognitively rooted than other children's, and that they are no more anxious or depressed when living as affirmed, transitioned children. These research efforts continue, and represent a widening trend across the psych sciences to be more inclusive of transgender and gender-nonconforming children.

Related to these developments, the latest edition of the *DSM* has changed the terminology from "gender identity disorder" (GID) to "gender dysphoria" (GD), in part to remove the stigma of "mental disorder" from transgender identity.[76] Reparative or "conversion" therapies for LGBT youth are opposed by the American Psychiatric Association (APA) and have been banned in nineteen states and counting. In addition, one of the leading researchers on childhood gender noncon-formity, Dr. Kenneth Zucker, was required to shut down his clinic in Toronto, Canada, due to allegations of conducting conversion therapy.[77]

On the biomedical side, several major gender clinics have been estab-lished across the United States, including in Boston, Los Angeles, San Francisco, and Chicago. Beyond providing pediatric and endocrino-logic expertise, including hormone therapy for kids, these clinics often connect parents to affiliated specialists in mental health, the law, and education and advocacy. The use of hormones and puberty blockers on children has been another source of debate, including when to admin-ister them and what health risks they may pose. Originally, many re-searchers, particularly in the Netherlands, advised waiting until at least age twelve to consider social transition, including using puberty block-ers, and until age sixteen for cross-sex hormones. These protocols were known as the "Dutch Model."[78] But, as I learned, these recommenda-tions were unpopular stateside, and have faded as the use of blockers has become normalized among clinicians.

Today, many advocates believe in transitioning a child whenever they assert the desire for this (well before twelve years old in some cases), es-pecially since using blockers alone does not cause any known medically permanent changes for the child. Practitioners may also endorse the start of cross-sex hormones at a time that achieves "peer concordance" with the rest of the child's cohort (sometimes sooner than sixteen years of age). Fundamentally, the reigning medical approach is to treat each child on a case-by-case basis. As one of the physicians I interviewed explained, who is considered an expert in the medical management of transgender children in the United States: each child is so unique, both physiologically and psychosocially—and gender is such a "highly subjective" experience—that every case is carefully assessed on an indi-vidual basis.[79]

Despite these affirmative trends, some clinicians are more reserved about early childhood transitions, in part because of the longitudinal statistics I have described: most childhood gender nonconformity does not "persist" into adult transsexuality, as it is often put, but allegedly "desists," resulting most commonly in "just" homosexuality, if anything nonnormative at all.[80] In 2012, for example, two leading mental health practitioners issued the following precautions in a special issue of the

Journal of Homosexuality: "There are no reliable screening instruments that differentiate between young children in whom [gender dysphoria] will desist and those in whom it will persist," and "Some clinicians believe that facilitating childhood gender transition may increase the probability of persistence into adolescence and adulthood."[81] As another psychiatrist wrote in a 2015 *New York Times* op-ed, "If anything marks what a child really is, it is experimentation and flux. Why, then, would one subject a child to hormones and gender reassignment if there is a high likelihood that the gender dysphoria will resolve?"[82]

These concerns were echoed more recently in 2018 in a high-profile article in *The Atlantic* by journalist Jesse Singal, "When Children Say They're Transgender." Singal opens with the story of fourteen-year-old Claire, who tries to pursue medical transition despite the reservations of her parents, but who eventually reneges months later, believing "that her feeling that she was a boy stemmed from rigid views of gender roles that she had internalized."[83] The piece stirred widespread controversy over the idea that trans-affirming approaches have gone "too far," especially when it comes to transitioning young kids. Many commentators felt that the piece dangerously inflated transition "regret narratives," fueling an anti-trans agenda. Others felt it was more measured and balanced, offering a welcome consideration for the experimentation that childhood should be allowed to reflect. Regardless, sex-deterministic, cis-normative logics undergird all of these precautionary tales and debates: *Should you formally transition a child, and if so, when? Is there an age that is "too young" or "too soon" to do this? Does one risk (over)determining a certain gendered outcome for a child? Should you really believe your child when they tell you they're different? Why uproot your child's sex category until you're "absolutely sure"? What if you get it "wrong"?*

All of these controversies surrounding gender-nonconforming children—including the longitudinal statistics that have dominated their psychiatric lore—make up the clinical and cultural background of the parents in this book.[84] However, within this fraught terrain, parents have forged an extensive support community. Thanks to the internet and social networking, contemporary parents and advocates of gender-nonconforming children have connected rapidly over the last twenty years. They find each other through major advocacy organizations, their related online forums and web pages, and within parent blogs, as well as at regional support groups, summer camps, and conferences through-out the United States and Canada. These groups started with a hand-ful of families, but their followings soon grew by the hundreds. Now, families are increasingly turning to more local LGBT organizations and centers, whose advocacy on behalf of transgender children is expanding. Through these online searches and their ensuing interactions, parents encounter proliferating infrastructural supports, where childhood gen-der nonconformity is addressed *not* as a problem to be corrected, nor necessarily as "proto-homosexuality," but as a matter of *gendered* differ-ence, and, in many cases, as transgender.

LGBT/Q Rights

Alongside this clinical history, the modern-day "gay rights" movement has made LGBTQ identities increasingly visible on the sociopolitical stage. Several major federal decisions reflect the growing normalization of gay identity in US society. This includes the repeals of the "Don't Ask Don't Tell" policy and the Defense of Marriage Act in 2011 and 2013, respectively, and the historic Supreme Court decision in 2015 that legal-ized same-sex marriage in all states.[85] By some accounts, successes in gay rights have helped precipitate advances in transgender rights, which the proverbial "LGBT" moniker suggests. Reflective of these associa-tions, the May 2014 cover story of *Time* magazine, "The Transgender Tipping Point," opens with the caption, "Nearly a year after the Supreme Court legalized same-sex marriage, another social movement is poised to challenge deeply held cultural beliefs."[86] The "transgender move-ment," as the author calls it, has gained momentum, with figures like Chaz Bono, Laverne Cox, Janet Mock, and Caitlyn Jenner giving trans identity a very public face.

Indeed, at multiple government levels, as well as within both pub-lic and private bureaucracies, trans-related policies are expanding and improving. This includes identity documents, health care coverage, and employment nondiscrimination protections. The majority of states, for example, no longer require the traditional surgical or medical criteria of "sex reassignment" to change identity documents. Moreover, as of the writing of this book, at least fifteen states now provide for nonbinary designations on licenses and/or birth certificates. Trans-exclusionary health care policies are being rewritten as well, although a majority of states still do not offer specific protections against trans-exclusionary care.[87] These changes have also included traditionally sex-segregated institutions: as of June 2015, all of the Seven Sister women's colleges allow transgender students to enroll.[88]

But the notion that "LGB" rights necessarily mean progress for the "T" is flawed. First, the expansion of trans rights is hardly uniform, but varies considerably between states, municipalities, employers, and health insurance plans. This has created a complicated, and often contradictory, legal patchwork for trans persons to navigate. Nor do these formal legal protections necessarily address the routine harassment, policing, and violence that gender-nonconforming persons face in everyday life, including in bathrooms, on public transportation, and at security checkpoints, to name but a few scenarios.[89] Moreover, the Trump administration, installed after the 2016 election, has hauled in a reactionary, anti-trans agenda, challenging if not rescinding key protections in housing, health care, education, and the military.[90] In 2018, for example, a White House memo indicated that the administration might try to redefine "gender" strictly according to biological criteria at birth (i.e., genitalia), causing widespread concern about the implications of this for transgender rights under Title IX. This memo has been described as an attempt to "erase" trans persons from legislative existence.[91]

The limitations of "gay rights" for actual trans progress, however, have a deeper ideological history than these recent political challenges. As anthropologist David Valentine explains in *Imagining Transgender*, the linchpin of the mainstream LGBT rights movement is the idea that *gender* and *sexuality* are fundamentally *separate* parts of the self.[92] That is, "gay" is about *sexuality* and *sexual orientation*, "trans" is about *gender identity*, and the two should not be confused. On these terms, "gay rights" are indeed quite distinct from "trans rights"—they address different parts of human social experience and identity.

In contrast to these mainstream understandings, Valentine found that many low-income, marginalized, gender-nonconforming persons of color in New York City sooner identified as "gay" than "trans," including those assigned male at birth but who lived as women. Ultimately, Valentine argues that other social factors, like race and class, do not merely influence how "gender" and "sexuality" are experienced, but can fundamentally *shift* which parts of the self these categories signify. As Valentine says, "Age, race, class, and so on don't merely inflect or intersect with those experiences we call gender and sexuality but rather *shift the very boundaries of what 'gender' and 'sexuality' can mean* in particular contexts."[93] For his particular informants, "gay" signaled something as much about their gender as it did their sexual orientation. I return to Valentine's work in chapter 2.

Nevertheless, distinctions between "gender" and "sexuality" are considered part of the mainstream LGBT awareness canon, and they were reiterated throughout my interviews. As one mother advised, the "LGBT" acronym actually offends her; it erroneously lumps together two wholly different things, "gay" and "trans." Precisely because of these logics, many LGBT activists have argued that gay rights have been advanced at the *expense* of transgender issues. The Employment Non-Discrimination Act, for example, was plagued by these divisions and was stalled in Congress for years. Protections for "sexual orientation" were included, while clauses for "gender identity and expression" were routinely debated and struck out.[94] As the critics note, separating issues of "gay" from "trans" in these ways is remiss, given that instances of "homophobia" usually concern visible manifestations of gender nonconformity, *not* same-sex attraction.[95] And, of course, these statuses are hardly exclusive: trans persons can identify as LGB, and vice versa.

For these reasons, the mainstream LGBT rights movement has been criticized for succumbing to overly "assimilationist," "homonormative," and gender-normative approaches, primarily serving cisgender gays and lesbians and doing little to crack the real cultural ideologies that underlie sex- and gender-based oppression.[96] Nor do these approaches serve the most marginalized segments of the LGBT population, including and especially low-income, gender-nonconforming, trans-feminine persons of color, who experience alarmingly disproportionate rates of homelessness, joblessness, criminalization, and homicide.[97] The crucial roles of transgender activists within the movement have been overlooked, too. As historian Susan Stryker documents in *Transgender History*, the 1966 riots at Compton's Cafeteria in San Francisco marked the first concerted protests against police brutality toward gender-nonconforming persons in public, predating the famous Stonewall riots that occurred three years later.[98] Stonewall itself, considered the catalyst of the modern-day "gay rights" movement, was led by several trans women of color, a crucial part of LGBT history that has been "whitewashed" and "gay-washed" in its legacy.[99]

Starting in the late 1980s, these concerns galvanized a more radicalized, "queer" brand of LGBT activism, aimed at addressing the trans-exclusionary tendencies of the movement, as well as its racist, classist, and sexist undercurrents.[100] These "queer" political efforts have sought to shift the movement's priorities away from marriage equality and access to the military and toward issues like affordable housing and health care, access to job training and education, and criminal justice reform—matters that present more pressing life-or-death challenges for many LGBT persons.[101] Pursuant to queer deconstructionist theorizing, which has interrogated static and stable understandings of gender and sexuality, queer politics have also challenged exclusively binary and/or medicalized perspectives of transgender identity, ushering in greater awareness for nonbinary, gender-fluid, and/or more visibly nonconforming identities and expressions. This includes identities that do not reflect traditional body modification expectations or transitions.[102] In a related vein, "queer-of-color" and "trans-of-color" critiques have challenged mainstream agendas for privileging certain kinds of transgender subjects over others (i.e., white, economically stable, middle-class to upper-class, medically transitioned, binary-presenting, and holding legal citizenship).[103] Such "trans-normative" politics, these scholars argue, leave those who are most in need of advocacy the most vulnerable to oppression and exclusion, often at the hands of the state.

In short, both scholars and activists have argued that the mainstream LGBT rights movement has failed to address the real sources of precarity, and wider structural inequalities, that so often impact LGBTQ persons and experience, especially transgender, nonbinary, and gender-nonconforming persons. Today's generation of LGBTQ politics is thus increasingly trans- and nonbinary-aware, and deeply committed to more intersectional concerns of racism, classism, and nationalism.[104]

Many of the parents I interviewed had little familiarity with transgender identity early on. They confessed that their early associations with the terms "transgender" and "transsexual" entailed rather sensationalistic portrayals from daytime talk shows, as well as *The Rocky Horror Picture Show* or "show girls in Vegas."[105] All but one of the parents I interviewed were cisgender, and the majority were heterosexual-identified (forty parents) and/or in heterosexual marriages. For most parents, however, "gay" did seem to offer a familiar reference for "transgender," by "LGBT" association. Many participants, for example, had cisgender, gay-identified friends or family, whom they readily referenced in our interviews. In our first interview, Lorraine, a forty-six-year-old, white, middle-class woman and the one explicitly "queer"-identified member of the sample, commented on the "gulf" she had observed between parents of trans kids and the LGBTQ community, which she considers her home turf. This includes specifically trans and queer affiliations:

> A couple of things occurred to me about that whole process for them [heterosexual parents]: one, for the first time in my life, I felt like we [LGBTQ parents] were in a position of privilege, because that's our community, we don't have to go very far to get the information that we need, and we both have had to navigate the community already. . . . They not only have the experience of their child being transgender and having to figure [that] out . . . but they have to go out and find someone in their territory to get the information that they need . . . and for us, once we realized that Jamie is transgendered,[106] it wasn't that big a deal because, you know, we've already got so many friends in [our city] who are transgendered, [our city] is a mecca for transgendered folk . . . for once in our life, it's a good thing that we're queer.

Lorraine's commentary resonates with Meadow's observation of the "transgender activism, cisgender logic" of the parent movement, a thread I return to in chapter 4.[107] Like Lorraine, fifteen of the parents were nonheterosexually identified, which includes five same-sex partnerships and four heterosexual partnerships among them (and two who identified as "none" in heterosexual marriages). These parents could claim a more personal identification with LGBTQ politics and/or community. As Bruce, a white, upper-middle-class, gay-identified married man, said, "I was a child of the sixties . . . when genderfuck was alive." However, at the start of their journeys, most of these parents seemed no more comfortable with the prospects of transgender identity for their children than the rest of the sample. In fact, several LGB-identified parents confessed to feeling viscerally uncomfortable about their child's ensuing gender nonconformity and "cross-dressing" early on, and one described herself then as "borderline transphobic." Altogether, the ways in which LGBTQ paradigms and discourses did, and did not, impact parents' trans-affirmative journeys are an overarching focus in this book.

Overview of the Book

With these historical and cultural trends in mind, this book turns its focus to parents' logics for gender, sexuality, the binary, and the body, which often challenged LGBT advocacy discourses, as well as queer politics and theorizing, as much as they harnessed them. This includes parents' deliberations between "just gay" and "truly trans" interpretations of gender nonconformity; parents' negotiations with *binary* and *nonbinary* possibilities; and parents' *biomedical* frameworks for transgender embodiment. These dynamics are explored through parents' evolving practices and perspectives on childhood gender nonconformity, as they respond to their children over the course of early childhood development and as they become immersed in trans-affirmative education, discourses, and support networks.

Chapter 1 offers an intimate empirical portrait of the families that make up this study, including how these parents first come to view their children as gender-nonconforming and, ultimately, as transgender. Many stories have been shared about parents and trans kids, from media exposés to memoirs to documentary films, illuminating key themes and patterns across cases.[108] I include a chapter like this at the outset of my analysis so that readers can know more intimately the families that populated my project, as well as to provide a critical empirical foundation for the chapters ahead. This material showcases the *child-driven, child-centered* nature of this phenomenon, as well as the extension of "feminist" parenting it signals. I also note important differences and caveats across cases, challenging the notion that there is any one "profile" for a transgender child. Finally, I highlight parents' troubles with *female masculinity* and the "tomboy" epithet in the cases of transgender boys, as much as parents' troubles with *male femininity* and "princess boys" in the cases of transgender girls.

In chapter 2, I turn to the first key area, gender and sexuality, and examine parents' contrasts between "just gay" and "truly trans" explanations for childhood gender nonconformity. Given age-old statistics that link childhood gender nonconformity with adult homosexuality, these deliberations are no small part of parents' journeys, nor of the historical juncture they represent. As noted earlier, mainstream LGBT rights discourses assert a firm distinction between gender and sexuality—gender identity is one thing, sexual orientation is another. However, parents' deliberations often signaled something more fluid, and potentially permeable, between these two realms of self, gesturing to a morphing "spectrum" of possibilities. This conceptual labor, I argue, gives increasing intelligibility to explicitly *(trans)gendered* understandings, versus ones formerly understood within a grid of (homo)sexuality. In social-constructionist terms, this is not merely descriptive labor, but *productive* labor, helping to bring broadening transgender possibilities into being. Parents' perspectives also prioritize *child-rooted* shifts and understandings, in a way that further troubles firm distinctions between these two categories of self.

In chapter 3, I turn to the gender binary, and discuss parents' newfound awareness of *nonbinary* possibilities. These were often described as being "somewhere in the middle" of the "spectrum," where a child "doesn't have to be just one or the other." Despite increasing sociopolitical emphasis on nonbinary, gender-fluid, and/or genderqueer possibilities—especially those that defy some trans-normative, gender-normative ideal—most of the children in this sample were adamantly binary-identified. For many of these parents, nonbinary possibilities proved more of an attempt to evade "truly trans" outcomes than any reality of their children's authentic selves. In making sense of these options, parents often found themselves engaging in queer deconstructionist debates about the gender binary in parent forums, hearkening back to decades-old feminist polemics about "reifying the binary" or not. Ultimately, parents affirm the self-conceptions their children express, however "young" or "soon" this may mean for their child's transition. In this area, I also examine several follow-up vignettes, highlighting the complications of nonbinary identities for children assigned male in particular.

Finally, in chapter 4, I turn to the area of the body, and evaluate parents' biomedical accounts of transgender embodiment, which they often analogized to a "birth defect." These frameworks often answered to their children's own embodied sensibilities, and worked to protect their privacy and autonomy, but they also reiterated cisgender body logics as natural and normal, in ways that LGBTQ platforms would resist. For several of my informants, these frameworks signaled the potential erasure of a more politicized trans consciousness among these children as well—especially among those growing up within the relative safety and "normalcy" of middle-class and upper-middle class families.

In the conclusion, I synthesize these themes for a sociology of trans-affirmative parenting, highlighting the limits as well as the great liberating potential of the phenomenon. These themes exemplify parents' love and support for their children while at the same time troubling cherished LGBTQ tenets on several key fronts: Gender and sexuality do not necessarily present as inherently disparate aspects of the precultural self, but are more fluid and open to reinterpretation, given new cultural contexts, opportunities, and awareness. "Gender-expansive" child-rearing often looks, fundamentally, very binary and gender-stereotypical, despite increasing visibility around nonbinary possibilities. And normalizing transgender experience, for many of these parents, often entails highly medicalized frameworks for bodies and genders. These families depart from conventional understandings of sex, gender, and sexuality, but in ways that prioritize *child-rooted* shifts and expressions, not necessarily LGBTQ paradigms.[109] All told, their experiences prove new ground for understanding the mechanisms and parameters of the (trans) gender change afoot. That is a story worth sharing.

1

"She's Just Who She Is"

Identifying the Transgender Child

She was trying to find a way to describe it. . . . She said, "You know how when you put blue and red together and they make purple? Well, it's kind of like that, except it makes a color you've never seen before."
—Theresa, parent

It's very seductive to think we all have the same stories because there are so many parallels, but it's important to be aware that there are unique things, because especially those of us who have such young kids, we're all trying to predict . . . [but] I really think that there are unique differences.
—Bruce, parent

In many of my interviews, parents attested to harboring strong aversions to the idea of "transgender" early on, before they started their parenting journeys. Parents' early discomfort with this category was itself gendered: their only frame of reference involved trans-feminine or "male-to-female" transitions. Indeed, whenever parents described to me their early understandings of "transgender," the figure they inevitably conjured up was an adult "man trying to be a woman," the tenor of which they qualified as problematic and sensationalistic in hindsight. Nancy, a forty-three-year-old, white, middle-class, heterosexual-identified woman and mother of Mickey, an eight-year-old transgender boy, gave the typical response:

My only exposure to transgender was, I'm going to date myself here, but like . . . Sally Jesse Raphael or Maury Povitch, like those talk shows where they have these transsexual or cross-dressing men and they're like forty who suddenly divorce their wives and live as a woman, and I was think-ing, *Oh my God, like I don't want this to be my kid.* . . . I didn't have any-thing that said, four-year-old girls that wish they had penises.[1]

Parents indicated it was difficult thinking that this kind of adult image could be relevant to their young child. Claire and Rick, for example, a white, upper-middle-class, heterosexual-identified married couple in their forties, could not accept that the label "transgender" applied, even after switching pronouns for their child, Andy, as of age four.[2] At the time of our interview, they had embraced Andy as the six-year-old transgender girl she was, but Claire reflected on these early sentiments:

> I knew that I had a child who was really a girl but who was anatomically a boy . . . [but] I was resistant to the very basic fact that . . . this word applied . . . the term was something that we completely and utterly just didn't think applied to us. . . . [It] was still something in our minds that applied to older men who cross-dressed.

Rick added, "The problem is that the word 'transgender' to us had a definition that included a little picture next to it of a fifty-year-old guy in pumps and his mom's sweater, you know what I mean? That is an awful thing to say, but that is the stereotype of the term." Like many parents, Claire and Rick seized on descriptors like "gender-creative," "gender-nonconforming," or "gender-fluid" instead, so as to evade explicit "transgender" associations with others. I do not mean to regurgitate problematic accounts in these excerpts; I do mean to signal parents' problematic starting points, from which they underwent a massive transformation. These comments also signal parents' discomfort with *male femininity* specifically, a stark reflection of the cultural hysteria sur-rounding feminine boys, male femininity, and trans-femininity.[3]

Given these fraught early understandings of the category, how did these parents come to see their own children as transgender? In this chapter, I detail the ways in which parents first came to see their child as gender-nonconforming and, ultimately, as transgender. This material showcases the *child-driven* nature of the phenomenon, as well as the feminist par-enting legacy from which it extends. Prompted by my own questions at the top of the interviews—*"When did you first start thinking about 'gen-*

der issues' with your child?"—parents provided me with a wealth of behaviors, preferences, statements, anecdotes, and overall accumulated observations about their child, which had come to constitute their gender-nonconforming "profile." As one advocate put it, it is a "constellation of things" that leads parents to a transgender understanding of their child. Among parents' stories, key themes and patterns emerge, but there are also notable differences and caveats, challenging any one standard "profile" for a transgender child. The strictures of hegemonic masculinity are duly reflected in parents' stories as well, especially for parents of children assigned male.[4] However, this chapter also highlights the limits of *female masculinity* and "tomboy" categorizations for parents of children assigned female, sometimes at comparable ages. Altogether, this material serves as a rich empirical foundation for the chapters ahead, which address more complex terrain regarding parents' (re)conceptions of gender, sexuality, the binary, and the body, at various stages of their journeys.

Increasingly, trans scholars and advocates seek to resist describing a person's experience according to the person's assigned sex at birth.[5] I wholly respect this approach, especially outside of my analysis. In few other contexts is referring to someone's body, genitalia, or assigned sex at birth ever appropriate or relevant. However, this principle would challenge many of the observations presented here: trans-feminine "versus" trans-masculine childhood trajectories, effectively, or children assigned male "versus" children assigned female. This is because from a sociological and ethnomethodological standpoint, it seems impossible to evade the reference.[6] As demonstrated by Jayne and Glenn's story in the introduction, parents' experiences indisputably hinged on the "male" and "female" birth sex designations of their children, including the host of expectations, assumptions, and presumed pathways of development these particular categories carried. Indeed, this is what made children's expressions remarkable to parents in the first place—and differentially so, depending on the category. In so many ways, "biological sex" is at the origin of parents' stories, and is reflected throughout the catalog of experiences described here.

"So That Maybe Muddied the Waters": Feminist Foundations

Throughout their stories, parents' observations both resisted and co-opted the terms of the gender binary: highly stereotypical markers for masculinity and femininity were what they first noted, and what they later embraced, in the service of questioning, and ultimately abandoning, their children's assigned sex designations. However, many of the mothers I interviewed indicated that they first entered child-rearing with at least a modicum of "gender-neutral" parenting principles, not unlike many parents who came of age in the wake of the second-wave feminist movement.[7] As such, many of my participants tried to create at least a moderately gender-inclusive environment from the beginning, in a way that made room for some of their children's "gender-atypical" preferences, versus squashing them outright. Moreover, in several key instances, parents' gender-inclusive values held force at later stages, when children's interests presented as not so stereotypical for the "other box" either. This was especially true for transgender girls. In these ways, parents applied and extended the principles of "feminist" child-rearing to trans-affirmative ends. These principles, I argue, coupled with a fundamentally *child-centered* mode of parenting and listening,[8] provide a key social mechanism through which childhood transgender possibilities are realized and facilitated by contemporary parents.

Martsy's experiences exemplified these processes. Martsy, a thirty-six-year-old, white, upper-middle-class, heterosexual-identified married woman and mother of Cindy, a five-year-old transgender girl, was eager to contribute to my project.[9] I first met Martsy in person at her house, where we had arranged for a formal interview. She was in stretch pants and a loose T-shirt, her brown hair hastily pulled back, and her face a bit flushed from the flurry of the day's schedule, having just handed off her second child, three years old, to her mother-in-law. Martsy's husband, Marco, a thirty-eight-year-old, Mexican American, heterosexual-identified man, had taken a full-time position with a company just over the state line, which meant long days commuting and working outside the home. Martsy, in turn, was predominantly responsible for the daily care and child-rearing of their two young children, from morning to bedtime, and had put her own career on hold.

Martsy traced the first signs of Cindy's gender nonconformity to her adoration for a feminine cat shirt—"like sparkly, rainbow, puffy sleeves." Cindy had selected this shirt herself from the girls' section of the store when she was eighteen months old. Despite her initial attempts to shift Cindy's interests away from the shirt, Martsy recalled feeling proud that her "male" child would walk so comfortably into the girls' department: "I'm like, *Oh, that's cute, look at me, pat myself on the back, my child sees no gender boundaries, la-la-la.*" Martsy went ahead and purchased the shirt, and could barely get Cindy to wear anything else. Like many of the mothers I spoke with, Martsy entered her parenting career with at least a baseline consciousness toward feminist parenting approaches, especially regarding a critical rejection of idealized femininity:

> I am not a girly girl . . . while I was pregnant . . . I purposely didn't find out what I was having, I [didn't] want them feeling confined by any gender norms . . . so that maybe muddied the waters in the beginning, because I was going out of my way to make sure that all doors were open and that my child never felt this is just for boys, this is just for girls. . . . If I was having a girl specifically, I didn't want a closet full of pink, ruffly, lacy [things], because I'm not a girly girl.

Ultimately, these sentiments proved "ironic" to Martsy, in light of the transgender "girly girl" she eventually realized she had, who was all about the pink, the ruffly, and the lacy.

Martsy noted that Marco also subscribed to gender-neutral principles early on, and that he too praised himself for Cindy's feminine preferences in her toddler years:

> He was fine, and he was open-minded to, *We can raise kids that see no boundaries, and that will make them more sensitive as people when they're older*, which is what we were both thinking, that they're not going to feel contained or confined, and they're not going to do that to other people either. . . . He was fine with the cat shirt that had sparkles and frilly, and he would defend that. He was fine even . . . when [Cindy] picked out the princess high-heel dress shoes at *Disney on Ice*. And he even laughed about that and took pictures and kind of patted himself on the back, like, *Look at what a good job we're doing.*

Cindy's young age likely influenced Marco's openness to her "atypical" preferences, as for many parents and especially fathers. In his view, Cindy's interests were the stuff of "child's play" and childhood exploration, even if he had embraced them as part of a gender-neutral parenting philosophy. As Cindy grew, however, Marco's amused support faded into something a bit more uncomfortable and resistant, and at the time of the interview, he was far more uneasy about a "transgender" conception of their child than Martsy was. In fact, it was proving a source of strain and conflict in the marriage, and Martsy confided to me, tearfully, in our interview that she felt frustrated and alone in the process, on top of already handling most of the "regular" child care by herself. (When I connected with Martsy months later at a conference, she informed me that Marco was leaps and bounds from these original sentiments and that he was increasingly espousing her understanding of Cindy as transgender. This testifies to the fluid, developmental aspects of parents' journeys.)

Over time, Cindy's gender-nonconforming expressions proliferated and intensified, from toy and clothing choices to the kinds of things she would say to Martsy. At around four years of age, for example, Cindy made a wish on a dandelion, telling Martsy, "Do you want to know what I wished for? I wish that I could be a girl." Cindy's behaviors ultimately propelled Martsy into consulting a therapist, who advised her to start keeping a journal of her observations and to shore up the frequency to which Cindy seemed to gravitate toward more "female" things. Martsy said, "I laughed at her at the time. I'm like, it would be easier to write down the things that would indicate that my child is the gender they were born into [there were far fewer of them]."

Nevertheless, pursuant to the therapist's advice, Martsy started recording things in August 2012, which included recollections of incidents dating back to October 2011, excerpted from her journal here: "Slowly we progressed from [a girly clothing] style to a 'girl' toy preference. However, I still chalked it all up to our attempts to raise a gender-neutral child."[10] Along with toy and clothing interests, Martsy started recording Cindy's verbal statements as well: "[Cindy] began telling me that (s)he was a girl on the inside and a boy on the outside," and later, "I would say almost daily this week [Cindy] has brought up on 'her' own something along the lines of, *I am a girl on the inside—I wish I were a girl—I feel like a girl.*" These included specific statements about her body too: "Cindy told me that Ruti [a stuffed toy cat] had pushed her peepee in. . . . Mama then asked if Cindy wished that her peepee was pushed in all the way like other girls. Cindy said yes." While these entries mark deeply personal and private terrain, for both Martsy and Cindy, they offer powerful, near real-time documentation of her child's incipient transgender expressions and identifications. This is important in the face of those who might question the realities of trans childhoods or the undue "influence" of the parents. The journal entries also reflect Martsy's developing consciousness that her child's behaviors concerned Cindy herself, not the effects of her "gender-neutral" parenting.

Martsy told me that in hindsight, she thought her early subscriptions to feminist parenting may have "muddied the waters," as far as not fully recognizing or affirming Cindy for who she was sooner. Cindy was not "just a boy who liked girl things," Martsy came to realize, she was actually a *girl*. Similar sentiments surfaced among parents of the presumed "tomboys" as well, which I return to later in the chapter: seemingly open and progressive "tomboy" understandings of their children actually impeded parents' recognition of who their children were, and that is *boys*, not tomboyish girls. Nevertheless, Martsy's gender-neutral principles afforded Cindy critical early opportunities to start expressing her gender. This, coupled with Martsy's equally *child-centered* approach to parenting and listening, provided Cindy a trans-feminine platform on which to start asserting herself. Through these mechanisms, Cindy's self-expressions were accommodated, observed, and heard—and eventually logged—most seriously by her mother, versus rebuffed or refused outright.[11]

Other parents exhibited feminist parenting approaches, too. Kari, for example, a forty-year-old, mixed-race, middle-class, heterosexual-identified married woman and mother of Emma, a five-year-old transgender girl, told me: "I'm pretty open-minded. Before I even had children my goal was to raise more gender-neutral children anyway. . . . We had a play kitchen, vacuum cleaner, things like that." Similarly, Meredith, a thirty-nine-year-old, mixed-race, upper-middle-class, heterosexual-identified married woman and mother of Martin, a seven-year-old transgender boy, voiced: "I've always been really big about, society puts too many gender constraints on people, I've always been like, *Yeah, I was a tomboy, we're female, let's show them what we can do, let's break all the gender barriers!*"

To be sure, not all parents practiced gender-neutral principles unrestrained at the outset of their parenthood. Bruce, for example, father of Holden, a five-year-old transgender girl, originally refused to purchase girls' items from the store for his child, despite her "demonic" public meltdowns over women's shoes. Julie, too, a thirty-nine-year-old, white, working-class, heterosexual-identified woman and mother of Macy, a five-year-old transgender girl, was upset with her ex for allowing Macy to play with Barbie dolls during visits, which she would not allow. Moreover, parents' ostensibly "gender-neutral" principles often manifested in the form of subtle gendered compromises, or "gender hedging," as noted in the introduction, especially with children assigned male. Wendy, for example, a fifty-one-year-old, white, upper-middle-class, bisexual-identified married woman, advised that she and her wife pushed for a *red* snow suit when Hazel, their five-year-old transgender girl, had begged for a *pink* one. Notably, several parents, in separate interviews, described this kind of gendered boundary work as "walking a fine line," "walking a tightrope," or "a tightrope act."[12]

There were limitations among parents of children assigned female, too. Karen, for example, a fifty-year-old, white, middle-class, heterosexual-identified woman and mother of Izzy, a ten-year-old transgender boy, advised that she loved having a "tomboy," but that she avoided going "too over the edge 'boy,'" such as with ninja toys and action figures. These were too masculine for her "female" child in her view. Similarly, Sheryl and Richard, a white, upper-middle-class, heterosexual-identified married couple in their fifties and parents of Gil, an eight-year-old transgender boy, noted that Gil loved overalls, and that they thought a "tomboy" aesthetic was "cute." But they still insisted on dresses at formal events and holidays. As Sheryl said, "As a tomboy he was great, we got away with tomboy," but things like formal suits and tuxedos were crossing the line. Despite these limitations, however, gender-neutral parenting principles provided at least a baseline opportunity for gender-nonconforming expressions and interests among many of these children.

Toys, Clothes, Preferences: Early Observations

In recounting for me their developing understandings of their children, parents reported that their children exhibited a strong inclination toward the "other sex's" conventional toys, play interests, clothes, and wider accoutrements, from very early on. This included objects already found at home or those selected at the store. Wendy, for example, described "all the gender stuff" that started surfacing with Hazel around the age of three, from the kinds of dress-up to TV shows to birthday parties she desired:

> The third year we started seeing all the gender stuff come out, and we really didn't know what to think of it . . . just constantly . . . wanting to dress up, wanting only girl things to play with . . . she cried because she wanted [a] Cinderella birthday and we made her have a robot one . . . and then she cried again 'cause she wanted [a] Tinkerbell [birthday] and we made her have Thomas the train. . . . We had a dress-up box at home, [she] just pretty much wanted to dress up all day, and it was never the fireman, never the Batman, never the Superman, which we had in there, it was always the princess, the Tinkerbell, the Snow White. All of the [TV] shows that . . . she wanted to see were always . . . *Angelina Ballerina* and *Strawberry Shortcake*.

Wendy also recalled that during potty training, around the age of four, Hazel would change out of her boy underwear and into her sister's girl underwear, which featured Tinkerbell and princesses and which they started letting her wear on a daily basis. Of course, clothes, toys, underwear, and the like do not have to be for "boys" or for "girls." I list them as such here to capture the parents' experiences and perspectives regarding their child's gender nonconformity.

Similarly, Julie started our interview by listing a stereotypical stock of "feminine" interests and behaviors she had observed in Macy:

> In the very beginning what I noticed is that he gravitated at a very young age toward pretty things, flowers, he'd put flowers in his hair. . . . He was always grabbing at my jewelry . . . a certain blouse that I had, and when he was in preschool . . . very often he'd be dressed as a princess [from the dress-up box] . . . and he usually hung out with the girls.

Julie also perceived Macy's mannerisms as feminine: "He always would eat with his pinky up, or pick things up with his pinky up, always really kind of dainty, very gentle." In one memorable event, Julie recalled the first time Macy ever saw a bride, which she was excited about for days:

He's like, "When I am going to get married, I'm going to wear a dress like that," and I took out the computer and I showed him what he'd probably wear . . . and he said, "No, I'm going to wear a dress like that" (*laughs*), and so I knew something was up.

While Julie felt that "something was up," she was not yet thinking "transgender," though several friends had mentioned this possibility to her, to which she actually took offense. Like many parents at this stage, Julie actually wondered if Macy might be "gay" instead. I revisit this interpretation in depth in chapter 2.

Additionally, several parents claimed that their children made use of toys that were stereotypical of their assigned sex, but in gender-atypical fashions. Claire and Rick, for example, noticed that Andy would line up matchbox cars and trucks inherited from her older brothers (or that Rick had purchased for her as potty-training prizes) and pretend that they were chatting with each other. When they asked what she was doing with them, Andy would say she was "playing sisters" or "roommates" or having "tea parties." In a similar vein, Madalyn, a twenty-nine-year-old, mixed-race, working-class, heterosexual-identified woman, mentioned that Talia, a five-year-old transgender girl, dismantled a toy drum set from her grandfather and "used the silver rings to make tiaras." Like many children, both Talia and Andy drew on their mothers' or sisters' wardrobes for dress-up. Talia routinely wore Madalyn's old prom and bridesmaid dresses around the house and she filled her closet with these dresses. She also outfitted her room with feminine decor: "It basically just looked like a girl's bedroom when you walked in . . . fake flowers . . . ribbons . . . my old jewelry." At a certain point, Talia also insisted on wearing some of Madalyn's smaller dresses underneath her boys' clothes when they left the house. Meanwhile, Andy often wore her mother's and sister's large blouses and flowery headbands, and also used the headbands to adorn her toy trucks.

However, a child's near-exclusive interests in the "other sex's" accoutrements was not always the case. Linda, a forty-one-year-old, mixed-race, middle-class, bisexual-identified married woman and mother of Violet, a six-year-old transgender girl, actually checked me against this line of thinking in our interview, shortly after she had described Violet's love of cars and dinosaurs:

E: How else did she start displaying to you a preference for more feminine things?

L: She really didn't, you know, I think that's a difficult question, I'm not
sure if that's the *right* question. . . . Violet has always been herself. . . .
The term "transgender" is indicative to me of how primitive we still
are as a culture, as a literal societal framework, because she's just . . .
who she is.

Linda also noted that Violet consistently pretended to be "Valerie the
Velociraptor" during playtime, even though Linda tried to offer her conventionally masculine names for these characters. Several other parents
of transgender girls reported on their child's affinity for traditionally
"masculine" interests, such as cars, roughhousing, or sword fighting.
They indicated that these behaviors originally conflicted them about
how to understand their child or about which labels applied when they
began more research into the issue. But these instances also expose
important differences across cases, disrupting any one standard "profile"
for a transgender child.

Sociologist Andrew Seeber's distinctions between "bodies and behaviors," including between "sex and gender" identities, yield insight here.[13]
In *Trans* Lives in the United States*, Seeber offers a new schema that
emphasizes the differences between "sex identity" (bodies) and "gender
identity" (behaviors), where one's sex-categorical, *bodily* identification as
male, female, or other should be held independent from one's *gendered*
expressions, interests, and behaviors, allowing room for "noncongruent"
identities and transitions. In other words, a child's preference for "cars
and dinosaurs" should not be held in opposition to her sex-categorical
identification as female. As Linda demonstrates here, many parents
come into this awareness organically, through teasing apart just such
observations on behalf of their children. This is where feminist child-
rearing principles are extended in particularly trans-aware capacities,
especially for children who are transgender girls. I return to these observations in chapter 3, where they present in more complicated, nonbinary
capacities for parents of transgender boys.

Parents of transgender boys also recalled a stereotypical stock of
gender-nonconforming preferences and behaviors that they had observed since early childhood. Meredith, for example, cited Martin's ob-

session with a brown cowboy hat when he was three years old, including his corrections to others when he wore it: "One of the first examples that comes to mind is, he wore a brown cowboy hat for a year, every day . . . [in his] late twos, almost three, and anytime anyone came up to him and said, 'Oh, you're a cowgirl,' he would say, 'No, I'm a cow*boy*.'" Martin also refused to wear any clothing that was expressly from the girls' section of the store, including the plainest attire Meredith could find. Martin explicitly asked which section of the store items came from, and he vetoed them accordingly, which Meredith tried to oblige. Such a relationship between Martin and his mother further attests to parents' *child-centered* approaches to parenting, before transgender issues ever crystallized in their consciousness.

Like Julie's observations previously, Nancy also perceived masculine mannerisms in her child, including how Mickey kept his hair, sat, and ate:

> She just never wanted me to brush it or comb it or braid it [his hair] . . . it would just slide around her face and it would get all sticky and dirty, she was like a real grungy kid. . . . I'm just like, *Oh my God*, you know, like sitting at the table, eating really fast . . . I just thought, *What is wrong?* . . . It was so embarrassing, but if you look back, and you ascribe like, that's traditional boy behavior, it makes sense—but then again, is that just stereotyping? I mean, not all boys are sloppy—but my kid was just . . . [his hair] was always a big rat's nest.

As I observed among many parents, Nancy here checked the potential gender-stereotyping in her interpretations, to which she was becoming acutely attuned, but which she nevertheless shored up in her understandings of her child's gender.

Nevertheless, parents' early reactions to their presumably "female" children, especially to their clothing preferences, posed a stark contrast to the cases of transgender girls and well attest to the seeming freedom given to children assigned female. As one mom said of allowing her child access to boys' clothes, boys' toys, and boyish haircuts through the age of ten: "We just cruised."[14] Imagine the following commentary in the case of an assumed "male" child who wanted to wear dresses to school, issued here from a mom of a transgender boy. Marie, a thirty-eight-year-old, white, upper-middle-class, heterosexual-identified married woman and mother of Milo, a seven-year-old transgender boy: "I started to notice that he was getting very particular in the shoes that he would wear, the underwear that he would wear, the type of clothes he was comfortable in, and *I allowed him the freedom of his choice, I did not make him wear anything that he was not comfortable in*" (emphasis mine). Or, as Marie commented further: "I don't know if I could say that I was open about this, I was not even aware of 'transgender' terminology at the time, I was just open to letting my child explore whatever his interests were."

Halloween is emblematic of this differential: children assigned female were readily permitted stereotypical male costumes, from Peter Pan to the Hulk to various superheroes and ninjas, whereas children assigned male were rarely able to dress up as female icons (e.g., Ariel, Cinderella), at least not without parents' deliberation and negotiation. Karen, for example, pulled out a photo album during our phone call and plainly listed off Izzy's Halloween costumes, starting at age three: "Clown, Bob the Builder, Woody [from *Toy Story*], firefighter, knight, magician—a boy magician . . . hockey player, Captain Edward Smith of the *Titanic*." These were all costumes procured well before Karen had conceived of Izzy as transgender. For parents of transgender girls, in contrast, allowing girls' clothes was nothing they "just cruised" through, even on Halloween. Martsy's in-laws, for example, swiftly nixed an Abby Cadabby fairy costume for Cindy, which Cindy had spent weeks giddily anticipating. Having to recount this restriction was an emotional, grief-stricken part of the interview for Martsy.

Notably, one parent was so resistant to permitting girls' clothes, she sewed feminine appliqués (flowers, hearts, etc.) onto her child's otherwise masculine attire, instead of just buying girls' clothes already decorated like this. Interestingly, a parent of a transgender boy did the same thing, but with underwear: she found the plainest girl underwear she could find (white or blue), and sewed on superhero appliqués, versus simply buying ready-made superhero underwear from the boys' department. These two cases well expose the differences between parents of trans boys and trans girls: the former parent engaged in this practice with outerwear, whereas the latter parent had already started buying clothing from the boys' department. Nevertheless, that a parent would perform this labor for undergarments, which no one else would see, exemplifies the hold of gender-normative accountability on *all* parents, refracted differentially through male and female expectations.

One educator I interviewed, Gail, who has spoken to hundreds of parents, was very direct about how these gendered imbalances skew the ages represented among the children at her organization. She told me that the majority of trans girls fall under eleven years old, while the majority of trans boys fall over eleven years old. She unequivocally attributed this to society's allowances for gender nonconformity among children assigned female over and above children assigned male:

> We have a double standard, we *encourage* our girls to wear what you want, dress how you want, get out there, throw that football if you want, if you want to play with trucks, here, you can be president. With our natal boys, we're not doing that, they're not walking out of the house in a dress, they're not running giddily down the aisle of pink toys with their parents saying *whoo-hoo!* And we've had many discussions among ourselves as well as with [other organizations] and we do feel there is a strong difference because of cultural expectations for the transgender [boys]. . . . Most of them are just allowed to be, because they're called tomboys, and there's nothing pejorative about that term, but there is something pejorative about being a sissy.

In short, the differential treatment of "girly boys" and "tomboys," and the overbearing rigidity of normative maleness, to which even early childhood is not immune, permeate these parents' early observations and approaches.

Similar to the trans-feminine cases, however, several parents of transgender boys reported that their children enjoyed toys and play interests that were "typical" for their assigned birth sex, including baby dolls, dancing, fashion, musical theater, and/or boy pop stars. As Nancy said of Mickey: "Me and my mother called it 'the factory' . . . there was like six or seven of them [baby dolls] all lined up, and he'd go one by one, burping, feeding, changing them." Nancy confided that over time, she would cling to this as a sign that Mickey was not actually transgender: "That was his one thing that I held on to, *Oh, he's a girl!*" Nancy also stated, though, that whenever Mickey played with the dolls, he identified as the "dad," and that he explicitly stated he did not want to have (birth) his own babies as a grown parent. This also recalls Seeber's schema of "bodies versus behaviors."

Similarly, Carolyn, a forty-four-year-old, white, middle-class, bisexual-identified married woman and mother of Vic, an agender-identified twelve-year-old, described Vic's childhood as fairly stereotypically feminine. This included playing dolls and dress-up with their little sister and liking "cute" things, such as Hello Kitty and My Little Pony. As Carolyn explained to me, "I would buy dresses for them and there was never, *I'm not wearing that, I hate dresses*, there was never that." At one point she paused to say, "He wasn't overt at all, and I know that a lot of times . . . kids who were transgender started when they were really young and it was so obvious, but then I found out after doing research that that was not always the case." These cases further challenge the idea of any one standard profile or trajectory for a transgender child, boy or girl.

The "Tomboy" Problem

Not surprisingly, many of the parents of the children assigned female chalked up their children's behaviors to "just being a typical tomboy." In fact, this was often a source of pride for the moms, if they found it remarkable at all. As Karen said, she never expected Izzy to be a "girly girl": "Yes, absolutely, I was thinking 'tomboy' and in the very beginning I was enjoying it." She elaborated: "I'm not a girly girl, I wasn't looking for a girly girl. . . . Izzy's preference was for anything that rolled and moved. . . . I loved the fact that she gravitated toward the trucks and trains." Similarly, Tory, a forty-three-year-old, white, upper-middle-class, heterosexual-identified married woman and mother of Connor, a seven-year-old transgender boy, declared: "Truthfully, I didn't notice because I was a complete tomboy. Connor never came and said to me 'I'm a boy' or anything, I just thought Connor was actually typically female, just really, really tomboyish." Indeed, a preponderance of mothers identified themselves as "tomboys" growing up, such that I came to expect this self-characterization in interviews. Other than one parent (a mother commenting on her husband), I never encountered a father who identified himself as a feminine child, let alone unabashedly or proudly.

Given the latitude that is afforded children assigned female, and the fact that not all of these children could be described as exclusively or overtly stereotypically masculine by their parents, parents' ultimate abandonment of a "tomboy" understanding of their children was the subject of much probing in interviews. While the "problem" of male femininity almost always surfaces in parents' accounts,[15] the proverbial "tomboy" epithet eventually proved equally dicey for the parents of children assigned female. These parents testified to the eventual limits of the epithet's explanatory power—and perhaps sooner than one might expect—as their children's behaviors intensified and as parents started feeling like "something more," "something different," or "something deeper" was occurring, as they often termed it. Nancy, for example, started feeling that Mickey exhibited an "extreme" level of masculinity, more than any other "tomboys" she knew of:

> I didn't know anyone whose kid was that extreme. . . . I mean people would say like, *Oh, it's just a phase, she'll outgrow it, my daughter was a tomboy, now she's the prom queen*, you know, and I thought, *Yeah, but was your daughter wearing boxers?* My kid was taking it to a whole other level. . . . I see girls that'll go head to toe "boys," but then they'll have the pink sketchers, or they'll have their hair braided, or they'll have pierced ears, or they'll have *one [feminine] thing* . . . but Mickey was just like, camouflage wallet, the whole nine [yards].

In fact, many of these mothers indicated that they grew concerned about just how "male"-oriented their children seemed. They took pains to clarify that "girls can like these things too," as if to disabuse them of a male (mis)identification. Early on, this felt like part of their feminist, gender-neutral approach.

Ultimately, several key factors surfaced in parents' reasons for departing from a "tomboy" conception of their child: namely, their child's repeated self-identifications as a "boy" or the child's stated desire to be one ("I want to be a boy"), as well as their commentary about their bodies. Grace, for example, a thirty-five-year-old, white, upper-middle-class, heterosexual-identified married woman and mother of Nick, a seven-year-old transgender boy, cited Nick's ongoing requests for a penis as significant in her thinking this was "more than just a tomboy thing" (Nick expressed this desire as of age two). In fact, long before they had identified him as transgender, Grace said that it was a running joke between her and her husband that Nick's college fund would go toward "buy[ing] her a penis" or "whatever reconstruction surgery she wanted." By Nick's fourth birthday, Grace had started consulting a therapist about his apparent "cross-dressing" behaviors, as she understood it at the time.

Additionally, Monica, a thirty-one-year-old, white, upper-middle-class, heterosexual-identified married woman, said that perceiving Hayden's "shame" and secrecy about dressing up in his father's clothes after school was a major wake-up call for her. Hayden had asked her not to tell anyone when he did this. Monica's husband, Dan, a thirty-five-year-old, white, heterosexual-identified man, also cited a memorable comment Hayden once made at bedtime: "He said, 'When the family dies, I'm going to cut my hair so I can be a boy.'" Dan, who was originally much more resistant to seeing Hayden as anything other than a tomboy, advised that this comment was his major wake-up call that there was "something more" going on: "[These were] very heavy comments for a five-year-old to make, in my mind. . . . For me, that was the *OK, time out, yes, there is something going on, we need to explore this a little bit more.*"

I do not marshal these examples to suggest definitive, objective distinctions between "tomboys" and "transgender boys." It is possible to imagine some or all of the preceding behaviors, including the desire for a penis, occurring for a child who lives as a "tomboy" uneventfully in another familial context, well past the ages of transition for the children represented here (five to seven years old). But what matters socioculturally, relative to the social change occurring, is how these *parents* came to understand and identify these differences on behalf of their children. The parents cited these particular behaviors—including repeated self-identifications as "boys"—as key factors that pushed them to consider their child's gender nonconformity as something "deeper" than being a tomboy. The growing visibility of transgender children might well mean the circumscription of the "tomboy" category for childhood female masculinity, as other gender-variant categories and understandings gain traction and legibility.[16]

"He Said This and It Was So Freaking Profound": Verbal Declarations

Parents' departure from the "tomboy" category actually exemplifies a critical factor in *all* parents' developing understandings of their children:

the things their children *said*, more than the kinds of clothing or toys they liked. As seen in the stories of Grace and Dan, poignant comments from the children, both about their sense of self and about their bodies, proved highly significant in parents' journeys and understandings. Throughout our interviews, parents recalled numerous conversations during which their child verbalized a "cross-gender" sense of self, or at least challenged the category that had been imposed on them from birth (e.g., "I'm your *son*, not your daughter!"; "Say 'she,' not 'he'"; or "I'm girl with a penis"). These repeated comments from children heavily precipitated parents' considerations that there was "something more serious" involved in children's atypical expressions. Indeed, these kinds of identificatory declarations by children were considered a defining indicator of a "truly transgender" child by the professionals, parents, and advocates I spoke with, versus "just" a gender-nonconforming child.

Wendy's interview was replete with this kind of illuminating commentary from her child, Hazel, which became crucial to her understanding and approach. As Wendy said, "All of a sudden at the age of three and a half, Hazel just started saying, '*I'm a girl, I'm a girl inside and out, I'm a girl forever.*'" Wendy added, "She came up with the terminology herself, and I swear I almost fell over." Wendy also recalled several poignant dialogues, or monologues, during car rides, which Hazel initiated seemingly out of the blue from her car seat in the back:

> One day we're in the car . . . and she said, "Mommy, listen to me, rainbows are different, snowflakes are different, cars are different, and *I'm* different, *I am a girl.*" And that was almost one of the last straws for me. . . . [T]hat same week—this was the week before we transitioned— she also said, "Mommy, I feel dead in boy clothes," so after that we never made her have boy clothes on.

By this point, Wendy had started consulting a well-known children's therapist and "gender specialist" (parents' use of therapists returns later in this chapter). This specialist advised Wendy about major "signs" or indicators to look for in identifying a transgender child. These included identity-based statements (especially in the form of "I am" versus "I want to be"), body-based statements ("Why do I have a penis?"), and requests for a name change.[17] Wendy had observed Hazel demonstrate all of these quite explicitly between three and four years of age, and Wendy's consultations with the therapist added new classificatory weight to them. Strong feelings surfaced around Hazel's remarks about her body: "My God, right after [the therapist] told me about that [signs and indicators] . . . my Hazel, who is absolutely petrified of needles and going to the doctor, [asks], 'Mommy, can't the doctor just give me a shot and get rid of my boy peepee? Can I just have a girl peepee?'" The final clincher for Wendy and her wife, Rita, was Hazel's unprompted request for a new name, just as the therapist had advised:

> It was like, *Oh, my God*. I remember texting my two sisters and I said, "I feel sick to my stomach, I think I'm going to throw up," because that was the last thing that we were waiting for to see if it would happen, and she came up to us one night in the living room and said, "Can you call me Hazel, because that's a girl's name, and I just don't understand why . . . you would name me Nate when that's a boy's name."

Wendy's visceral reactions to these experiences—such as feeling sick to her stomach—do not necessarily signal her aversion to understanding Hazel as transgender. Instead, they testify to the significance and clarity with which she regarded Hazel's comments. Hazel was expressing herself in exactly the ways the therapist had flagged for transgender children. As such, Wendy's reactions signal the significance of the identification for her: she realized her child was a transgender girl, and she was going to embrace and transition her accordingly. For Wendy and Rita, this was a life-altering new understanding of their child, which caused strong "gut-level" emotions for them.

Other parents described a similar wealth of poignant verbal encounters. Claire cited one memorable moment when Andy said to her at bedtime, "'When you say I'm beautiful, say 'she' is beautiful.'" As Claire said, "I just felt like . . . you don't screw with someone's self-definition of beauty, like I am not allowed to mess with that, that just felt sacred and holy and absolute." Rick, Claire's husband, referred to this as a "crucible moment" in their developing consciousness about Andy: "Then wheels started turning for us." Nancy recalled that during Mickey's toddler years, he would frequently correct the pronouns she used when she referred to him to others ("say he not she"). These corrections tapered off over the years, which Nancy attributed to Mickey's constantly being dismissed and misgendered by others. However, Nancy recalled a "freaking profound" moment at the hair salon, when Mickey was seven years old. With her voice cracking on the phone, Nancy narrated the incident for me: She had finally agreed to letting Mickey get a more buzzed "boy" haircut. When it was finished, Mickey turned to admire himself in the mirror. Reflecting on his new look, he said, "This up here [gesturing to his head] matches this in here [gesturing to his chest/heart]." This was a critical moment in Nancy's understanding of her child's gender and his self-identification.

Grace described a similarly transformative moment in her family, when she was watching a Katie Couric television special that featured a transgender teenager. By this point, Grace had started researching about gender-nonconforming children on the internet. Nick, who had just turned seven, wandered into the room to watch it, and Grace purposefully did not say anything, waiting to see how he would react. His response to the program, delivered via Post-it notes, proved instrumental to Grace and her husband's trans-affirmative decisions moving forward:

> I just kind of watched him watch it . . . he said, "You mean I'm not stuck this way?" . . . I said, "Not if you don't want to be" . . . and then he ran over and grabbed a Post-it note and wrote on it, [which] said, "How do I get new private parts?" . . . and then he went over and wrote me another note and brought it to me and [it] said, "Mommy, I am a boy." *(Grace starts to cry)* And I just told him, "I know, honey . . . Mommy and Daddy have known for a long time."

Grace also recounted illuminating conversations Nick had had with their therapist: "[The therapist] asked, 'If you could be any age, what age would you be?' and he said, 'Zero' . . . and I asked him, 'Why did you pick zero?' . . . and he goes, 'Because then I would have started out as a boy from the beginning.'"

Another key dimension of these discursive interactions, which surfaced across interviews, was parents' observations that their child enjoyed being perceived as the "other sex" in public. This includes related pronoun attributions from others, which the child often did not want the parent to correct.[18] The following account from Marie is a clear example of this:

> There was a year in there that my child was *insisting* on telling strangers that he was a boy and that I was not allowed to identify him as my daughter, and he would get really angry with me if I said his name, so I would say between the age of five and six, I did not introduce him as my daughter anymore, and I did not correct people when they identified him as a boy, I just let it go. So that eventually led to [changing his name].

Over time, these kinds of public interactions helped parents to understand their child's desire for recognition as the "other sex," further laying the groundwork for transgender identifications and transitions.

Despite the plethora of poignant dialogues and verbal declarations in parents' stories, not all parents recall adamant "cross-gender" declarations from their children, and these parents offered various accounts for why that might be. Linda, for example, attributed Violet's lack of assertiveness about being identified as a girl to her husband's side of the family. As she said, "They will be polite until it makes you uncomfortable." But Linda also attributed this to the fact that no one was willing to recognize Violet as a girl. As Linda reflected, in anguish, on our call, "She was learning to squash that part of herself . . . a very, very fundamental aspect of one's self-expression as a human being [was] getting slowly choked to death by the environment." Similarly, Karen said that "Izzy was not saying, '*I am a boy!*' all the time, he was just saying it more through his choices and actions . . . so it's not like my son was demanding to be [transitioned at five or six years old]." Karen felt that Izzy's adopted status was what made him feel less secure in explicitly demanding a boy identification from her, as she feels he already has anxiety about his place within wider family relations.

Marie did not recall specific identificatory statements within her household either, only out in public: "I think he believed me when I told him that he was a girl, I don't think he wanted to challenge me on that . . . he has never insisted to me that he is a boy, but he's insisted that I identify him as a boy to others." In these instances, direct self-identifications from the children are lacking in parents' accounts, another important difference across cases. Nevertheless, the verbal declarations described here, and parents' candid dialogues with their children about their (trans)gendered sense of self, were consequential in parents' developing understandings of their children.

As seen in Wendy's experiences, children's commentary about their bodies was significant in parents' understandings as well. These kinds of comments also informed parents' decisions about medical options later in the children's lives, once it became developmentally appropriate, which I return to in chapter 4. A child's relationship to their body is highly personal terrain, and these were some of the data over which I deliberated most about sharing or recording. However, I asked parents about this information (*"Did your child ever say anything to you about their body?"*), if it didn't already surface on its own in our interviews, to capture the degrees to which "body dysphoria" impacted their understandings of their children.

Like other facets of parents' observations, there was variation and at times ambiguity here, both within and across cases—perhaps more so regarding the body than with any other variable. To be sure, according to parents' reports, almost all transgender children (and several gender-nonconforming children) indicated to their parents at some point that they had a desire for alternative anatomical characteristics. But most of these instances could not be characterized as extreme distress or "trapped-in-the-wrong-body" feelings. Kari, for example, felt that Emma was at once comfortable with her present anatomy and desiring of different anatomy in the future. This prompted Kari to consider a wider range of gendered and embodied possibilities on behalf of her daughter:

> I think that you should be allowed to be born a male and transition to a female and have male parts and still be a female. . . . This is not a blanket statement, this is particular for Emma right now, she does not seem uncomfortable having a penis, and I hope to continue that with her, because she *wants* to have a vagina, she's like, "Well, when I grow up, am I going to have a vagina?" and I said, "I don't know, you might" . . . but she doesn't—like I know of kids her age that [are uncomfortable with their bodies and she isn't].

Similar nuance was exhibited by Becca, a forty-four-year-old, white, upper-middle-class, heterosexual-identified married woman and mother of Bo. In our first interview, Becca claimed she had observed no body dysphoria in Bo, seven years old at the time, and explicitly cited this as the reason she had *not* yet identified her as transgender. As of our second interview, however, Bo was nine years old and living as a transgender girl, and was fully planning on pursuing hormone treatments, excitedly so. As these examples indicate, parents' awareness of their children's potential desire for body change was variable both within and across cases.

Other parents reported more explicit interests in body change from their children, starting in their toddler years. For example, when I asked Karen to give me specific examples of how Izzy expressed that to her as a young child, she answered me matter-of-factly: "Uh, how about, '*I want a penis*'?" Similarly, Julie said of Macy: "She would ask me questions her whole life about why she has a penis, and when I allowed her to start wearing dresses, she said, 'Is my penis going to go away? Did *you* have a penis? Why don't you have one?'" Interestingly, many parents also cited a child's stated desire for, or stated aversion to, having their own children when they are older—often in terms of having "babies in their own bellies." (Children assigned male expressed an interest in this, while children assigned female children tended not to in parents' reports.) While these sentiments could well be true for cisgender children, too, parents paid specific attention to these aspects of children's sensibilities, and sometimes expressly inquired about them. All told, children's verbal declarations about their sense of self, and about their bodies, marked substantial factors in parents' developing understandings of their children.

Coming to "Transgender"

Despite holding at least a baseline regard for gender-neutral parenting principles, all parents met a critical demarcation within the norms and expectations of the gender binary, where their children's self-expressions became overly uncomfortable or troublesome for them, or at least warranted more concerted attention. This is seen clearly in Martsy and Emilio's story earlier in this chapter, as well as Jayne and Glenn's in the introduction. Their children's interests seemed to demand more than parents' principles could accommodate or make sense of, especially when it came to children's "cross-gender" identity statements. Several of the poignant comments and conversations detailed earlier mark that critical threshold for parents. In seeking guidance and input, parents often turned to professionals, either mental health professionals or starting with their main pediatrician.

Alongside these efforts with clinicians, however, parents also started conducting internet research. I learned from parents that their forays into trans-affirmative parenting often started with a Google search, to the effect of "boys who want to wear dresses" or "boys who like girl things." As noted in the introduction, parents quickly discovered an extensive virtual community of other parents with gender-nonconforming children online. These networks, including the regional support groups they led them to, proved highly formative in parents' journeys and approaches, often more so than the therapists they consulted. As recounted by Patrice, a fifty-year-old, white, upper-middle-class, bisexual-identified woman and mother of Casey, a nine-year-old transgender girl, "I don't really remember what changed my mind [about Casey's gender], I think it was maybe realizing there were other kids just like Casey. . . . My [ex-wife] helped to start the [support group] here in [town] . . . so that Casey could find other kids like herself." A similar process occurred for Julie: "After one meeting, I decided I'm going to let him wear some more things . . . and after the second meeting . . . I just decided I'm going to let him buy a dress." Through online research, support group interactions, and eventual conference experiences, parents became immersed in a gender-expansive consciousness, discourse, and "diagnostic community."[19] In this community, all of parents' observations and experiences with children over the years start becoming intelligible as a matter of "transgender."

The exogenous influence of all this parent-led training and education offers parents what medical and mental health practitioners were often hesitant to endorse: a clear understanding of a child and, in turn, the practical steps forward that such an understanding entails. Given parents' initial associations with "transgender," the affirmative, normalizing effects of this community on parents' understandings are profound. Claire told me that our interview reminded her of their own "transphobia" when they started their journey, including toward trans terminology. It was actually the moderator of one of the online listservs who told Claire that "transgender" is indeed relevant to Andy, at which point she and Rick started using the term. These communities also expose parents to the prospects of nonbinary, gender-fluid, and gender-queer gender identities, which I discuss more fully in chapter 4.

The impact of this community on parents' developing understandings was also evident in their frustrations with the therapists they were consulting off-line. It was not uncommon for parents to find these initial consultations frustrating and unhelpful. Several parents told me that their original doctor or counselor told them "not to worry," that it was "just a phase," or to attempt more middle-ground, "gender-neutral" options with the child. This approach seemed nonviable in the face of their child's unwavering "cross-gender" self-expressions, which often brought a mounting sense of conflict, antagonism, and/or unhappiness, for both parents and children. Parents felt that these professionals had little to no experience with childhood gender nonconformity and were not versed enough to guide them either way. As Wendy said:

> The thing that discourages me most is the education of the . . . mental health professionals. It is outrageous, we go to [a big research hospital], it is like the cutting-edge teaching hospital, it's supposed to be the most innovative, forward, progressive kind of hospital there is . . . [but] there was not one person in there that had any gender experience.

In addition, a few parents worried that the clinician was eager to get their feet wet in new therapeutic terrain and was using their child's case as training wheels. Karen, for example, was first advised by a therapist to consider dressing more femininely herself, as a model for Izzy. Indeed, many parents told me it was these kinds of encounters with inexperienced professionals that motivated their participation in my project, so that future parents could avoid them.

Several mothers were frustrated that their initial consultations did not give them the definitive answer or "diagnosis" they were looking for, which felt especially important in the face of skeptical family members. Grace, for example, was very upset with their first counselor, who was still uncertain about seven-year-old Nick's gender nonconformity. The counselor did not yet want to rule out homosexuality as a possible explanation and recommended more "data collection." Grace, however, felt that she had plenty of "data" since they first took Nick to see him at age four, and ultimately pursued other options through her own therapist. Martsy and Meredith were also hoping for some kind of official designation, but were dismayed when their psychologists hesitated to make claims either way, citing the limited long-range research on transgender children at the time. These frustrations indicated that parents had already developed their own strong transgender understandings of their children, based on the other parent-advocacy networks, and were seeking a definitive stamp of assurance from the professionals who were vested with the authority to give it.

In fact, both Martsy and Nicole were familiar with the gender dysphoria diagnosis from their own graduate studies and had a copy of the *DSM* in their households. They started consulting it when they first started wondering about their children's behaviors. As recalled by Nicole, a forty-six-year-old, white, upper-middle-class, heterosexual-identified married woman and mother of Sadie, a twelve-year-old transgender girl: "[That] really solidified—I kind of diagnosed her [at three years old], before I took her to the specialist . . . it was life-altering, when I read that, like, *We definitely have a problem and I need to get her into somebody*." Indeed, the "constellation" of behaviors, preferences, and verbalized self-expressions parents cataloged over the years closely align with the *DSM*'s criteria for gender dysphoria, but they were used here by these parents as a framework for affirmation, support, and transition, not correction.

For many parents, it took several trials and referrals before they found a counselor they felt was familiar enough with the issues to assist. Based on the geographic regions represented within my sample, I sensed that there were one or two forerunning therapists who treated the bulk of an area's families with gender-nonconforming children. These specialists' names spread quickly within parents' support group networks. One such therapist I spoke with provides children with a "gender worksheet" of sorts, where children complete statements such as, "I was born with a (boy/girl) body, I think I have the heart of a (boy/girl), I think I have the brain of a (boy/girl)." Unlike parents' original consultants, these therapists advocate "following the child's lead," and honor the identities and expressions the children claim, including if this means a formal social transition.

Along with searching for a therapist who seemed versed in childhood gender nonconformity—and who was open to a transgender "diagnosis"—parents also rallied other professionals to learn the terrain.

Marie, for example, along with a group of other parents, organized a medical training for doctors in their region, whom many parents found resistant to, or unfamiliar with, hormone therapy. These parents recruited one of the leading specialists in the United States to conduct this training, and helped push for the formation of one of the now major US medical clinics. In a similar vein, Trish, a fifty-one-year-old, white, middle-class, heterosexual-identified married woman, brought their pediatrician several articles she had researched on the use of hormone blockers for children, as a means of convincing him to pursue them for Joe, her eleven-year-old transgender boy. In these ways, parents took a direct hand in educating the professionals or "gatekeepers" from whom they were seeking authorized treatment for their children, not unlike the approach that many transgender adults must resort to in health care.[20]

With social transition, children are formally recognized and affirmed as the sex category with which they identify, by their parents and by other adults in their lives whom their parents inform—including principals, teachers, extended family, neighbors, old friends, and others—and they are newly enrolled in school as such. Social transition also includes new pronouns and new names, if requested, and full permission to wear whatever clothing, hairstyle, and so forth, the child desires. For neighbors, Karen wrote a letter explaining the transition and requesting that they refer to Izzy by his affirmed gender and pronouns, which she kept on tiny cards that were easily dispensable when she saw them around the neighborhood. It was also not uncommon for parents to send formal letters to other parents at their children's school, explaining what gender nonconformity is and requesting respect for their decision.

A few parents in my sample came into their awareness of "transgender" through alternative avenues. Several parents in my study were referred to outside resources or professionals by friends, coworkers, or teachers, who had observed their child as significantly gender-nonconforming on their own. Harmony, for example, a forty-year-old, white, upper-middle-class, heterosexual-identified married woman and mother of Baldwin, an eight-year-old transgender boy, was asked by teachers to speak at a staff training regarding her gender-nonconforming child. Baldwin had been presenting as a boy at school and often told peers he was a boy, before Harmony was even aware of childhood transgender possibilities. At the training, she met the moderator of a local

support group. She started attending the group, which eventually catalyzed her identification of Baldwin as transgender. Harmony told me
that in hindsight, she felt this was part of the teachers' tacit "plan" to
educate her about her child.

These experiences mark a clear contrast from those I cataloged during my first interviews in 2009, in which parents recalled feeling utterly
alone in the social landscape and that no one had heard of childhood
transgender possibilities. No friend or teacher in their midst recommended that they look into their child's "gender issues" more concertedly or referred them to a particular therapist or support group—let
alone invited them to a staff training on gender-nonconforming children. On the contrary, they were the ones who often pushed schools for
staff training or organized support groups in their communities from
scratch. This testifies to the rapidly growing advocacy infrastructure
that has developed around gender-nonconforming and transgender
children, including in schools, communities, hospitals, and other institutional milieus across the United States and Canada.

Conclusion

This chapter captures a rich tapestry of experiences that parents had
with their children, from the clothes, toys, and activities their children
preferred to children's repeated articulations about their sense of self.
This detailed inventory of experiences proves a key means through
which parents validate and legitimatize transgender identifications for
their children, and it showcases the *child-driven* engine of the phenomenon, versus any forced "agendas" on parents' parts. Some have used
the notion of parents' "influence" on their children to question parents' trans-affirmative decisions.[21] My detailed reporting of the data
here is intended in part to honor and reiterate these rich, *child-rooted*
accounts.

Starting with at least a modicum of "gender-neutral" principles in parents' approaches, these stories demonstrate the profoundly *child-centered*
nature of the paradigm. The *children's* actions, expressions, and preferences in these contexts—contrary to the normative expectations of their
assigned sex—are what lead parents to consider, quite seriously, if there
is something "more" to their behaviors that warrants exploring. However,

these stories also demonstrate the significance of the parents' active—or reactive—role. These parents provided a developmental environment that offered at least a baseline level of openness to gender nonconformity, wherein opportunities for children's "cross-gender" expressions and identifications would be possible, versus totally disallowed. It is the adult figures in these children's lives who then observed and listened to their children in these significant ways, from agreeing to the first princess costume or haircut to ultimately seeking trans-affirmative counseling, education, and support. Here, through everyday interactions, the children reveal who they are, and their parents "scramble," as one mom put it, to ultimately understand, facilitate, and affirm that sense of self. In these ways, parents' efforts are duly emblematic of broader cultural trends in child-centered, intensive, and bidirectional parenting.

Parents' observations and experiences were heavily inflected by the birth sex assignments of the children. Children assigned female could live and express themselves rather unremarkably in a more masculine "tomboy" space early on, in a way children assigned male could not in a feminine capacity. Per many parents' stories, children presumed to be little "boys" simply did not have access to a comparable, problem-free, gender-variant space. However, parents of transgender boys testified to the eventual limits of the "tomboy" epithet, too, which could not explain or account for the "extremity" of their child's masculinity, as Nancy put it. Tellingly, Grace was taking Nick to a therapist as of age four. Nancy, Karen, Monica, and Dan were feeling concerned by the time their children were five years old. In these ways, these parents' stories complicate the narrative that children assigned female necessarily have more leeway; at a certain point, their behaviors seemed like just as much of a "problem" as the behaviors of children assigned male, sometimes by comparable ages (four to five years old).

To be sure, there were noticeable patterns and similarities across cases, which are what bring parents like these together in online forums and live support groups, as well as to my own research project. But there were also key exceptions and caveats, challenging the idea of any one uniform profile for transgender children. Not all children had unequivocal appeal for the "other sex's" stereotypical accoutrements, even though these kinds of observations prove crucial to many parents' understandings. Indeed, several parents listed playtime preferences that were quite "stereotypical" for their children's assigned birth sex, such as trucks, cars, and dinosaurs for the transgender girls or baby dolls for the transgender boys. Not all children were vocal or adamant about a "cross-gender" identification either, or demanded this of their parents. And many children's degree of body dysphoria, loosely defined, presented in more complex and varying forms than "I'm in the wrong body." In a few notable cases, parents did not perceive any embodied discomfort at all. As various institutional agents and structures, including schools and the health professions, are called upon to support transgender children, it will be important to attend to the array of experiences that might constitute a transgender childhood, lest a parent or professional "hang their hat" on things a child did or didn't say, or did or didn't do, that do not "fit the profile," as one advocate put it to me.

Many scholars have challenged the traditional gender stereotypes that adult transgender persons have been subjected to, particularly by the "gatekeepers" of the medico-psychological establishment. Historically, one's claim to a transgender identification, and related medical treatments, hinged on one's ability to present as a (hetero)normative man or woman to professionals, with stereotypically masculine or feminine interests and expressions.[22] In other words, assigned females had to present as conventionally masculine men who liked women, and assigned males had to present as conventionally feminine women who liked men, to get the treatment they desired. One of the first parents I ever spoke with, Clarise, a white, middle-class, heterosexual-identified married woman in her fifties, interrogated just this kind of gender-normative scrutiny.[23] She felt that, many years prior, she and others had risked exacting these stereotypes on her own transgender son, who enjoyed many stereotypically feminine things as a child. Clarise asserted that her son's feminine interests should not be taken as at odds with his male identification, echoing precisely Seeber's interventions about bodies, behaviors, and identities:

> I'm not sure who decided what was girly and what wasn't. . . . I happen to be the mother of many children [five]. I really found that if I was able to offer my children different choices . . . or just be open to whatever they chose . . . if I had dolls and trucks and blocks and art supplies . . .

they didn't seem to gravitate toward what they were supposed to do according to their gender, and I don't think children will, actually, I think that's really a social thing that we're very unaware of a lot of times that we do to children. So why did my [trans] son like to wear skirts? Well, *pfft*, why not? They're pretty cool. . . . I don't have a problem looking back at his childhood, seeing the dresses and whatever and saying, *Well, he [can still] be a transgender person.* . . . I struggled with that at first because people were telling me what the transgender narrative for childhood was and it didn't fit my child . . . there seems to be so much emphasis on, *What did your child play with, how did they dress, did she say she was a boy?*

Expanding what transgender can mean and look like for any particular child extends a gender-inclusive, feminist parenting agenda for *all* children, widening the range of "masculine" and "feminine" options that are available to anybody, and any body, be they cisgender, gender-nonconforming, or other. These principles do not presume any set of behaviors, interests, or expressions for any body *or* identity. They also allow for a range of embodiments for children that further disrupt the sex/gender binary. While these principles may be clear to gender-inclusive parents, scholars, and advocates, they may not be as clearly realized or practiced outside of the childhood transgender scenario. In this way, trans-affirmative parenting may help usher in for all families the true "revolutionary" potential that feminist parenting beckoned decades ago.[24] Though certain strains of feminism have been hostile to transgender identity—dubbed "TERF" or "trans-exclusionary radical feminist"—this chapter highlights the truly trans-inclusive potential of feminism's legacy.[25]

In the chapters ahead, I shift my focus to the three main conceptual areas outlined in the introduction, starting with *gender and sexuality*. In making sense of their children's gender-nonconforming expressions, parents also grapple with divergent interpretive grids for understanding what they mean, often in terms of gender identity ("truly trans") and sexual orientation ("just gay"). As Julie expressed earlier, she originally wondered if her child might be gay, not transgender. In the next chapter, I examine the ways in which parents compared and contrasted these different grids of interpretation, both for their children and for others. These newfound conceptual reckonings between "gender" and "sexuality" are shifting and lifting deep-rooted cultural connections between gender nonconformity and homosexuality, to particularly gender-expansive ends.

2

"Our World Has Been Rocked"

Gender and Sexuality

I know that the research that we have until this point, from
what I've read and you may correct me if I'm wrong, but one
in four [kids] essentially at this point continues on the transgender path and maybe two out of the remaining three wind
up to be gay, and I guess that's a majority, but I don't think
that's going to hold true over the coming years.
—Janice, parent

Throughout my conversations with parents, "gender-nonconforming"
broadly described a child whose self-expressions significantly contrasted with the expectations of their assigned birth sex, but who was
not necessarily "transgender." As my interviewees said, there is a whole
"spectrum" of gendered variation, and only some children on that spectrum are "truly transgender"—as one advocate put it, those "further
to the right on that spectrum." However, parents' distinctions between
"gender-nonconforming" and "truly transgender" carried fluid connotations and associations, sometimes referring to matters of binary and
nonbinary *gender identity*, other times referring to *sexual orientation*.
For example, "further to the right on the spectrum" sometimes implied
a child who is more *binary*-identified than a *nonbinary* child "in the
middle," and other times it implied a child who is more "transgender"
than "just gay." As such, what distinguished "gender-nonconforming"
from "truly transgender" was up for grabs in our conversations. The
proverbial "spectrum" my participants invoked allowed for *both (trans)
gender* and *(homo)sexual* possibilities.

In line with mainstream LGBT rights discourses, my interviewees
held *gender identity* and *sexual orientation* as fundamentally, ontologically distinct parts of the self.[1] However, as indicated in the instances

above, "gender" and "sexuality" were *not* always conceived as radically separate spheres of the self, but surfaced instead as a morphing *continuum of possibilities*, with room for negotiation and reinterpretation. Sometimes gender nonconformity was a matter of *sexuality and sexual orientation* ("just gay"), other times it signaled something about one's *gender identity*, and other times maybe both were relevant. But this is precisely what the concept of a "spectrum" allows for—fluidity, ambiguity, and change, versus fixed and finite categories. This marked one key area, I argue, where parents' practices and perspectives actually troubled and shifted reigning LGBT rights discourses—to gender-expansive ends.

The history of "just gay" and "truly trans" outcomes for childhood gender nonconformity is a well-documented facet of this terrain, as noted in the introduction.[2] In this chapter, however, I seek to emphasize the *generative, productive* potential of comparing these outcomes, through which parents imagine, expand, and legitimize *(trans)gendered* possibilities along a "spectrum" of meanings, versus simply distinguish them from *(homo)sexual* ones. Of course, these constructions carry a host of caveats. Many advocates would reject the notion of a simple, linear spectrum in which "transgender" is imagined as something "more" nonconforming than "just gay." A multidimensional matrix would make more sense, with separate axes for gender identity, gender expression, sexual orientation, and embodiment.[3] Moreover, my participants well understood that "gay" and "trans" were not mutually exclusive. A trans person, for example, could also sexually identify as gay, queer, or bisexual. Nor does the "spectrum" necessarily preclude cisgender and/or heterosexual possibilities. Overall, I encountered much more nuance and sophistication than that in my participants' understandings. This chapter, however, focuses on those instances when my participants explicitly compared "just gay" and "truly trans" as divergent outcomes for—and possible meanings of—gender nonconformity. Through these deliberations, *(trans)gendered* interpretations gain meaning and significance.

Parents' distinctions between "truly trans" and "just gay" are arguably at the crux of the trans-affirmative model: to raise a child as categorically "transgender" hinges on seeing their nonconformity as a matter of gender and gender identity, *not* sexuality and sexual orientation. Gender-based interpretations help to relinquish assigned sex designations; sexuality-based ones do not. Heather, for example, a fifty-six-year-old, white, upper-middle-class, lesbian-identified married woman and mother of Samantha, an eleven-year-old transgender girl, lamented the associations between gender nonconformity and homosexuality, especially for young children: "If you started talking about a four-year-old's 'sexual preference' with any number of people, they would look at you like you needed to be institutionalized." Given these understandings, some advocates would question devoting a chapter in this book to the topic of sexuality and sexual orientation. Some parents, such as Heather, might find it borderline offensive.[4] But from a sociocultural perspective, homosexuality is intimately tied to the story and to the historical juncture it represents. This includes, precisely, parents' rejections of it as a relevant explanatory framework.

Contrary to contemporary LGBT distinctions, the relationship between "gender" and "sexuality" marks a deeply entwined, cross-cultural legacy. As Valentine wrote in *Imagining Transgender*:

> In much contemporary social theory and grassroots political activism, it is a matter of faith and theory that "gender" and "sexuality" are distinct—if related—arenas of human experience. . . . [But] "gender" and "sexuality" are neither self-evident experiences nor natural explanatory frameworks. Rather, they are also categories with complicated histories and politics, and which deserve critical attention.[5]

In the nineteenth and twentieth centuries, for example, the "homosexual" was first conceived as a "gender inversion" condition among Western European psychiatrists.[6] Visible forms of gender transgression marked the emergence of gay subcultures in the United States and later of the gay liberation movement.[7] And various scholars from anthropology, sociology, and history have demonstrated that what is understood as "gay" or "trans"—or "straight," for that matter—in one culture or time period is not so easily translatable to another.[8] Many of Valentine's low-income informants of color, for example, sooner identified as "gay" than "trans," including those who were assigned male at birth but who lived and presented as women. Because of this, Valentine theorized shifts in meaning for "gender" and "sexuality" across ethnoracial, cultural, and class boundaries, where the meaning of one category ("sexuality") is not necessarily *distinct from* the other ("gender"), but may actually *leak* or *shift into* it.[9]

Broadly, I characterize these lines of scholarship as "social construction-ist." The "constructionist" theoretical paradigm underscores the social, historical, and discursive factors that help shape "gender" and "sexual" possibilities in any given cultural moment, versus their biological roots.[10]

Bryant's scholarship on "gender disorders in childhood" diagnoses is also instructive here. Bryant argues that these diagnoses have had *productive* and *generative* functions for expressions of gender and sexuality, as much as they manage or diagnose them.[11] In other words, the development and application of the diagnostic criteria have helped to *produce* certain ideas about what homosexuality and transsexuality can look like, versus simply identified and treated them. Bryant also argues that these diagnoses serve as sites of contestation and resistance among practitioners, as much as they serve to medicalize and pathologize gender nonconformity.[12] Bryant's perspectives resonate with the parental deliberations examined in this chapter, in which parents contest and re-ject the "authority" of longitudinal studies on gender-nonconforming children. On these terms, "gender" and "sexuality," "gay" and "trans" are as much open to contestation and reinterpretation as they are objective realities to be identified, distinguished, and managed.

Gender theorist Judith Butler's concept of the "heterosexual matrix" further emphasizes the inextricable link between "gender" and "sexuality." Butler argues that heterosexuality depends upon the notion of *gendered* binary "opposites"—that is, on masculine males and feminine females, who are expected to be "naturally" mutually attracted and to reproduce.[13] In effect, normative sexuality in modern Western culture helps produce the idea of normatively gendered subjects, deviations from which raise the specter of homosexuality and often result in dis-ciplinary consequences. Indeed, people still often read—and harass—gender nonconformity as a matter of homosexuality, particularly for males, such that "homophobia" might be better understood as transpho-bia.[14] The use of the "gay panic defense" by perpetrators of transgender hate crimes is another stark cultural referent for this.[15] Similarly, parent-ing guides and experts have long regarded gender-atypical preferences in children as an indicator of adult same-sex orientation.[16] Concerns about "gay" outcomes are often what lead parents to address these be-haviors in the first place, especially for children assigned male. Tellingly, one couple in my study was reported to Child Protective Services (CPS) for allegedly "forcing a child to be a homosexual." And as noted in Jayne and Glenn's story, a family friend plainly asked them at a family gathering how they would feel about raising a "gay son."

In short, it is hard for contemporary parents of gender-nonconforming children to avoid the "gay" reference. Teasing apart the interpretive grids of "gender" and "sexuality" is thus no small part of parents' journeys. It is the ideological bedrock of their approach, and the means of navigating the ontological chaos and confusion their children's behaviors represent, both now and in the future. I harness the insights from the preceding scholars to analyze the ways in which my own research participants actively construct, produce, and normalize *(trans)gendered* understandings of their children, in ways that are distinct from "just gay" and that were unavailable to previous generations of children. In "constructionist" terms, these distinctions are not merely descriptive, but *productive,* helping to imagine and expand the very categories of being that they name. To be clear, this analysis does not mean to question the identifications of these children, or of anyone else, past or present. I believe, as these parents know, that a child is only what they express themselves to be, at any given moment. I do mean to show how, through the discursive and deliberative processes available to them, my participants give *transgender* possibilities increasing credence and viability on "the spectrum," for their kids and for others.

Gender and Sexuality at a Crossroads

In the following sections, I address four major areas in which distinctions and deliberations between "trans" and "gay" permeated the interviews: (1) parents' early thoughts about their child's gender nonconformity as an indicator of an incipient gay orientation; (2) critical evaluations of previous research on gender-nonconforming children; (3) cisgender, gay-identified adults in parents' lives; and (4) parents' "openness to change" about their child's identity over the life course. In some instances, "trans" and "gay" are indeed held up as fundamentally, ontologically distinct aspects of the self, and thus as different types of gender nonconformity—one is a matter of *gender identity*, the other is a matter of *sexual orientation*. In other instances, however, something murkier presents, such that the boundaries between these separate realms of self become more porous and permeable. In these moments, "gay" kinds of nonconformity, as these were originally perceived or conceptualized, are reinterpreted as "trans" kinds of nonconformity after all. Through this deliberative, discursive, and conceptual work, *(trans)gender*, and not just *(homo)sexuality*, becomes an increasingly legitimate grid of understanding for gender nonconformity.

Early "Gay" Interpretations

Not surprisingly, many parents originally wondered about their child's gender nonconformity in terms of sexual orientation. Janice, for example, a thirty-eight-year-old, white, working-class, gay-identified woman and mother of Eileen, a seven-year-old transgender girl, recalled an early incident when Eileen was crying in her crib. Janice said that Eileen seemed consoled by the prospect of matching curtains and decor, displaying an interest in interior design that struck Janice as atypical for a "boy": "I thought, *Oh the kid's going to be gay* . . . so I really wasn't thinking gender at that point, I was thinking more [sexual] orientation." She added, "I didn't even know gender identity was a *thing*, I still didn't think this was a matter of gender identity so much as a future [sexual] orientation issue." Similarly, Julie recalled that her friends originally mentioned the possibility of her child being transgender to her, but she resisted, thinking she might be gay instead: "I said, 'I'm kind of worried,' and they said, 'You know, maybe he's transgender,' and I was like, 'No he's not!' I thought maybe he would be gay." I heard similar considerations among parents of the presumed "tomboys," too. As Monica said, "I actually thought for a long time that Hayden was just a lesbian. . . . I was actually hoping for that, but I started reading books."

Monica's comment reflects the sentiments of many parents once they started encountering transgender explanations for their children's behaviors—that "gay" would be the preferable, "easier" outcome, for both parent and child, compared with transgender. Karen grew quite impassioned about this position in our interview:

> I can deal with gay; if you're gay you can still use the bathroom, you can still wear your clothing, you can still keep your name and your mother

doesn't get called to the county for abusing you, you know what I mean? . . . I signed my kid up for swim lessons and I had to bring him home in his wet suit in the car in the snow because we don't feel comfortable in any [public] bathroom. This is an incredibly difficult life . . . our world has been *rocked*. What's *gay*? I don't care.

These comments refute the notion that parents embark on transgender transitions for their children because they are subliminally "homophobic," an argument that has surfaced in public discourse and debate about the phenomenon.[17] A few parents, however, claimed that "gay" was never on their radar, in part because any sexual orientation at all seemed irrelevant to their young, prepubescent child (like Heather's earlier comment). Nevertheless, ongoing research regarding their child's persistent "cross-gender" expressions ultimately led parents to reject a sexuality-based grid of interpretation, as exhibited in the following testimonials.

Notorious Statistics

For both parents and professionals, the statistical legacy of the research on gender-nonconforming children is well known: most gender-nonconforming children grow up to be cisgender and "just gay" while transgender is a rare outcome.[18] Parents readily encounter the lore of these studies through online research, in parental forums, and from the professionals they consult. This oft-cited body of research, and the notorious statistics it has produced, proved a major site where distinctions and deliberations between "truly trans" and "just gay" surfaced in interviews. However, the ways in which this research was deemed irrelevant to a transgender child varied. On the one hand, some parents argued that these studies really only addressed "gender-nonconforming" children, versus categorically "transgender" children like their own. In other words, these studies refer to the *type* of gender nonconformity that is *not* transgender, and thus the studies are irrelevant. As Wendy said, "I couldn't find anything on transgender children, just more gender-variant and gender-nonconforming. . . . They didn't even use transgendered kids, they were just taking gender-nonconforming kids and considering them as transgendered." Similarly, Nicole advised:

It's a very small fraction of people that become adult transgender people, there's [many] more gay, lesbians than there [are] transgender, so chances are if you have a kid that's gender-nonconforming, the odds are they're going to be gay more than they are transgender . . . [but] it was very obvious with [Sadie], there was just no doubt, there was so much more than gender-nonconforming going on there.

On these terms, the children from the studies did not turn out to be transgender because they represented a different kind of gender nonconformity in the first place—the kind, at least implicitly, that is more likely related to *(homo)sexuality* and *sexual orientation*. Other parents echoed a "fundamental difference" between gender-nonconforming children, the likes of those most frequently reflected in the studies, and their own transgender child. As Bruce said:

I was aware of studies that say that large numbers, like 80 to 90 percent of boys who are gender-nonconforming, end up becoming gay men, and when I read that that was very familiar to me because I am a gay man. . . . I had my own sort of long history with pushing at gender, [but] when my child did it at such an early age and really with very few examples— like we're two gay men, and we're gender-conforming gay men, we do not have dresses in the house, we do not have earrings in the house—I thought, *Wow, this is something to take note of*, but then it wasn't just sort of play, it just seemed so in her *core being*.

Here, different types of gender nonconformity fracture between the realms of *(homo)sexuality* and *(trans)gender*.

I encountered notions of distinct types of gender nonconformity among the professionals and advocates I interviewed as well. As Neil said, "Some of the numbers that get reported about persistence of who does end up being trans, and oh 'three-quarters of them will end up being gay,' that's a skewed population . . . we're talking about apples and oranges, we're talking about different kids." Several other advocates noted how wide the net is cast, too, for the kinds of children captured in the studies. This implied that *any* gender-nonconforming child could be included and assessed, especially a male child, versus those who are "truly trans." As Gail, another advocate, said, "What do we mean by 'gender-exploring'? So a boy throws on a dress . . . [or] puts on a pair of sparkly shoes that are pink, it draws attention. Girls get those Michael Jordan sneakers, nobody even knows." All of these claims work to dismiss the relevance and authority of the "just gay" body of research, especially in terms of referring to a different *type* of gender nonconformity altogether.

On the other hand, however, my informants also levied incisive methodological critiques about the studies, which they believed rendered them flawed and unreliable anyway. On these terms, the irrelevance of the studies was a matter of flawed research, not a matter of different types of kids. Wendy, for example, also said, "A lot of the kids weren't even available for the follow-up, but they still counted [them] in their studies, so their statistics were way off." As she explained to me, without robust and accurate follow-up by the researchers, no one can really know the veracity of the alleged "just gay" outcomes. Similarly, Meryl, another advocate, said:

> I think that part of the problem with these kinds of studies is that the people that they're talking about . . . were not followed long enough. In other words, when you look at adult transgender people, you can see that some don't come out until their forties, their fifties, their sixties, their *seventies*, so how long were those people followed? . . . [J]ust because somebody hasn't come out as transgender by the time they're twenty-five doesn't mean that we can dismiss [that possibility].

Neil also cited factors that compromised the studies' merits, including their reparative and corrective practices: "Many of the people [who] showed up at the clinic for help were sent to that clinic because there's a lot of pressure to fix it. There's like a whole group of kids who never went . . . or who were very turned off by what was emerging as essentially a reparative approach. I just tend to dismiss that [research] entirely . . . it's so old, the research protocols were horrible." In these instances, factors *other* than essentially different types of gender nonconformity were raised. The kind of nonconformity once written off as "just gay" could well be a matter of "truly trans" after all; it was just poorly studied.

In addition, several of the professionals I interviewed discounted the key "signs" that were often cited for differentiating "just gender-nonconforming" and "truly trans" children, including the kinds of identity statements that a child might make (e.g., "I feel like a girl" or "I *am* a girl"). Some trans children just don't make such statements, they explained, even though many parents wait to hear them. As Gail said:

> I'm basing it on the hundreds and hundreds of intakes I've done, and I'm going to go to the lower end of the age range, particularly the under-sixes, it's just not what I'm hearing, I'm hearing a lot about a parent who . . . [thinks the child has] to say it, they've got all these other signs . . . but they never uttered those exact words. . . . Many parents will say, "He's never said I'm a girl, he's never uttered those words." . . . And it's not definitive of anything . . . sometimes kids don't say it because they don't know they can say it or they don't know, they don't have the verbiage for it.

She continued, "And you have to keep in mind the age of the child and how on board the parent might be or not be in having a transgender child. . . . I think there's a lot of factors that go into the descriptors you use for your child."

These comments resonated with those of Charlotte, a therapist I interviewed, who described a range of children's "temperaments," as well as the retrospective accounts of adult transgender clients. Some children are more adamant about recognition, while some persons do not realize they are transgender until decades later. These factors can also variously affect, and expand, the ways transgender identity might appear in the population:

> I mean . . . young kids, some of them don't really know, it totally depends on temperament, some kids are very clear about what they want about everything, and other kids are not, and so if the child's more anxious or more inhibited in general, [that] is going to play out in this, too, as far as asserting it. . . . [And] what level of consciousness is this? . . . [J]ust with my anecdotal experience with [transgender] adults, and their awareness of this as children, some were fully aware but their parents didn't listen, some were fully aware but didn't know what to do about it, some were not aware and just held off, and they didn't realize what it was until they were adults, some were not aware of *anything* [until adulthood] . . . so it's just

such a broad spectrum of when this becomes very conscious and very uncomfortable . . . enough to . . . do something about it.

All of these insights further muddied firm distinctions between different kinds of childhood gender nonconformity, including how these may be captured in clinical studies or by the parents who observe them. On these grounds, more and more forms of childhood gender nonconformity become relevant to "transgender" assessment and consideration. This recalls Bryant's insights on gender disorder diagnoses as sites of contestation and debate; parents and professionals here contested the longitudinal claims about gender-nonconforming children, such that "just gay" may not be the likely outcome at all. Indeed, despite her firm distinctions earlier, Nicole also gestured to the "blurriness" all of these factors might mean for distinguishing different types of gender nonconformity:

> It's a really, really blurry line between a kid that might just be gender-variant or gender-nonconforming and [a kid who is] transgender, because being transgender is very rare, so I really think you have to analyze that kid and reanalyze and super-analyze and put them under a microscope and ask them a lot of questions before you transition. That should be like the last resort.

While Nicole still posits "truly transgender" as a statistically rare outcome, she also signals the proliferating ways this prospect might be observed, captured, and realized by the parents and professionals supporting any given child. This, in fact, expands and increases the viability of transgender possibilities on parents' interpretive radar, as much as it clarifies and specifies them.

Distinctions and debates between "just gay" and "truly trans" understandings consumed my interview with Leigh, who was one of the first founders of a support group for parents of gender-nonconforming children in the late 1990s. Leigh's principal focus was on children assigned male. Leigh feels that (male) childhood gender nonconformity is almost always a matter of homosexuality, just as the prior longitudinal research has implied. In fact, Leigh's whole impetus for establishing the group was to help other parents become comfortable with gay outcomes and to avoid the repressive measures that she and her husband had practiced with their own gender-nonconforming son in the 1970s and 1980s. This included enrolling him in corrective psychotherapy and forbidding gender-atypical play, which she now considers child abuse.

Even though Leigh had heard about transgender prospects (and actually met with some of the original researchers of gender-nonconforming children in the United States), she told me that the idea of raising socially transitioned, transgender-identified children was virtually nonexistent at the time she started the group. Nor did the term "transgender" ever surface among the mental health professionals she consulted about her own son; it was always about "gay" or not. Despite the wariness and resistance she and her colleagues experienced in trying to publicize the group—supporting "girly boys" or "gentle boys" still felt so taboo at the time, she explained—Leigh learned that the group's web page received more hits than any other page on the hospital's site. As she told me, "You see it was out there, but people didn't know what to do with it." The group's web page reiterated what the research had long suggested—that early childhood gender nonconformity most often results in a gay sexual orientation, not transgender identity. (I sensed this was one key place where parents learned of this statistical legacy.)

Since this time, the group has grown to include children assigned female and transgender-identified children. Leigh expressed concerns to me, however, about the advent of trans-affirmative parenting: "I feel like gay little boys are getting lost again, first of all we didn't let them be gay little boys, and now we're transitioning them all to transgender." Leigh compared the relatively new trans-affirmative paradigm to other "fads" in mental health, which practitioners eventually move away from: "I mean we are prone, as you know, as a society, to look for quick fixes, and then we always overdo it a little bit too much. Some good comes out of it. . . . If we can identify the [transgender] kids early, that would be great, but right now everybody's assuming [they're transgender]." Leigh told me that she has radically retreated from advocating in this domain due to these concerns. In her last e-mail to me, she wrote, "I get too upset about all the kids that are transitioned so early. There is hardly any mention anymore that one-third of gay boys were gender-nonconforming in childhood, even higher with girls. This just breaks my heart."

Leigh's general principle is to tell parents to avoid transitioning until the child is nine or ten years old, unless there is extreme duress and/or body dysphoria. Parents should push the "there-are-all-different-kinds-of-boys" message, versus proposing the option of being a girl "prematurely." Indeed, many of the parents in my sample attempted to reiterate just such messages to their children early on, for both male and female children ("Boys can like those things too"). Over the years, I occasionally heard Leigh's group characterized as one that is more oriented to gender-nonconforming, and not transgender, children. But these impressions varied as to whether this was a matter of the children's authentic identities or if it was the parents themselves who were resistant to explicit "transgender" identifications. Leigh's perspectives, as well as these varying characterizations of her group, are duly emblematic of the often-fraught distinctions between "just gender-nonconforming" and "truly transgender" I encountered among my informants, which were differentially mapped onto *(homo)sexual* and *(trans)gender* grids of interpretation.

For all parents and professionals, a child's perceived level of distress, anxiety, and unhappiness stands as a significant factor in determining their transgender status or not. Given the mental health risks associated with transgender youth, including high rates of suicidality, most advocate that a child who seems severely distraught should be allowed to socially transition.[19] It is worth noting, however, that the new gender dysphoria diagnosis in the *DSM* was devised in part to acknowledge that *not* all trans persons experience distress and that trans experience itself does not necessarily mean distress or warrant psychiatric care.[20] As such, parents waiting for the appearance of extreme distress might rely on a narrow, if misleading, indicator as well, similar to waiting for certain verbal declarations or other "signs" to arise.

I marshal the preceding comments because they expose areas where ostensibly "distinct types" of childhood gender nonconformity were suddenly more permeable or relevant to each other, or at least up for debate. As my informants variously articulated: there wasn't enough follow-up done in the research so several of the cases could be "truly transgender" after all; some of the parents from the old studies might have had reparative aims, actively inhibiting a transgender outcome; our culture's proscriptions for maleness and femaleness impact who gets noticed and researched anyway; some transgender children may be less vocal about their identities and thus less identifiable; and some family environments, not to mention wider sociohistorical contexts, are more receptive to transgender possibilities than others. All of these factors, by parents, professionals, and advocates alike, forge an ever-evolving body of discourse that counters the authority of prior research and legitimizes transgender possibilities. Here, on the imagined "spectrum" of possibilities, formerly "just gay" understandings shift into the realm of "truly trans."

The (Cisgender) Gay Adult

Another site where *(trans)gender* and *(homo)sexual* possibilities converged in our conversations involved cisgender gay-identified adults in parents' lives. These persons surfaced as key figures in parents' growing understandings of their children. Indeed, while transgender adults function as key signifiers in the parent-advocacy community,[21] cisgender gay- and lesbian-identified adults appeared equally if not more significant in my interviews with parents. They either validated what parents had observed as some LGBTQ-related difference in their child, or helped them to distinguish their child from future "just gay" outcomes. Notably, I never explicitly asked parents about gay-identified friends or confidants in their lives. Rather, these adults surfaced organically in parents' accounts. Grace, for example, mentioned a close lesbian friend, whose childhood retrospective stood as a touchpoint for Grace and her husband early on, when they first considered Nick's behaviors as "proto-homosexual":

> G: We were doing more research along the lines of homosexuality and traits and we have a good friend who is a lesbian, so we talked to her about him wanting the boy clothes, saying he was a boy, he would pee standing up outside . . . and our friend said "Oh, yeah, that was me as a child, I wondered why I wasn't a boy," so we kind of thought, *OK, this is how lesbians think, like they do wish that they were boys.*
>
> E: How do you make sense of that now, then?
>
> G: And I told [my husband], I said maybe she is transgender and doesn't really know it, or maybe some lesbians *do* think that way, but there definitely is a difference. . . . Someone who is just a lesbian knows that

they are a certain sex, and they have qualities and like characteristics of the other sex. . . . Like my lesbian friend knows that she's a female but she may like male things, likes to dress more masculine . . . whereas Nick, he yearns to be able to [pee standing up], not out of convenience, because he feels, as a man, as a boy, that he should be able to do that.

In these evolving deliberations, Grace once wondered if her friend was not transgender herself, and originally thought her own child might be a lesbian. Yet, in the face of highly similar childhood profiles and "traits," Grace has ultimately distinguished two kinds of gender nonconformity, where "there definitely is a difference." For her friend, gender nonconformity is a matter of taking on certain gendered qualities that do not affect her female sex identification, whereas for her son, these are a matter of feeling and being *male*. This is an example of parents' intellectual work in carving out explicitly *(trans)gendered* kinds of knowing and understanding along a continuum of possibilities.

Several other mothers confided that they had wondered if gay-identified friends were "really transgender" or if they wanted to be. Tory, for example, mentioned a lesbian friend, with whom she has conversed about gender nonconformity:

I have a friend who is gay who said to me, "If all these options were available when I was small, who knows, I may have transitioned." Even now, she goes, "I still feel like a boy, but you know, it doesn't make me unhappy to have the body I have, and I have a good relationship." And she looks like a boy, 'cause at school the kids will say, "Are you a boy or a girl?" She dresses like a boy, like she has short hair, and I think to myself, well you know what, who knows, maybe Connor will be there, maybe Connor won't, but it just shows that you can be anywhere on the spectrum. I don't know how far to the edge Connor is, only Connor'll know that.

In Tory's musings with her friend, distinctions between gender identity and sexual orientation merge and change on the "spectrum" of variation, and Tory does not rule out a cisgender, gay outcome, even as she now raises Connor as a transgender boy. In these instances, what was once understood as a matter of sexuality is reconsidered as, potentially, a matter of gender too, and vice versa.

Similar comparisons among parents occurred regarding transgender girls and adult gay men, though the planes of reference seemed far stauncher in these instances, signaling a rigidity around maleness to which femaleness seemed less subject on the spectrum. For example, Shella, a forty-three-year-old, white, working-class, heterosexual-identified woman and mother of Tegan, a ten-year-old transgender girl, recalled one interaction she had with a parent at a summer camp for gender-nonconforming children. This other parent surmised the kids were all "just gay":

> [This other mom] said, "You know, I look around and I look at all these boys, and I just think they're gay, that's all." [But] having grown up around a lot of gay people, I've asked a lot of male gay friends about this, none of them say that they ever denied their physical parts, so to me, the difference between a trans person and maybe like a gay boy is that gay men, they love their anatomy. That's not the issue for them.

Here, Shella defines the desire to change or "deny" one's sexual anatomy as a substantial differentiating factor between a transgender child and a gay person. Indeed, all three of the preceding examples indicate parents' attention to their children's embodied sensibilities in making these critical distinctions.

Shella went on to define "gay" as strictly a matter of sexual desire and attraction and irrelevant to her prepubescent child:

> 'Cause when [my daughter] was younger people would say, "Well do you think he's gay?" And I would say, "Well, I don't know." I mean there were no hormones then, how do you know if you're gay? Gay is how you, who you're attracted to, right? That has nothing to do with your identity, but people get that confused, and I understand, so this woman making that blanket statement, I think that's fascinating and it may be true, I mean, Tegan could still turn a corner, she might end up being a gay man. I doubt it, though, because she does not want her body parts.

Shella's thoughts are emblematic of the kinds of intellectual work, and key observations, that parents engage in to differentiate "just gay" from "truly trans" (indeed, Shella indicated that she has asked "a lot of" gay men about this). However, even as she defines them as having "nothing to do with" each other, Shella is careful not to completely discount the former as a future possibility ("She might end up being a gay man"). Evidently, parents come to understand their children as transgender through, in part, extended comparisons to cisgender gay adults. But differentiating "gay" and "trans" in these ways often occurs along an imagined "spectrum" of LGBTQ possibilities, where both realms of gender and sexuality are intermittently relevant, possible, and permeable. This deliberative, discursive process expands how some nonconformities can be coded and understood, in increasingly trans-affirmative ways.

Interestingly, many parents often mused about potential hereditary relationships to other gay-identified family members. Bruce confessed to wondering about his own genetic influence on his child: "And don't you know that there's a part of me that wonders if somehow I passed on the gene for gender nonconformity." Grace revealed similar musings regarding her father-in-law, who now identifies as gay: "I wonder if it's a hereditary thing. My husband's father is gay. Is it something that maybe is in his bloodline, or just in [our] DNA?" In these ways, homosexuality was often contemplated as a potential genetic source for a child's gender nonconformity, relinking these two separate spheres of self at the earliest stages of development. The double helix of DNA, bridging disparate strands of material in the womb, serves as a fitting metaphor for the ways in which these parents deliberated between *(trans)gender* and *(homo)sexual* grids of interpretation: gay is different from trans, but it still holds powerful potential in accounting for early childhood gender nonconformity. These ruminations also demonstrate parents' biological explanatory models for gendered and sexual difference.

Open to Change

One of the more profound reckonings between *(trans)gender* and *(homo)sexuality* was observed in those instances when parents cited being "open to change," as I coded it in the data—that is, when parents voiced awareness that their child, affirmed as they are now as transgender, could grow up to be a cisgender feminine male or a cisgender masculine female and possibly gay-identified. Of course, parents would not wholly discount the possibility that their children could grow up to identify in cisgender-heterosexual capacities either, but given statistical associations between childhood gender nonconformity and adult homosexuality, not to mention wider cultural associations, they were conscious to include "gay" in the realm of possibilities. While parents felt strongly that their child will always be transgender, they intimated, almost as a moral imperative, that they understood that the "other box" may not always be their child's identification. As Wendy said, "We can't become too comfortable with the [female] box, we have to be prepared for that, we know that we need to be aware of that."

This presents a remarkably open, fluid, and *child-rooted* perspective on the mutability of gender identity and sex category over the life course—and not just of gender expression. There was nothing tentative or playful about the ways in which these parents were honoring their child's "cross-gender" sense of self, including vis-à-vis school administrations, extended family, doctors, and others. Nevertheless, many parents explicitly articulated this potential for change, which is significant in the face of doctors and experts who have publicly opined that these parents risk doing damage by forcing something "too soon."[22] In many ways, these parents embrace the approach of "parenting here and now," even if that means a formal social transition now and a change in that course down the line. On these more fungible, *child-driven* terms, there is nothing to get "wrong." Marie typified this outlook:

> I call him a transgender child right now, but who knows what he will be feeling in the future. My child is attracted to females, so yes, it's possible [he could be gay], and yes, I identify my child as being, you know, butch, and yes, I identify my child as also being transgender. I think that my child is interwoven with all of those, just the word "transgender" is maybe the way I identify him right now. All I really know to be honest is that *today* he identifies as being a boy and he's attracted to girls, so if that makes him a straight transgender boy, then that's what it makes him today, but I don't really know what the future holds for him, I feel that anything is possible, he's only seven.

While parents of transgender boys seemed more open to ambiguity between trans-masculinity and adult homosexuality than parents of transgender girls, awareness of future gay possibilities surfaced among the latter group as well. Claire and Rick, for example, still regarded male homosexuality as potentially relevant to their young transgender daughter, based on research they had found. As Claire said:

> We were also doing research at the time because we still thought—OK, and we still do think—that there's a chance that we're raising someone who will eventually be, you know, identify as a male, possibly, who knows, and gay—so we were looking at the older brother effect, saying look, this is still statistically, she fits this profile.[23]

Similarly, Michelle, a forty-two-year-old, white, middle-class, heterosexual-identified woman and mother of Rian, a five-year-old transgender girl, mentioned a close friend who has a son, eleven years old, who both Michelle and her friend think will be gay as an adult. She and this friend often discussed whether Rian is more like him than transgender. When I asked Michelle how she decided her child is transgender, versus "just" a more "feminine pink boy" like her friend's son, she responded matter-of-factly: "Well, I don't need to know that. Why do I need to know that? I'm supporting Rian where Rian's at now, who Rian needs to be [right now]."

Of course, allowing for the possibility that a child may grow up to identify with their assigned sex is not necessarily a radical viewpoint; for some, it might be a holdout for a more cis-normative outcome. But it also demonstrates parents' endeavors to practice a more fluid perspective on gender and sexuality, especially when they would feel far more comfortable in a fixed, determinate space than wading and waiting through categorical uncertainty. Of all areas up for grabs, no parent expected their child's gender identity to be one of them. In short, while parents embrace their child as the "other sex" in childhood, they do not entirely refute the possibility that their child could grow up to identify as a cisgender, gay adult. This signals lingering associations between, if not openness to, childhood gender nonconformity and adult homosexuality on the "spectrum," even while parents mark "gay" and "trans" as separate entities of the self.

This crossroads between *gender identity* and *sexual orientation* was perhaps best exemplified during my interview with Trish and her eighteen-year-old daughter, Vanessa, the sibling of Joe, a transgender boy. Trish advised that she was offended by popular associations between "gay" and "trans" that the LGBT acronym creates. The former is a "sexual thing," she explained, and unrelated to her son's gender nonconformity:

> I personally don't like "LGBT." LGB is a *sexual* thing, T is a *gender* thing, and they don't belong together in my mind. . . . I think it's disrespectful to transgenders when they're lumped together that way. I understand the history, but I still would love some day for it to be separate so that the general population understands it as separate.

Trish went on to say that she never thought Joe was a "lesbian" "because lesbian is sexual and he was eleven! That's not fair!"

As an example of these distinctions, the family described to me a gay-identified male friend of Trish's, who would often dress up in women's clothes and dance around the house. But Vanessa clarified that "he didn't want to be a girl," it was "all just for fun"—as she said, "it was a sexual thing, it wasn't a gender thing, and that's so different." However, several hours later in the conversation, Vanessa troubled these very distinctions, demonstrating more openness and ambiguity in interpreting these expressions in light of her newfound transgender awareness: "My eyes are more open. That boy wants to be pretty today and have fun? Is it a sexual thing, or a gender thing? That's what I feel has changed for me." Here, what was once so clearly demarcated as "just gay" and a "sexual thing" is now suddenly open to—if not more appropriate for—*(trans)gendered* interpretations, understandings, and ways of knowing.

Conclusion

In line with mainstream LGBT rights discourses, my participants reiterated critical distinctions between gender and sexuality: gender identity is one thing ("trans"), sexual orientation is another ("gay"). However, the sections presented in this chapter also expose instances when those conceptual realms become less fixed and firm, and more porous and open to reinterpretation—just the kind of fluidity and flexibility that the notion of a "spectrum" permits. These deliberations between gender and sexuality, "trans" and "gay," are at the nexus of the gender change occurring among these families and, I would argue, of the social change at large. They are where, and how, *(trans)gender* gains traction as the relevant interpretive grid for nonnormative expression and sensibility—for these parents' kids and for others. This contrasts with the presumptions of parents and professionals during Leigh's parenting career, wherein *(homo)sexuality* was the dominant, if not sole, interpretive grid. Janice actually mused, unprompted, about just such a paradigm shift:

> I know that the research that we have until this point, from what I've read and you may correct me if I'm wrong, but one in four essentially at this point continues on the transgender path and maybe two out of the remaining three wind up to be gay, and I guess that's a majority, but I don't think that's going to hold true over the coming years.

As observed earlier, my interviewees worked to carve out distinct types of gender nonconformity. Previous research that speaks to a "just gay" outcome, for example, did not pertain to their own gender-nonconforming child—and necessarily so, their child is *transgender*, a different *type* of gender nonconformity. In these distinctions, parents identify and define key differentiating criteria, including the desire to modify sexual anatomy (albeit not necessarily) and the articulation that one *is* or *wants to be* the "other sex." Furthermore, several parents claimed that "gay" would be irrelevant to a prepubescent, "prehormonal" child anyway; the latter is strictly a "sexual thing," the other, a "gender thing." With these understandings, parents construct and legitimize a distinctly "transgender" understanding of their child's gender nonconformity, and they allow their child access to the "other box" accordingly, in a way that "just gay" understandings would preclude. Here, "not gay" is definitive and constitutive of "truly trans."

At the same time, however, close cultural associations between gender nonconformity and homosexuality lingered throughout, if not pervaded, parents' conceptions and distinctions. Indeed, "gender identity" and "sexual orientation" are the two realms of interpretation, differentiation, and understanding available to these parents for making sense of children's behaviors. To identify certain kinds of gender nonconformity as "truly trans" demands, at least in part, comparing them to other forms that are "just gay." Emblematic of these associations, several parents wondered if gay-identified family members passed on quintessential genetic material to their children. In these moments, gender and sexuality are not conceived as radically separate realms of the self, but one is actually imagined as the biological source of the other.

More notably, longitudinal studies on gender-nonconforming children were frequently and incisively critiqued for their methodological flaws. Several professionals noted that, for example, a transgender child can express him- or herself in myriad ways, some less overtly than others, which are not always well captured by the research. They also explained that the labeling of a child as "transgender" may be contingent on a host of extrinsic factors, including cultural, familial, and biographical. In all of these instances, parents and professionals were not necessarily referring to distinct types of gender nonconformity but, rather, were opening up space for reinterpretation and reconsideration, where cases formerly understood as "just gay" could well be "truly trans" after all. Parents' intermittent references to gay-identified adults in their milieu, whose nonconformity now struck them as something potentially *(trans)gendered,* too, were further indicative of a deliberative, malleable relationship between these otherwise distinct arenas of self. This is where, on the imagined "spectrum" of possibilities, *transgender* gains significance and opportunity, even as it is distinguished as a rare, specific type. As Vanessa said, "That's what I feel has changed for me." "Just gay" shifts into the realm of "truly trans" understanding.

Biological factors that would explain gender and sexual variation, especially pertaining to genetic influences or prenatal hormones (including hereditary relationships among LGBT-identified family members), are inconclusive, and parents certainly did not have such markers available to them during their journeys. Geneticists, neuroscientists, and endocrinologists, including one I interviewed, would reiterate these uncertainties, even though plenty of scientific inquiries and findings—such as the "gay gene"—have been debated and implicated here for decades.[24] Similarly, there are no clear biological markers for gay, trans, or cisgender-heterosexual "outcomes" to childhood gender nonconformity. Notions of the transgender or transsexual "brain" are gaining popularity, and they support other legitimizing "born-this-way" discourses of the LGBT rights movement.[25] But as of the time of the interviews, no parent had pursued neurological scans or testing of their children (a few did have their children's hormones checked; all tests came back "normal" for children's natal biology). Regardless of their reliability, biological platforms raise questions about what such markers would mean for the decisions of parents and practitioners—would a child with the "wrong" kind of brain, genetics, or physiology be denied transition? Based on the *child-centered, child-driven* approach I observed, I doubt parents would allow such tests to trump their child's earnest declarations of self. This was not the kind of child-rooted affirmation they practiced.

In the end, these parents must proceed without the biological "proof" anyway, supporting their children as best they can "today," as Marie put it, despite the ambiguity that the realms of *(trans)gender* and *(homo) sexuality* entail for age-old statistics and long-term projections. Indeed, several parents were keen not to dismiss the possibility that their child could "still" grow up to be a cisgender, gay-identified person, or perhaps nonbinary or genderqueer, even as they have affirmed them now as transgender girls or boys. These perspectives entertain a remarkably fluid, mutable perspective on gender and sexuality over the life course, wherein the identity categories claimed and expressed are as much a matter of the progression of time, the inevitable morphing of child-rooted developments, the seizing of different discourses and conceptions as they become available, as they are essential types of difference and identity. And one is no less true than another. These parents have decided that whatever debates or potential "outcomes" arise, these should not impact their parental responses here and now: today, their children express themselves as transgender boys and girls, or something less binary altogether, and should be recognized as such, regardless of what the future brings.

In a society that is increasingly LGBTQ-aware—but that comes with a legacy of associations between gender nonconformity and gay identity, as well as profound resistance to sex-category changes—these parents find themselves newly defining and carving out *(trans)gendered* subjectivities for their young children. They do this in a way that at once legitimizes transgender possibilities, but that does not preclude other forms of gender or sexual diversity either. These considerations also signal room for negotiation between "gender" and "sexuality" that expands one's options in self-determination over the life course. Through this discursive, deliberative, and conceptual work, parents open up a seeming proliferating range of LGBTQ-spectrum possibilities for their young children, and perhaps for others, too. This is the social construction of these categories at work, helping to bring (trans)gender-expansive options into being. In the next chapter, I turn to the second key conceptual area, *the gender binary*, and examine another valence between "transgender" and "gender-nonconforming" in the interviews: *binary* and *nonbinary* possibilities.

3

"Picking the 'Other Box'"

Troubling the (Non)Binary

It's nice to have your kid fit in a box, even if it's the other box.
—Wendy, parent

As of July 2019, twelve US states and counting provide for "third gender" or "nonbinary" identity options on driver's licenses and/or birth certificates (and without the traditionally prerequisite doctor's note).[1] These options not only are emblematic of society's growing transgender awareness, but also reflect mounting sociopolitical emphasis on genders that fall outside the "male-female binary" altogether. Binary categories of any kind seem to be of waning relevance to a new generation of youth at the vanguard of a "gender revolution."[2] In 2017, for example, a national survey indicated that increasing percentages of millennials identify in nonbinary capacities, including as agender, genderqueer, and genderfluid.[3] Indeed, over the past several years, I have observed many of my own peers and students embrace the "nonbinary" label, and related "they/them" pronouns, in some ways replacing "trans," and perhaps "queer," as the nonnormative umbrella category. In short, *nonbinary* identities and possibilities, in their own right, are marking radical new ground in the law, culture, and politics.

For the parents I studied, nonbinary possibilities marked an inevitable part of their trans-affirmative education and enlightenment. Being "somewhere in the middle" of the spectrum, as they often put it, was a possibility they soon learned about and considered on behalf of their children. This chapter thus explores a different valence in parents' deliberations between "transgender" and "gender-nonconforming": *binary* and *nonbinary* possibilities, respectively. In these instances, the imagined "spectrum" invoked in our interviews included gender-fluid, genderqueer, two-spirit, "boygir" (as one child coined it), and/or more ambiguous gender expressions and identities that cannot be defined firmly as "boy" or "girl." These also include "agender" identities like Vic's (twelve years old), which resist any relationship to the binary, male or female, masculine or feminine.

Of course, the analytic distinctions I have sought to outline amid these various considerations were not so clear-cut among parents, but inevitably overlapped, morphed, and shifted in our conversations: "gender-nonconforming" as something about *sexuality* and *sexual orientation*, or "gender-nonconforming" as something indeed about *gender* but in *nonbinary* capacities, both of which were distinguished from "truly transgender" or "going all the way" in parents' minds in a *binary* and sex-categorical capacity on the spectrum. These proliferating categories, and their slippages across a widening "spectrum" of possibilities, signal a multiplicity of meanings for "gender" and "sexuality" that are increasingly up for grabs and that fall outside the normative "heterosexual matrix."[4]

Binary and nonbinary possibilities, however, were not regarded equally or neutrally by my participants, nor were they experienced as such. The majority of parents' children were firmly binary-identified, and transitioned as transgender, by the time of my second round of interviews. This includes children from the earlier cohort who were originally identified as "gender-nonconforming" but who had since transitioned as transgender girls, which I detail in follow-up vignettes later in this chapter. In fact, for many of these parents, nonbinary options proved more of a crutch against "going all the way" than they were relevant to their children's authentic identities. Nonbinary possibilities were thus ultimately abandoned by most of my interviewees in the service of affirming their binary-identifying children. As much as parents strove for the "purple" possibilities "in the middle," their children largely aligned with the proverbial "pink and blue." As Bruce said of his transgender daughter, "I have this child who is *so* conformist, just against her own birth sex." And parents almost always framed the binary outcome as "easier" in the end. As Wendy said, "It's nice to have your kid fit in a box, even if it's the other box."

This marked another key area where parents' experiences and perspectives challenged LGBTQ paradigms and discourses, especially in terms of queer, deconstructionist, and/or nonbinary potentials. Of course, LGBTQ advocacy efforts have never denied binary identities and possibilities. On the contrary, many trans and queer activists have argued that the mainstream LGBT rights movement privileges more binary and gender-normative identities. And the message at the heart of all these advocacy efforts is to be free to be one's most authentic self, in whatever form or direction that takes. But parents' affirmative efforts inevitably confronted more expansive options "beyond the binary," as reflected in popular discourse and culture, which their children simply did not claim. Their children were, plainly, boys and girls. Parents often felt compelled to consider nonbinary possibilities for their kids, and sometimes felt pressured to defend themselves against them, especially in the name of early childhood exploration.[5] On several occasions, I heard parents were confronted with questions to the effect of, *"Are you sure you're not just picking the 'other box' because it's easier? Why do you have to transition? Why can't you explore more gender-nonconforming options, especially while they're still so young?"*

In fact, many of the parents from the original cohort seemed admirably hell-bent on exploring these options for their children, however new and unfamiliar these options were to them. I say "admirably" not to valorize nonbinary identities over others, but because for so many of these families, nonbinary options seemed nearly impossible to realize in the long term. Nevertheless, these parents were actively resistant to "truly trans" presumptions for their kids over fears of defaulting prematurely to "just another box." This was especially true for parents of children assigned male at birth. In their view, childhood gender nonconformity demanded a critical reappraisal of binary options in the first place, and "truly trans" was often framed as a potentially overly simplistic, compensatory choice. Shella exemplified these sentiments in our first interview, when her child Tegan was seven years old: "Tegan's just everything, he's not limited, and I think part of it is that gender thing, there's no boxes for him. . . . I just want to keep it that way, I don't want the world to crush him." (By our second interview three years later, Tegan had transitioned to living and identifying full-time as a girl, and relatively seamlessly in Shella's view.)

Several of these parents regarded "truly trans" as the "scarier" outcome, too. This was tinged, I sensed, with fears over "sex change" and body modification, aspects that were central to parents' early understandings of "transgender." As Sara, a fifty-six-year-old, white, middle-class, lesbian-identified married woman and mother of Jackie, an eleven-year-old gender-nonconforming child, said in our first interview, "I don't want her to have the operation, I don't want her to take hormones . . . here's this baby that I feed organic food to, you know? I don't want her pumping hormones in her body . . . all that stuff really scares me."

For the majority of parents in the cumulative sample, however, whose children were firmly transgender-identified at the time, binary identities and transitions seemed to afford some relief from the prospects of gender ambiguity. As scary as it seemed at first, parents confessed that "going all the way" felt ironically "easier" in the end. To be clear, all of these transitions were directed by their children's own sensibilities and expressions, to which parents' (non)binary outlooks gave way. The sociohistorical context seemed to influence parents' perspectives as well. "Transgender," as a childhood option, and as an "industry," seemed so much more viable and conceivable just a few years further into the research project.[6]

Parents' shifting perspectives in these ways, as well as the LGBTQ discourses they engaged with, hearken back to age-old dialectics in academic theorizing of gender, as well as in queer and trans politics: binary versus less binary identities, the viability of which is constrained by the limits of the male-female binary itself. Broadly, there are two dimensions of these dialectics, which reverberate throughout parents' commentary in this chapter. The first is a moralizing strand that frames nonbinary genders as more progressive, radical, or enlightened, with binary transitions and identities framed as a kind of "false consciousness" or a "dupe" of normative gender ideology.[7] Biologist and trans activist Julia Serano refers to this as "subversivism," or the "practice of extolling certain gender and sexual expressions and identities simply because they are unconventional or nonconforming . . . [and] 'subvert' oppressive binary gender norms."[8] Similarly, Seeber refers to these political schisms as "hierarchies of stigma" or "transer-than-thou" discourses.[9] While contemporary advocates and academics alike would reject the hierarchizing of genders according to their alleged "progressive" potential, this was an undeniable strain of thought that parents confronted, both within their own support group networks and with other persons.[10]

Another dimension calls attention to the difficulties of living out nonbinary genders in the first place, without necessarily any valuation, in a world so accountably ordered around "two and only two" options.[11] As decades of sociological scholarship have demonstrated, the gender binary undergirds countless macrostructural, institutional arrangements, from the family to the workplace to the economy.[12] The gender binary is also reinforced as a fundamental ethnomethodological metric in everyday "micro" interactions.[13] So long as binary sex categories—male or female—are "omnirelevant" to social life, nonbinary expressions remain susceptible to social sanction and scrutiny.[14] Not surprisingly, nonbinary persons continue to experience challenges to recognition and inclusion, in both social interactions and social institutions and especially within schools.[15]

These dialectics are further impacted by the inequalities between the male and female categories themselves. As discussed in chapter 1, male femininity and female masculinity are valued differently, in large part due to the esteem, and rigidity, that normative masculinity carries.[16] This is why Serano defines most "transphobia" as really a matter of "trans-misogyny" and "effememania": "Our society tends to single out trans women and others on the male-to-female (MTF) spectrum for attention and ridicule. This is not merely because we transgress binary gender norms per se, but because we, by necessity, embrace our own femaleness and femininity."[17] She adds, "In a world where masculinity is assumed to represent strength and power, those who are butch and boyish are able to contemplate their identities within the relative safety of those connotations."[18] Feminine gender expressions from persons perceived or identified as "male" mark particularly precarious terrain.[19]

Of course, more visible forms of gender nonconformity are *not* necessarily nonbinary; persons perceived by others as gender-nonconforming may well identify in binary capacities.[20] However, parents' reckonings with nonbinary possibilities inevitably collided with more visible forms of gender nonconformity, especially with male children (e.g., boys who wanted to wear dresses). These accounts also confront Seeber's critical distinctions between "bodies and behaviors," in which one's gendered behaviors (i.e., wearing dresses) are held distinct from one's self-identification (i.e., male). While scholars like Seeber recognize that these different self-expressions should not be seen as contradictory or incompatible, these kinds of prospects troubled firm "boy" and "girl" identifications for parents. Such (non)binary troubles appeared in a range of scenarios: a transgender boy, for example, who prefers girl toys and clothes; a transgender girl whose play preferences and comportment strike her grandparents as stereotypically masculine; and a gender-nonconforming child who moves seemingly easily between stereotypically masculine and feminine modes of interaction. Here, parents felt compelled to consider seemingly murkier, less binary parts of the spectrum. In the following sections, I examine these shifting encounters with binary and nonbinary possibilities among parents and their children, in both trans-masculine and trans-feminine cases.

Binary and Nonbinary Possibilities

Whenever the nonbinary kind of gender nonconformity surfaced in interviews, it was almost always in terms how much "harder" such a child would be to support than one who is transgender. Indeed, "harder" versus "easier" was the dominant frame through which binary and nonbinary possibilities were discussed. The unique struggles of the parents of nonbinary children came up across interviews and conference workshops. Wendy typified this outlook, which she had gleaned from one conference experience:

> Because it is easier for us as parents—as hard as it is for us to have the transgendered child—to have her walk into a school and someone says, *"Oh, what a cute little girl!"* . . . as opposed to if she was still "Nate" and only wanted to wear dresses. . . . I mean there you're setting yourself up for the school bullying. I can't just have the principal change the gender marker, you know? . . . The girls aren't going to want to play with her, and the boys aren't going to want to play with her, and she's going to be somewhere in the middle. And when we listen to parents at the conference . . . those people in the middle [whose] kids have flip-flopped, we're like, *Oh my God*. I mean we have to be prepared for that, but *oh, what a scary thing*! [Because] it is nice to have your kid fit in a box, even if it's the other box.

I often heard that these parents did not feel fully supported in advocacy forums and workshops either, as reflected in the following comment from Nicole:

The other thing is the parents that have kids that are gender-variant or gender-nonconforming or don't fit into any box, they feel like . . . they're in the minority . . . they feel like people forget about them . . . like, *"We don't feel welcome here in this group . . . you're always talking about transgender this, transgender that . . . well I have a kid that was male and now female and back to male . . . we feel very excluded from the conversation . . . your kid's one way or the other and mine, I don't know if they're gay or what."* . . . I think [those parents] feel very alone if their kid is not transgender.

Both Bruce and Wendy intimated feeling the "jealousy" of parents of gender-nonconforming children because their own children "fit within the binary," effectively making school, basic social interactions, and other aspects of everyday life "easier." Bruce actually romanticized the rebellious potentials of the nonbinary "messy middle," as he put it, which nevertheless did not resonate with his own "conformist" girly-girl:

[Originally], I was just thinking a gender rebel! And I hear all these parents who are so jealous of me because my child has at least fallen on one side of the binary, and I would *love* to have a child who just messed with the binary, who just was gender-pushing every boundary. . . . I'm envious of the people who have children who are this messy middle that the world is so intolerant of, and I feel like I would be such a good parent to that child because I would say, *Well, the world is wrong,* but instead I have this child who is *so* conformist, just against her own birth sex.

Here, like Martsy, Claire, Wendy, and many other parents in the sample, Bruce advised that his child was not just girl-identifying, but adamantly, stereotypically feminine, almost against his own wishes, and that she had no interest in more fluid possibilities. In fact, at one point he described her as the "most normal girl in the world," and said that raising her has been an "amazingly easy" experience.

Even so, while parents expressed sympathy toward the parents of gender-nonconforming children, they also often confessed that they were uncomfortable or "freaked out" by the prospect of a nonbinary child when they were still coming to grips with their child's gender nonconformity. The following exchange with Martsy exemplifies this:

> E: Did you ever consider . . . maybe she's somewhere on a spectrum
> versus she identifies as a girl?
> M: I did for a while, and it freaked me out . . . that freaked me out
> more than being transgender . . . because I think that that's a little bit
> harder. Transgender, you can tell other people, "Look, it's like having
> a girl's brain in a boy's body," it seems like you can simplify it for
> those that are able to hear it. . . . So that freaked me out because I felt
> like that was going to be harder for people to understand or digest . . .
> and harder for me to explain to others in some ways.

Nancy was also very candid about her discomfort with nonbinary possibilities, which she revealed later in the interview might be more relevant to her transgender son than she originally thought:

> The therapist [in the support group] talked about—which is another
> thing that freaked me out—was like . . . some kids feel like they're
> both and some kids feel like they're neither, and I struggle with that
> concept. . . . I feel for those people but I cannot *imagine*. . . . In theory
> it sounds great if you've got these really artistic parents that can support that, but I think that would drive me nuts. . . . I just can't wrap
> my head around that concept because . . . I was brought up traditional,
> and it's like there's two genders, and the whole thing was really hard
> for me to grasp.

Heather, whose daughter, Samantha, was living as a gender-nonconforming child at the time of our first interview and as a transgender girl as of the second, reflected on how impossible living "in the middle" seemed to her, even though her child lived as such for several years:

> My thinking about it would be different if the genderqueer option seemed
> more doable. Like how do you—I know the answers to, how can I make
> my body not be a boy and how can I look like a girl, that's straightforward. But how can I be who I am and still live a happy, well-adjusted life
> in the middle? I don't know how to do it. . . . I've listened to panels and
> I've listened to people say it all the time, but that seems really hard. It
> seems like every morning when you wake up you have to make all these

choices and decisions. . . . "*How do I fit into the world today?*" That seems like it would take a lot of energy to be that, especially for kids.

Heather was not yet convinced about her daughter's new transgender status: "She self-identifies as a girl, she's asked to use feminine pronouns, she's changed her name, and I see her as a girl. However, she is still very—for lack of a better word—*un-adamant* about it. . . . Could she be one of these kids who's in the genderqueer category, who's just going to go back and forth? Bottom line, I don't really know." Heather also cited examples of other kinds of nonnormativity in her children's lives, which she imagines affects Samantha's development and sense of self:

> Even today, there's a teacher at school who's either trans or has hormone issues, so she has a beard but she identifies as a woman and I believe is biologically a woman, and the kids can't stop staring at her. . . . [But] that kind of image, I think, is off-putting to a really feminine boy . . . no kid wants to stick out. . . . The analogy I sometimes use is, we have a friend who has a port wine stain on pretty much the whole side of his face, and I said, "Look, he can't hide that, that's something he has to live with." And we talked about, "*Did he get teased because of it? Do people make fun of him? Do people stare at him? Yes, they do. Well how does he live with that? Well, that's who he is, that's just who he is.*" And so I wish that [it] was a little more OK for the binary to be more fluid . . . because there's no other space.

Heather's thoughts resonated with the recollections of several other parents, who recounted painstaking efforts at trying to exercise more gender-neutral or gender-ambiguous compromises before accepting a binary, transgender identity for their children. As Linda expressed to me emphatically on our phone call:

> The thing of it is, when you're trying to find gender-neutral clothing for your transgender child or your gender-creative child . . . it was awful, Elizabeth, it was like ripping, slowly pulling your entrails out of your stomach, going into Kohl's and going into Target and going into Gap Kids and trying to find the clothes that look like boy clothes but could be

girl clothes, it was agony, agony for me. I was just miserable, depressed, ashamed, crying in my car.

In a similar vein, Karen described her child as a "total misfit" when she attempted a "gender-neutral" year at school, in the midst of the school's highly gendered practices:

> For the whole fourth-grade year I was trying not to use any pronouns. . . . He was wearing pants [boys' uniform] . . . but he was also wearing the vest that the girls wear [girls' uniform], and I felt as though . . . we were walking a tightrope, and it was so easy to fall off, and [it] was probably a big source of anxiety for Izzy. . . . I [once] saw Izzy's class walking . . . in boys' and girls' lines, and I saw Izzy walking along, clunking . . . in the girls' line . . . looking like a total misfit.

While Karen and Linda have both come to recognize their children as a boy and a girl, respectively, their previous pained attempts exemplify the challenges that many parents faced trying to facilitate more nonbinary possibilities at the start of their journeys—possibilities their kids nevertheless rejected. Indeed, attempting more neutral or middle-ground options for a firmly "cross-gender," binary-identifying child was part of the agony and the conflict for these parents—it was constricting their child's most authentic sense of self.

Several parents, although by far the minority of the sample, could speak more personally to raising a gender-nonconforming or nonbinary child, and in some ways testified to the "jealousy" sensed by Bruce and others. Dana, for example, a thirty-five-year-old, white, working-class, heterosexual-identified married woman, articulated for me the daily struggle that her child's identity entailed. At the time of our interview, Skylar, nine years old, identified as two-spirit, an indigenous term Skylar had adopted from a book Dana shared with him, and was using male pronouns.[21] As Dana recalled:

> It's really uncomfortable for me in the grocery store to have to explain this to random people I don't know, because I've just said *"Come on boys"* and obviously someone appearing *female* follows me. . . . Even just going

to the park to play with random people, I have to adjust my speaking to remove pronouns.

Dana also surmised that Skylar's gender nonconformity had turned away potential renters of a spare room in their house (a source of extra income for the family). Dana felt compelled to tell potential tenants about Skylar's gender and how her family accepts him for who he is, but she reported that she did not hear back from about "75 percent" of those who had expressed interest: "A few times I've had comments, one specifically sticks out in my mind of, 'Well, I don't want your child to confuse my child, so I don't think that this will be a good fit for us.' That one just sort of sticks with me." By comparison, Dana considered the experiences of parents of transgender children a "luxury."

In one unique instance, Janice advised that she became familiar with nonbinary prospects only after she had formally transitioned her child, Eileen, and had become more immersed in the parent-advocacy community. She confessed, in turn, that she has wondered if she should have tried to "stay in the middle" longer, had she been aware of those possibilities sooner. At the time of our interview, Janice was embattled with her in-laws, who did not allow Eileen to present as a girl in their home. They claimed that they did not observe the same feminine preferences (and related identity statements) that Janice had observed of Eileen for years, and they did not support a transgender identification or transition. Buttressing their claims were Eileen's "boy mode" behaviors, which she seemed to easily oblige at her grandparents' house—including being "physically aggressive, kicking, hitting . . . simulating martial arts punches in the air," per Janice's descriptions. Janice told me, "Seeing that she can move fluidly like that makes me wonder."

On the other hand, Janice wondered if Eileen was "just picking the lesser of two evils"—getting to see her grandparents as a "boy" versus not getting to see them at all. On these terms, Eileen's "masculine" behaviors were just a crutch against full sex-category relinquishment in her grandparents' eyes, an unbelievable "compromise" and calculus for a child her age to bear. But Janice also confessed that she was "extremely uncomfortable" in a nonbinary, gender-fluid space prior to Eileen's transition:

J: It's kind of like going through a really blinding rainstorm. . . . It's one of those situations where if I had known a little bit more, I probably would have let us stay in the middle a little bit longer . . . but I was extremely uncomfortable with the middle.

E: Known more about what?

J: Known more about gender-nonconforming kids. . . . To me at that time, I only—and again, I know this sounds really crazy, but I only knew, or at least could conceptualize . . . the two polar ends, and I didn't realize that there was this whole group of kids that kind of live in the middle, and I never, *never* pressed for a [binary] transition, because again, like I've said multiple times, Eileen was there way faster than I was, and I was not ready for the transition when it happened. . . . But I might have liked to stay in the middle a little bit longer, only because I see how easily Eileen moves back to boy mode when she has to see her grandparents.

Janice is confident that Eileen is living as the girl she feels herself to be, and this excerpt reiterates how *child-driven* these social transitions are for parents and their kids. But learning about gender-nonconforming children who occupy more "middle" spaces, in tandem with her in-laws' observations, was troubling for Janice. While Eileen's seemingly "masculine" behaviors around her grandparents should not compromise her "girl" identification for others, they proved highly conflicting for Janice in trying to defend a social transition to the "other box."

Interestingly, parents' fraught encounters with male femininity, in ways that made them confront nonbinary prospects too, readily surfaced among the parents of transgender boys, which I came to code as "gender-nonconforming in the other box." Early into our follow-up interview, for example, Sheryl and Richard informed me that their transgender son, Gil, eleven years old, enjoyed things that many would consider "effeminate" for a boy, including nail polish, bright clothing, baby dolls, and *The Wizard of Oz* (Gil was a fanatic, and impressively knew every line). Gil had also recently told his parents he thinks he might be gay (attracted to other boys). This was true for at least five other trans-masculine children in the sample.[22] As Sheryl said, "He would tell us, 'Well I'm not like the other boys,' so he did feel really bad that he felt like he was stuck in the middle. Girls didn't want him, boys didn't relate to him." That these children felt safe enough to vocalize things like thinking they might be gay to their parents, as early as eight years old, is a testament to how open and communicative these parent-child relationships are. This further reflects the *child-directed, child-centered* roots of the paradigm—even among parents like Nancy, discussed next, who expressed more ambivalence about gender-progressive, LGBTQ-informed positions.

Throughout our interview, Nancy was extremely self-aware about her discomfort over her son's nonconformity, both before and after transition. Nancy felt that her "traditional values" background complicated her feelings about gender nonconformity, including nonbinary identity. Like Gil, Nancy's transgender son, Mickey, exhibited a host of "effeminate" interests, including liking Justin Bieber, Barbies, and girl playmates. When Mickey first told Nancy that he thought he might be gay, she thought to herself, *"Absolutely not . . . you're not going to live multiple, alternative lifestyles."* As she confided, "I've got to be *honest*, it was a little embarrassing for me because . . . I'm telling [my friends] that my daughter feels that she's a boy and she's got the wrong body, so I'm going to raise her as a boy, and now she's Mickey—*however*, she likes boys, or *he* likes boys, and he plays with Barbies."

Nancy described multiple instances in which Mickey's behaviors did not live up to normative masculinity, in a way that agitated and discomfited her. She expressed uneasiness, for example, when Mickey played dress-up after socially transitioning: "Seeing a boy dressed like a girl . . . in my traditional mind, that's not right, you know?" She also mentioned the time Mickey confessed that he had secretly wanted new Barbies at the toy store, but felt pressured to ask for army action figures instead: "I was kind of frustrated with him for getting the wrong toy, but I think it's more about like, *Fuck, what are you, are you a boy or [what]? 'Cause I'm having my own trouble with this."* Nancy, of course, ended up buying Mickey some Barbies, which he played with frequently. Nancy also recalled the time Mickey got hurt and cried at the skate park. She told me she had to work hard to restrain her thoughts about "sissy boys" in front of him:

The thing that almost came out of my mouth was, *Boys don't cry . . . .* [P]art of me kind of felt, *You're at the skate park now with a bunch of teen-*

age boys, don't be a baby, don't be a sissy.... I had to just really bite my tongue because I was angry at him, like, *Well, you wanted to be a boy, so get tough now!*

As Nancy's stories exhibit here, and as for many of my participants, trans-affirmative parenting was a matter of constantly confronting and putting aside their own gendered hang-ups, at various points on the spectrum, for the sake of honoring their children's most authentic self-expressions.

In other moments, Nancy bemoaned the hardships that masculinist stereotypes have caused for her son, including getting teased at school for being "a fag" and wishing he could dance with the girl groups at the school talent show, which she knew he secretly wanted. This was the part of the interview in which Nancy's slightly humorous, irreverent edge slipped into a deeper grief and pain, palpable through her tears on the phone: "I just felt so bad . . . we live in this world where you have to be just like this or that at this age, and you know I'm the same way, because I know in my head I would probably be cringing if my kid was up there dancing to Justin Bieber with the girls." Nancy felt "envious" of other parents whose transgender boys were more stereotypically masculine and binary-presenting: "Because . . . then you're fitting into my little box."

Nancy's comments immediately reminded me of my first interview with Lorraine, in which she mentioned that her own transgender son, Jamie, had started playing with dresses at home. Despite her strong affiliations with queer identity and politics, Lorraine joked to me, "Be a girl or be a boy, but *please God* don't be a boy wearing dresses . . . it's getting to be too Victor-Victoria for me." These examples further expose the trouble with visible, transgressive forms of "male femininity" or "girly boys" in our culture, including for transgender boys. Although parents harnessed the insights of gender-neutral or feminist child-rearing, as noted in chapter 1, they continually faced their limits with the "male box." Tellingly, these kinds of post-transition, gender-nonconforming anxieties were virtually nonexistent among parents of transgender girls, save Janice. While one's gender *identity* should be held separate from their gendered *behaviors and expressions*—Gil, Mickey, and Jamie identify as *boys* and happen to like more stereotypically feminine things—the limits of the male sex category strained otherwise firm, and binary, identifications and transitions for their parents. In short, the strictures of normative masculinity compelled several of these parents to contemplate less binary identities and possibilities, too, which might better contain the kinds of mixed expressions and sensibilities their children displayed.

In all of these moments, parents attest to nonbinary identity as something nearly impossible to understand or "grasp" conceptually, let alone facilitate or manage practically in everyday life. A gender-nonconforming child—versus a categorically transgender one—means "not knowing" and, in the words of several parents, is cause for feeling "freaked out." Janice's analogy of the "really blinding rainstorm" was particularly reflective of many parents' sensibilities about trying to navigate nonbinary terrain on behalf of their young children. Moreover, the material shows that parents' anxieties around nonbinary identity are intimately related to anxieties around "male femininity," where one implicates the other. However, for the majority of the children represented here, nonbinary did not really reflect their self-identifications—they were, plainly, boys and girls, just "transgender" ones, according to their parents' schemas for sex and gender.

Parents' (Non)Binary Politics

Apart from the immediate matters of their children's own identities, I learned that parents reflected on the gender binary in markedly politicized and intellectual ways, both in our interviews and with each other. Their reflections echoed a legacy of fraught debates across feminism, queer theory, and the social sciences about "reifying the binary" or not in transgender and transsexual transitions.[23] Many parents were familiar with narratives that frame genderqueer, gender-fluid, and/or nonbinary identities as more "progressive"—precisely what Serano would call "subversivism." Indeed, being aware of distinctions between a binary-identifying, transgender child and more gender-nonconforming, nonbinary possibilities proved important for parents in defending themselves against the notion that they are "just pushing their child into another box," or, put differently, that they might be formally transitioning a child "too soon." Parents are only affirming what their children continually express themselves to be, they told me, which happens to be the "other box." If their child were truly less binary, which they know that some are, of course they never would have facilitated the transition, to paraphrase the resounding response. Parents' experiences with firmly binary-identifying children contrast with stories from other persons who later embraced nonbinary identities once they learned about them, as well as with burgeoning nonbinary visibility in the culture at large.[24] While some of these children may well change their identifications later in life, they were strongly binary-identified in early childhood, often against the more neutral or fluid attempts of their parents.

Claire grew impassioned during our interview about this strain of debate, in some ways defending her family's decision to socially transition a child "as young as" four years old:

> The other one [debates among parents] is between parents who . . . have truly gender-fluid children and parents who have transgender children . . . so we get the squeeze from the right, which is saying, *Tell your kid to put on their goddamn pants and put an end to this and you're screwing your kids up and it's all your fault,* and then the left, though, can be equally as dangerous, and the left is squeezing us with, . . . *You're just forcing your child to be a girl because you can't stand the idea that gender is a binary, that it's a social construct, and you're just playing into it because you guys are white . . . so it's easier for you to have a girl than it is to have a genderqueer child or a gender-nonconforming kid and if you just had the cajones . . . blah blah blah.*[25]

She went on to give a specific example where this surfaced:

> So one woman just was on the transgender listserv saying, "This is really tricky for me because, you know, gender's just a construct," and we were like, *No no no no,* the pink and blue is random, that pink is one thing and blue is another, but when you wake up in the morning and you know you're a girl . . . [or] you know you're a boy, that's not just made up from society, that is your identity, that's important.

Claire advised she has specifically encountered this line of argument from lesbian-identified acquaintances and/or academics at social gatherings, in which she felt burdened to defend her child's social transition. Rick, Claire's husband, added that while they had been aware of the "social constructs" of gender, such as men's and women's stereotypical "roles," their experiences with a transgender child were teaching them about the "science" of gender, which is more a matter of "your identity, your sense of self." In their household, for example, Rick was the stay-at-home parent and primary caretaker of their four children while Claire was the primary breadwinner. Rick felt he often had to educate his male friends about full-time parenting, including that it is *not* the "easier job." This, for Rick, is the "social" side of gender. But there is nothing "constructed" about *feeling* that you are a boy or a girl, he explained, that is a biological, precultural fact. The "constructs" are what society determines boys and girls should do, like, act like, and so forth (e.g., boys play with trucks and girls play with dolls). Gender identities, in contrast, are biologically driven and untouchable. Like Claire and Rick, many parents embraced biological, scientific accounts of gender identity. This is wired in "during that first duplication of cells," as one parent told me. In these ways, parents learn to abandon strictly binary *and* sex-deterministic possibilities for gender, but not precultural, essentialist explanations for them.

In contrast, Tory confided that she feels that many parents are "*so affirmative*" regarding transgender identities and transitioning that they ignore nonbinary possibilities (precisely the kind of argument that irks Claire and Rick):

> It just surprises me that people are so affirmative and it's so 100 percent one way . . . it's like some of the parents look at it as completely binary also, it's like she was a girl, now she's a boy, and there couldn't possibly be anything in between. I get the impression that some people are somewhat black-white thinkers. . . . I think the ones that think like me are probably more reserved in saying anything [in the forums].

She gave an example of one parent who expressed reservations online about pursuing a formal social transition for his child. Tory felt that many parents "jumped in" to warn him about "losing his child" if he delayed the process, insinuating, in her eyes, that he might be in denial about or unsupportive of transgender options:

> It just seems like a lot of political—when I talk about political dogma, that's kind of [what I mean], I can see the huge split between the people

that . . . jump right on the bandwagon and never question it, and then the people that want to learn more and are open to more than one opinion . . . and it does seem that if you're not completely affirming [in a transgender capacity you're criticized].

Tory had embraced Connor as a boy (although she was using female pronouns frequently in our interview). However, Tory wanted to afford Connor as much "latitude" as possible, and was mindful about the potential for change down the line, including Connor's living as a masculine-of-center female as an adult:

> I don't believe in 100 percent commitment to anything. Having said that, I don't think there's a definite way to be a boy or a girl, so, if you're more flexible in thinking, maybe it wouldn't be such a big deal, even to Connor. . . . It's great to know you're a boy, but if you don't have to conform to what society thinks a boy is, would you really feel the need to change for anybody and just be yourself?

Tory's sentiments exhibit remarkable openness toward gender and sexuality on behalf of her child, but they also risk regurgitating arguments that many would argue have plagued trans identities and communities for decades (i.e., *Just be your own kind of male or female. Why do you have to transition?*).

I encountered similar dialectics quite intimately within one family's story during my follow-up interview with Lorraine. In our first joint interview, Lorraine was partnered with Sam, who identified as butch and gender-nonconforming.[26] They both had affirmed Jamie, their child, as a transgender boy when he was five years old. However, as of our second interview several years later, I learned that Lorraine and Sam had since separated and were in the midst of a major conflict over the prospects of Jamie's medical transition. Lorraine wanted to pursue hormone blockers while Sam and her new partner were adamantly opposed. For these reasons, Lorraine and Sam were embarking on a "medical custody" battle over Jamie, who was eleven years old by this point. Based on conversations with Jamie, Lorraine felt strongly that hormone blockers were "a perfectly appropriate track to put him on" and were "protocol," since Jamie had indicated that he did not want to go through "female puberty."

But Sam and her partner, she advised, did not get this impression from Jamie and did not want him pursuing body modification. Lorraine felt that they wanted him to be a "poster child" for "genderqueer" instead:

> Jamie is caught in the middle [of us], and I feel sorry for the poor dude. I mean, really, I could care less except when he's with us, he says, "I don't want to go through female puberty," [and] when he's with them, they talk about how awesome it is to be genderqueer and that he doesn't have to do anything to his body and he can just be as he is and he can still be male with a female body—which is absolutely true. There's nothing they're saying that is wrong about that, except that, it's not how Jamie feels, and he is afraid, and he told us flat-out on numerous occasions he is afraid to disagree with [them]. . . . I don't know, maybe he's afraid to disagree with us too. . . . They seem very bent on, from my perspective, making Jamie into a poster child for being genderqueer. . . . They've stated repeatedly in writing that Jamie is not averse to going through female puberty, but when I asked him about that, he's *horrified*, he wants nothing to do with female puberty, he knows he's transgendered, he'll label himself as transgendered.

Jamie's stepfather and Lorraine's new partner, Cory, was present for our follow-up interview. Like Lorraine, Cory was white, middle-class, and forty-six years old. Cory was also the one transgender interviewee in my sample and identifies as heterosexual. Cory offered me his perspectives on the developing landscape of trans-affirmative parenting, which was nonexistent when he was growing up, he explained. Cory also admitted that he does not understand, or relate to, nonbinary identities and that he is quite binary-oriented in his worldview:

> You know, it's a new world, and I can't even possibly begin to understand it. I'm an older guy, I'm from [a] very conservative state, I went to Catholic school, I'm really just kind of an old fuddy-duddy in comparison to Jamie, and that's OK . . . but I really just try to relegate myself to answering questions. . . . If I had had his choices [i.e., early childhood transition and hormones], I definitely would have taken them. . . . I had my fantasies and my prayers to God at the age of six or whatever to make me a boy . . . but I mean . . . that's water under the bridge, that was forty years ago. . . . I'm a conservative guy, gender-wise. . . . I don't even understand

the twenty-somethings who are genderqueer, I don't get it, but that's the new thing. . . . I like my stereotypes right where they are, I like my binary genders right where they are . . . and I understand that people want to be fluid, [but] that's not what I want for myself.

Lorraine added: "Elizabeth, it took me a very long time in our relationship to understand that I'm not in a relationship with somebody who's queer, I am not in a relationship with somebody who is trans, I am in a relationship with *a man* whose maleness was sustained with medical intervention." It was clear that Lorraine was considering a similar perspective for Jamie.

Evidently, parents find themselves immersed in political, ethical, and/or intellectual debates about transgender "versus" gender-nonconforming identities for their children. These processes at once give voice to *nonbinary* options, but they also validate and normalize *binary* identities and transitions for children as authentic to who they are (inclusive of body modification, if desired), not as a kind of "sellout" to the gender binary. These testimonials showcase the prevailing conceptions of, and struggles with, nonbinary possibilities that these parents confront, both politically and ideologically and practically and experientially. The "messy middle," as Bruce called it, strikes parents as "harder," scary, and stigmatizing, especially for "boys in dresses." At the same time, awareness of its potential compels parents to consider these options for their children before pursuing a binary social transition, lest they risk "pushing their child into the other box" just because it seems "easier." As difficult as the "messy middle" seemed, however, I also sensed that some parents clung to these prospects early on in the hopes of evading "truly trans" outcomes for their children or of "going all the way." In the next section, I examine several longitudinal vignettes from the study, wherein parents had to wrestle with these "debates" in more concrete ways on the ground, as they realized and facilitated their children's most authentic sense of self in both transgender and cisgender directions.

Follow-Up Vignettes: Movement across the Spectrum

The follow-up cases showcased here refer to parents I first interviewed in 2009–11 and whom I formally followed up with several years later, in

2012–13. During this time, their children's identifications *changed* from explicitly "gender-nonconforming" to "transgender" *or* toward something more cisgender. Using four representative vignettes, I discuss nine such follow-up cases in my sample, all of which refer to children assigned male at birth. Of the thirteen follow-up cases total in the sample, all of the longitudinal change occurred among these nine children assigned male: four had transitioned to identifying as girls full-time, while the other five developed in more cisgender directions (although I would not characterize them as "gender-normative," as I discuss later). For the children assigned female, there was no formal change in their identifications, according to parents. As noted throughout this book, these vignettes include instances in which parents are using the wrong pronouns and markers relative to a child's later affirmed identity.

Of course, these four vignettes cannot exhaustively capture every element of change in these stories over time; however, using a small number of vignettes allows for more detailed attention to the processes involved and, in turn, sharper analytic clarity of the overall themes they represent.[27] The four cases selected duly illuminate the dynamics parents navigated between gender-nonconforming and transgender possibilities, particularly for children assigned male, in ways that are perhaps more "tangible" than the parents' discussions and debates presented earlier. They showcase quite intimately children moving in both transgender and cisgender directions out of less binary, more fluid spaces, as well as parents' differing impressions about those developments. These vignettes include notions of both internal, organic gender authenticity and external social norms and pressures, as well as child-directed and parent-facilitated dynamics, themes I encountered across all cases.

When I first interviewed the parents in the original cohort, they seemed nearly consumed with "gender-nonconforming-versus-truly-transgender" distinctions. They were determined, admirably so, not to bypass possibilities "beyond the binary" for their children, however unfamiliar these were. In some ways, their interests in nonbinary options struck me as deflections of "truly trans" trajectories, which several parents described as "scary" or the "scarier" outcome. But in other ways, these efforts imagined a wider array of gendered subjectivities on behalf of their children, even if transiently, and challenged the merits of the male/female boxes altogether.

From a methodological standpoint, I wondered if I just happened to capture the first cohort when they were in the thick of those early deliberations—at a certain earlier snapshot in time along a more general "journey to trans" (or journey to cisgender)—and just happened to capture the second set after that stage, when those deliberations were largely behind them. However, a comparison of the children's ages at the time of the interviews challenges that supposition: all of the children who now live as girls full-time were six or seven years old at the time of the first interviews, whereas the majority of the transgender girls from the new sample were fully socially transitioned and affirmed by that age. In other words, the "newer" cohort did seem to move to transgender categorizations sooner in their children's development. The follow-up parents, in contrast, seemed to have lingered a little longer within more nonbinary spaces. It also seems the new set of parents were making decisions within an infrastructural context that was readily and rapidly more aware of childhood transgender possibilities. For all of these reasons, I detail some of these follow-up vignettes, wherein parents and children were actively trying to live out gender-nonconforming spaces "somewhere in the middle."

"Gender-Nonconforming to Transgender"

Four of the children who were assigned male at birth and were first identified as gender-nonconforming now live and identify as girls. Parents' accounts of these transitions were divergent and not so clear-cut. In two of the cases, parents seemed certain about their child's girl identification, as an authentic gender identity they had come to realize and recognize. Parents in the other two cases, however, exhibited a modicum of uncertainty about their child's new status, precisely due to the challenges around nonbinary identities articulated earlier in this chapter. Here, I discuss one of each of such cases to capture these divergent parental impressions.

ALLY AND ELIAS

Ally, a fifty-two-year-old, white, upper-middle-class married woman, was one of the first parents I interviewed for the project, first on the telephone, and later in person with her husband, Elias, a Mexican

American man.[28] Their child, Raya, was seven years old at the time of our first interview. I came to regard Ally as the "armchair sociologist" of the sample; our interviews seemed as much a heady philosophical riff about "gender" as about her own parenting experiences with Raya. (She also once told me she wished she could consult a "clinical sociologist" of sorts about her child versus the typical medical or mental health professional.) Ally presents as somewhat gender-nonconforming herself and identifies as bisexual. She told me that had the term "genderqueer" existed during her high school days, she likely would have seized it.

Raya exhibited strong feminine preferences from early childhood, including in fashion, dress-up, dance, and pink cowboy boots, as well as with wearing towels on her head to simulate long hair (a common observation from parents across trans-feminine cases). Raya also had an impressive mastery of cars at a young age, being able to identify the make and model of any vehicle on the road, which Ally boasted about in our interview. Like many of the parents from this cohort, Ally actively considered nonbinary possibilities for Raya, in part because she had observed a seeming dexterity in Raya in both stereotypically masculine and feminine modes of play and interaction, similar to Janice's observations of Eileen. One minute Raya was swordfighting with the boys, the next she was gabbing with the girls about Hannah Montana. As Ally explained, "I just noticed how he would sort of flow from one to the other, it was very situational." She also advised, "I sometimes wonder whether what we're looking at is just another intersex condition of sorts, that is much more subtle." Ally mused about possible "other spaces" that were not so sex-typed:

> He says, 'I'm more girl than boy, so I'd rather they . . . think of me as a girl.' What remains kind of unanswered is, if he could have it exactly the way he likes, would he rather have a whole other space opened up for him that doesn't have to be just girl, or just boy, and he can just kind of be?

Informing some of these deliberations, Ally did not recall explicit "cross-gender" identifications or verbal declarations from Raya early on: "None of that [i.e., 'I'm a girl!'], which is partly why I kind of hang back, and I'm in this watching mode. . . . I'm like, did I just totally miss something before? Or do I really have a gender-fluid child?" During this time, both

Ally and Elias were avoiding using any pronouns around Raya, at Raya's request.

Ally does remember, however, other kinds of statements from Raya, such as, "I'm going to get out of the *girls'* side of the car." As Ally explained, "She started putting a 'girl' label on *everything* and claiming it." Over the years, Ally also felt that she had observed Raya consciously amplify her femininity so that her peers were less likely to question her behaviors as a "boy": "I got the impression toward the end of the school year that he had drawn a few conclusions . . . one was that people weren't going to let you be a blend, they were going to insist that you had to be one or the other . . . so he has decided it's just easier if everybody says he's a girl."

As of our second interview, Raya was eleven years old, and Ally and Elias had embraced her as a transgender girl. They reported that she had formally socially transitioned in third grade, when she "edited out" the remaining boy items from her wardrobe. However, after attending a conference that included several genderqueer teen speakers, Ally felt that Raya returned home to experiment with more fluid clothing choices and modes of socializing, much the way she did as a younger child: "[These teenagers were] kind of 'dress however you feel like it,' one day to the next, [and Raya saw that] she didn't have to have a consistent gender presentation that was carefully crafted for the world." But Ally observed this quickly ceased again soon into fourth grade: "And then it was really noticeable—*boom*, back to the closet again. My theory is that she got pushback, she found that, *Oh, we're back in [our hometown], we can't do that here.*"

Ally has always bemoaned the polarizing forces of the male-female binary, especially among young schoolchildren. She wondered, and worried, if these pressures influenced Raya's trajectory, especially in light of her observations of Raya's fraught experimentation with more fluid interests and behaviors years prior. On her back patio, Ally reflected on these conundrums as the "sociological component" of the issue:

> So that is always in the back of my mind . . . would we get a different arc of development for her if we were magically transported to a place where gender is perceived differently and not so polarized? Because she really, really cares about belonging. So, yeah . . . I think a lot about the sociologi-

cal component . . . because I don't know how much of her identity is actually being shaped by the culture and its language, and what the acceptable categories are in her age-group.

Even as Ally now embraces Raya as a transgender girl, she ruminated on the potential allure of a "simplistic" transgender narrative for gender-nonconforming children a narrative that Martsy, in contrast, had embraced quite candidly precisely for its simplicity. To preface her ruminations, quoted in the following excerpt, Ally asked if I had connected with another potential interviewee in town who, in Ally's opinion, had transitioned her child "blazingly fast." Ally described this as the "bleeding edge" of the issue—she feels that parents seem to be transitioning their children at younger and younger ages, in ways that echo some of the cohort differences I observed among my sample. She joked that this was her "talking-trash-about-the-other-parents" part of the interview:

"Gender-variant" was always an awkward term. It was what we seized on first, and it had more—it was more stretchy. But transgender identity is more tightly bound, and, OK, I'll go there, this is my thing with [some parents]. . . . I'm thinking it might be, in a way, easier to explain to yourself that, *Oh, we just had him in the wrong box, some people, somehow, are cross-wired, and they're in that box, not that one.* And [this way], you can conceptualize your kid . . . but to tear down or weaken gender categories, eh, that's harder. So is it a relief to be told that, *Hey, not very many people know this, but there are some babies that are just born with, for whatever reason, their brain got cross-wired, and they're the opposite of what you thought, and . . . their brain is not in line with the rest of their body?* . . . I guess I wonder [about] being quick to say, *Ah! That's it! We have an explanation here! He's just transgender. OK, done* . . . [versus exploring the] uncertainty about what you've got here, and having to deal with the unpredictability of your kid not developing on a clear trajectory, and not being able to look forward to, *Ten years hence, we're going to be on blockers.* . . . I sometimes see the narrative of the transgender person as "merely cross-gendered" as temptingly simplistic.

As Ally's comments indicate, some parents harbored agnosticism about their child's developing gender status, wondering if external binary pressures, and the seeming impossibilities of a more nonbinary life, hampered a more authentic identification, especially for children assigned male. These concerns were outnumbered, however, by the rest of the sample, who were more confident about their child's transgender status—that it is *not* a kind of acquiescence to the gender binary, but is true to how they feel. This kind of certainty was exhibited by Becca and Nathaniel, presented in the next vignette.

BECCA AND NATHANIEL

In our first interview, Becca and Nathaniel, a white, upper-middle-class, heterosexual-identified married couple in their forties, felt strongly that their child, Bo, seven years old, was *not* transgender, but was gender-nonconforming. They were actually honoring the label that Bo had derived for herself at the time, "boygir." As Becca said, "In terms of like, the identity part of it, I think he identifies himself as a boy or, you know, this slightly other category." Around that time, Becca had been blogging about her child's gender nonconformity as a "girly boy" (this is how I first found her), writing and thinking earnestly about nonbinary possibilities. At one point, she sent me a link to a web page she had discovered that defined all new terms and identity categories, including "neutrois," one that really piqued her interest. Like several other parents at the time, Becca cited Bo's seeming comfort with her body as one of several key signs that she was likely *not* transgender: "I don't think that he's truly transgender, from what I understand . . . like when it comes down to it, there's no dysphoria, there's no body issues . . . there's none of that." She added, "He wasn't necessarily like all out saying, *I'm a girl, I'm a girl, I'm a girl, I'm a girl!*"

In addition to her more feminine interests and performances—such as self-curated fashion shows and dance routines, the creativity of which blew Nathaniel and Becca away—Bo had started experimenting with more masculine expressions from time to time, wearing all boys' clothes to summer camp and bonding with other boys her age. During our interview, Nathaniel marveled at Bo's ability to hang with both the boys and the girls competently, referring to her as a kind of gender "double agent":

> You know, to me, he's like a spy, and he snuck into the world of women and he's in there, and he's got 'em figured out, he's got 'em nailed, you

know, there's no question that he speaks "girl," and that part fascinates me because now . . . it feels like, even though he's a boy, he snuck over to the boys' side, and he's checking out that side of the plate, and getting them all dialed in and figured out, and [he's learning], how do you fart and burp and hit people and do stuff so that you're acceptable on that side of the world, too, when the world seems to have this binary construct. It's like he's a double agent, and he's somewhere in between, and he's just constantly picking up on stuff . . . and it's just *amazing*.

As of our second interview several years later, Bo was nine years old, and Becca and Nathaniel reported that Bo was living as an affirmed transgender girl. Admittedly, I was struck by how this seemed almost like a foregone conclusion in their responses, in sharp contrast to their initial emphasis on possibilities "beyond the binary," which they had felt strongly applied. With some difficulty, I probed them to chart for me key developments that led them to this new understanding of Bo. They advised that Bo had started presenting as increasingly feminine at school, where all her peers knew her as a "boy." As of third grade, however, Becca and Nathaniel starting observing distress, anxiety, and behavioral issues in Bo. This largely catalyzed their decision to formally socially transition Bo as a girl. Specifically, Becca and Nathaniel recalled a pivotal moment when they asked Bo how she wanted to be enrolled in school at the start of fourth grade—as a girl, or something else. "Writhing on the floor," distressed, and frustrated, Bo shouted back, "*I just wanna be a girl!*"

At first, Bo requested female pronouns but not a change in her masculine birth name. But after a short time, Becca and Nathaniel felt compelled to say that that name was confusing for her peers and that she should use her chosen gender-neutral name instead. Becca sensed that Bo was hesitant to change her name due to fears over an explicit "male-to-female" transition among her peers—that maybe, in Bo's eyes, keeping her old name would make things more subtle and smooth for others. In this case, a conventionally masculine birth name, coupled with female pronouns and a female presentation, proved socially untenable for Bo. In many ways, this is symbolic of the challenges mentioned earlier with nonbinary and/or more visible forms of gender nonconformity, wherein the gender-nonconforming person, rather than surrounding persons, feels pressured to accommodate. Ensuing disagreements with the school administration over Bo's use of the girls' restroom—despite its former embrace of her gender nonconformity—ultimately resulted in the decision to enroll Bo in another school privately, meaning that only a few key staff persons were aware of her transgender status. Contrary to her early days blogging publicly about childhood gender nonconformity, Becca told me then, "There's more [of] a resolve in my mind that really nobody needs to know this."

Years later, in 2018, I touched base with Becca again on the phone. Bo was fifteen years old at the time, thriving as a teenage girl in the tenth grade, and several years into hormone therapy. Due to Bo's "running with the wrong crowd" at the new district and engaging in risky behavior (including drinking in middle school), Becca and Nathaniel had decided to reenroll her in her old school. By this point, her transgender status was no longer very private; many students were aware, and among some peer groups, it was a status symbol and source of popularity. Although Bo did occasionally encounter bullying and teasing remarks from other kids, Becca felt that most of this left her unfazed. In Becca's eyes, Bo is a remarkably confident go-getter, unflinching in her career interests in modeling (which her height and stunning facial features assist with). Bo seeks out social settings that value her, not put her down, Becca explained.

Like several parents, Becca emphasized that because growing up as transgender has been so "normal" for Bo, connecting to a wider transgender community or politics—let alone one rooted in a sense of historical oppression—did not call to her: "We have to *drag* her to the trans marches, we have to *drag* her to the conferences." Becca went on to say, however, that she observed a shift in this stance with the advent of a new gay-identified friend in Bo's life, who is deeply committed to the LGBTQ community. Becca also senses that the sudden passing of a trans-identified peer has effected Bo's newfound interests in the LGBTQ community.

Toward the end of our call, Becca emphasized one research area that she feels is critical for researchers to study in this terrain: the seeming preponderance of behavioral "comorbidities" among transgender children, including attention deficit disorder (ADD), attention deficit hyperactivity disorder (ADHD), autism-spectrum disorders, and other neurodivergences. This signaled to me a more medicalized understanding of gender nonconformity, which I return to in the next chapter. Becca half jokingly ruminated about her cravings for spinach, too, during Bo's pregnancy—as opposed to her cravings for hamburgers with her cisgender son—insinuating that diet might have affected Bo's gestation. Given the origins of our conversations—a newfound ideological unpacking of the gender binary, in the face of a highly expressive, creative child, who seemed to her parents to play within and around "the boxes" with verve and aplomb—I was somewhat surprised to end on this note with Becca. It seemed to emphasize the private, medical matters of transgender identity as much as it did a sociopolitical critique of gender-binary ideology. Of course, for all parents, these are not exclusive or opposing frameworks and approaches. But I sensed that coming into a firmly binary understanding of Bo's identity as a girl, and the related medical technologies that assisted that, shifted these parents' conceptual orientation.

"Gender-Nonconforming to Cisgender(ish)"

Similar to the parents of transgender children, the parents of the children who developed in more cis-normative directions had differing accounts for these changes, with parents in three of the cases attributing at least some of the change to social pressures, while parents in the other two cases were confident that their child's status is authentic to who they are. "Gender-normative" feels like an inaccurate description for these children, as none of the parents would characterize them as stereotypically male or masculine. These children have not formally departed from their assigned sex category, male, but they still experience or express moments of gender nonconformity. One child, for example, at the time of our second interview, was still wearing his hair long and was still often sex-categorized as female in public because of this (despite wearing all boys' clothes). Another child still occasionally wore pieces of girls' clothing (e.g., hot pink pants, but never skirts and dresses like before). Notwithstanding, for all of these children, parents reported that their conventionally feminine expressions and interests had waned over the years, especially outside of the home.

LAURIE

Laurie, a forty-three-year-old, white, upper-middle-class, heterosexual-identified married woman, had interviewed many parents herself before I found her. She was one of the first parents to blog about gender-nonconforming children, and she and her husband went on to write a related children's book. When we first spoke in 2009, Laurie identified her nine-year-old child, Phillip, as gender-nonconforming or a "pink boy." He was wearing dresses to school throughout preschool and kindergarten, which a letter to other parents explained on his behalf, and had asked for feminine bedroom decor, among other toys and objects. Laurie said that he had voiced the idea of starting kindergarten "as a girl," but Laurie felt strongly that this was a strategy for avoiding questioning from peers, versus something authentic to his identity, just as Ally had wondered about Raya. As Laurie recalled, "When we were going to start kindergarten, he said he wanted to go to school as a girl, and we said why, and he said, 'Because then people wouldn't ask me questions,' and I think he just wants to be himself."

Since that time, Laurie reported, Phillip developed in more normative directions, including preferring boys' clothes full-time and having more boy friends and conventionally masculine play interests, such as Star Wars and Legos. As such, Laurie came to see Phillip as more of a "purple boy," her code name for a nonstereotypical cisgender male child (e.g., he loves opera and hates sports). As of our second interview, Phillip was eleven years old. Despite his more masculine presentation and clothing style, however, Phillip was still often read in public as a girl due to his long hair and quasi-feminine physique. In fact, as of our second interview, he was not allowed to use public restrooms alone because of these frequent misattributions. Laurie is confident that Phillip developed in ways authentic to himself versus succumbing to social pressures. However, Laurie did note that Phillip requested that his parents use pen names for their book, to avoid association with the project and being mocked by peers, which he experienced in his elementary years.

During our second interview, Laurie was very forthright about the difficulties she has observed among other parents who are trying to raise nonbinary children "in between":

I think people are super-uncomfortable with in-between. I have a friend whose kid is now trans, and who for a long time we just thought was gender-nonconforming, and she's transitioned at school. . . . . I remember how *uncomfortable* my friend was in that period of not knowing, and she's sort of *relieved* now that this kid is trans—she is *not* a person who pushed her kid into being trans in any way, she was totally open . . . but now she's relieved, and even though it has its own set of challenges and she's meeting with endocrinologists about blockers and that's freaking her out . . . I just watched that discomfort and the not knowing, and I see that in so many parents. It's *hard*, it's like . . . *shit*, it's hard to dwell right here . . . it's hard not to know.

Laurie also lamented all the focus in popular discourse currently, in her view, on transgender children, which she feels eclipses the need to open up the (cisgender) boyhood box, just as we have permitted for "tomboys." She wishes there was more room in our culture for the "pink" and "purple" boys like her son, not unlike Leigh's concerns in chapter 2. She intimated that perhaps all the hand-wringing she's observed among parents over different shades and meanings of gender nonconformity— "just gay," "gender-fluid," "truly transgender," "somewhere in the middle"—would not exist if we simply normalized male femininity from the start. As she said, "I think that part of trying to parse this language so thoroughly is discomfort in our culture about 'pink boys.' We don't spend time doing that with girls, we don't go, *Well there's the tomboy and then there's the Thumbelina.* . . . They're just tomboys, or they're not even talked about." In this way, Laurie articulated a provocative constructionist take on the trans-affirmative parenting paradigm, which might obscure other (cis)gendered possibilities for male children.

BETH AND BARRY

Even over the phone, Beth charmed me immediately with a kind, bubbly, and humble disposition. Beth, a forty-one-year-old, white, upper-middle-class, heterosexual-identified married woman, was hesitant to use any specific label or category to identify her child, but her experiences with him fully resonated with my project on parents of gender-nonconforming children (she had found my research blurb on a parent's blog site that she had been following). Beth cited an exemplary host of gender-nonconforming interests to describe Tim, who was five years old at the time of our first interview. This included asking for a "princess party" for his fourth birthday, wanting women's purses and Barbie toys, as well as wearing a hoodie on his head, which he referred to as his "hair." Tim was also obsessed with an Ariel mermaid costume, which he often wore around the house—at first with matching jewels and heels, but later without. Beth admitted that the accessories proved "too much to handle" for her and her husband, Barry, so they eventually confiscated them. Beth confessed to me that she actually gave the shoes to the dog to chew on the sly, so that she would not have to explicitly relay their discomfort about them to Tim. Evidently, while Beth herself was uncomfortable with some of Tim's nonconformity, she was compelled to muzzle that discomfort in front of him.

Like many parents during these early years, Beth attempted delicate gendered "compromises" with Tim, and hedged around his preferences. For example, Tim really wanted a Disney princess bike, but Beth and Barry were uncomfortable with him using this in the neighborhood. As a "compromise," Beth suggested to Tim a plain, solid-color bike, which she could outfit with a detachable Barbie basket. Beth fashioned similar compromises regarding dressy shoes for Tim. Instead of formal girls' shoes, she bought him Crocs with Disney princesses on them, which he was allowed to wear "if he goes over to a girlfriend's for a playdate, but he can't wear them to [summer] camp, he can't wear them normally." At one point, Beth described these efforts as "heartbreaking," but they felt necessary to protect her child from potential judgment and harm.

Beth also recalled one memorable conversation when she was talking to both her children about what it is like to be a boy or a girl. Tim said that he knew what is was like to "feel like both." As Beth told me:

I said, "Well, I sometimes wonder what it would feel like to be a boy, that's natural," and Tim told us, "Well, I know what it feels like to be both a boy and a girl," and so I said to him, "Really, what does that feel like?" And he said, very matter-of-factly . . . "The same, just both the same."

As of our second interview several years later, Tim was eight years old. Beth reported that Tim had "toned it [femininity] down, by his own choice": "I think he started in first grade being much more self-regulating." When I asked Beth why she thinks this change was a matter of self-regulation and restraint, versus an authentic development of who Tim was, she replied, "Because he's sort of extreme about it." For example, she explained, "He's very cautious now that his favorite color's blue, and that he *only* wears blue." In a separate phone interview, Barry, a forty-two-year-old, white, upper-middle-class, heterosexual-identified man, advised that he too had observed some "repression" of Tim's feminine side, but that he felt this was part of a careful strategy on Tim's part to navigate the world with less ostracism and scrutiny: "We try to do the best . . . we can to balance everything. . . . We certainly want him to be who is and be comfortable with who he is . . . and to not have . . . inner conflict, inner turmoil, but [we] also . . . of course don't want [him] to have external turmoil or conflict either." I sensed that Barry felt it was his role, as Tim's father, to let his child choose this kind of self-preservationist approach. Beth echoed this stance: "I think maybe we've accepted [Tim's new expressions] now . . . it's kind of his way of being . . . but he still has that . . . [sense of] relating to girls."

Beth felt that Tim was uncomfortable engaging in his more "flamboyant" behavior, as she put it, around his father and his brother, but he allegedly did a fashion show for the babysitter while they were out. Tim also enjoyed doing workout videos with Beth, provided the other two family members were on a different floor of the house. Interestingly, Beth reported that Tim once described being excluded from the girls at school as "gender discrimination": "He's really smart, and he said it was discrimination, because they had studied Black history month, and he was like, 'You know that discrimination still exists in the world, with gender?'" Beth also advised that Tim experienced anxiety issues, for which he was attending therapy. Beth felt that some this was related to his "gender stuff": "I think if you know instinctively that you don't fit in somewhere, like how can you not . . . feel anxious? It's got to come out in some way, you can't sublimate the whole [experience]—he obviously does not fit in with the typical boys." Beth told me that she would love to find literature that might help her with Tim, but that so much of it strikes her as "extreme," including being explicitly "transgender"-focused:

> I'm constantly wishing there was a book just for the layperson, [but] there's nowhere I can go. . . . It seems like everything else is just, there are a lot of extremes, and so it's hard to get in that conversation if you feel like your kid is definitely this way, but they're not wearing lipstick and dresses to school. . . . I mean he wouldn't grow his hair long and wear dresses to school.

Ultimately, Beth and Barry recognized a range of potential "outcomes" for Tim's identity and expression, including those on the LGBTQ spectrum. They did not want to make any presumptions, though, and they wanted to let him lead the approach, even one they perceived as "self-regulation." They feel that only time will tell. In this way, these parents are also striving to "follow the child's lead."

All told, the children from the follow-up cohort have developed in divergent directions, and parents' accounts of those trajectories differ. Some parents reported the child's distress and anxiety as a catalyst for newly realizing their child's gender, wherein the parents took on a more active facilitator role, as in Becca and Nathaniel's case. Others described a relatively seamless transition to girl that was largely child-directed. Some attributed at least a modicum of the changes to "social pressures" around the gender binary, for both trans and cis trajectories. Others, in contrast, were more confident that their children's status reflected them authentically (even when bullying and teasing were part of the story). The present childhood "outcome" is perhaps less sociologically pertinent than parents' different perspectives and processes for understanding them. Parents identified multiple and varying factors, both internal and external, that were potentially influential in their child's growth and identity development.

Conclusion

This inventory of parents' experiences offers a compelling demonstration of the complicated character of the gender binary and the power of the social organization around it. Either through their own children or through the experiences of other parents they have observed, these parents come to understand gender not only as a matter of cisgender or transgender possibilities, but also inclusive of nonbinary possibilities, which cannot be easily reconciled with male or female, boy or girl boxes. As Janice said, "I only knew, or at least could conceptualize . . . the two polar ends, and I didn't realize that there was this whole group of kids that kind of live in the middle." Through these deliberations, parents recognize that there are possibilities all over the map, or all across the proverbial "spectrum," producing a nascent set of interpretations that were unavailable to previous generations of children, including and especially ones that do not mean "just gay." These parents are realizing that while the "middle" may be "messy," both conceptually and practically, there is indeed a nonbinary "middle" ground to be reckoned with in the first place.

As parents develop a new gender-expansive consciousness, they find themselves thinking through familiar polemics and debates about binary and nonbinary possibilities. That these parents find themselves deliberating and intellectualizing about the gender binary on behalf of their children, as they come to newly understand the world so ruthlessly ordered around a rigid and polarizing binary, is remarkable, in multiple senses of the word. Now that many of these parents have come to recognize their children firmly as boys and girls, they might not think that their child was ever "really" gender-nonconforming, but rather that they were trying to express themselves in more gender-fluid spaces.

Fundamentally, these parents are only affirming and responding to what they believe their child is expressing at any point in the life course—which is often the "other box." And for many of these parents, a formal social transition ends up feeling like a relief relative to more nebulous gender prospects "somewhere in the middle." However, even as they move toward more distinct identifiers for their children, parents demonstrate that arriving at these designations is not easy, that there are signposts and turning points and reinterpretations along the way, not to mention fears of either the unknown or the very much known. Following their child's lead, regardless of the new possibilities and perspectives they were learning, was the compass that held force.

It would be remiss to conclude that nonbinary, genderqueer, and/or gender-fluid possibilities are so difficult to manage, for both young children and their parents, that they are quickly abandoned for a "box," either the assigned one or the "other" one. Indeed, some of this material indicates that parents' early efforts with more genderqueer possibilities—particularly for children assigned male—was in part a *deflection away* from more binary outcomes, not the other way around. Parents' early stigmatizing conceptions of "transgender," as noted in chapter 1, would also challenge the idea that any of them would be "quick" to facilitate such a transition. And no parent—as much as it pains parents, advocates, and professionals alike to admit—enthusiastically or unthinkingly jumps for a full "cross-gender" transition just because it is the "easier" thing to do. As Gail, an educator, said when the notion of transitioning "because it is easier" came up in the interview:

> Why would a parent—and this is, you know, *ugh* (*sighs heavily*)—why would a parent think that this would be so awesome (*laughs*), like having your child go through this process, having your child go through surgeries and everything, having your child go through marginalization and prejudice, why would a parent sign their kid up for that, like, *really*? . . . I have not known a parent yet that would not step off of their child transitioning, given that information from the child . . . there's not a parent I've ever worked with that wouldn't do it, *ever*.

At the same time, it would be remiss to overlook the pressures that all of these possibilities mean for male children specifically, who are ever subject to the oft-ruthless consequences of gender accountability. The two sides of the binary are far from equal, and the process whereby one locates oneself (or one's child) somewhere along the "spectrum" appears far more fraught for males than for females, including for transgender boys.

This discussion cannot speak for the children's own "authentic" sensibilities, about why they felt drawn to one particular identity or expression over another, nor would I venture to project any ultimate authentic "outcome." Indeed, I would sooner interrogate the notion that there might be any finite "outcome" at all, versus an array of gendered possibilities, which are as true and authentic as they can be at any particular moment in the unfolding of a life course. I can only interpret parents' accounts of those revelations, as they come to pass in the daily experiences of child-rearing. Nevertheless, these parents are the principal agents who facilitate their children's identifications, whether or not that means a formal, binary, social transition. As such, parents' active assessments of these developments, amid a seeming proliferation of gendered options, both now and in the future, present a key social mechanism in the story.

In the next chapter, I turn to parents' negotiations with privacy and (non)disclosure on behalf of their children. As I will discuss, these efforts in privacy are related to parents' *biomedical understandings* of transgender embodiment. Parents often analogized their child's "contradictory embodiment" to a disability or a "birth defect," which is nobody's business other than the parents and clinicians who manage it. I examine the intersection of these themes—privacy, the body, and biomedicine—to explore how a new generation of parents attempts to normalize transgender experience in the twenty-first century, in the most compelling ways they know how, but in ways that risk reiterating traditional cisgender body logics for sex and gender.

4

"A Regular, Normal Childhood"

Privacy, Protection, and Medical Interventions

I know a lot of people don't feel that way . . . but I think
something went wrong, your brain and your body don't
match, it's not right, and it's not easy.
—Karen, parent

As parents moved further into embracing and recognizing their children
as transgender, deliberations over whether to disclose that identification to others, in myriad scenarios, took on a dominant force in their
lives. At the time of our interview, for example, Martsy had not yet told
her mother-in-law that they had formally socially transitioned Cindy
as a girl and had enrolled her in school as such. When I arrived for the
interview, Martsy's in-law was still standing in the driveway, picking up
their other child. Martsy did not want to have to explain to her who I
was, so she very subtly told me to make myself scarce. Well attuned to
parents' privacy negotiations, I immediately understood Martsy's subtle
gesturing and aimlessly walked back down the driveway, pretending to
be lost in the neighborhood. Later, when our interview ran long and her
in-law returned, I ran to hide in the bathroom (the in-law proceeded to
use the bathroom anyway, so Martsy and I just pretended that I was a
visiting neighbor). In this case, few people at school knew Cindy was a
transgender girl, and few people in the extended family were aware she
had been embraced as such. As Martsy explained to me that afternoon,
"More often I feel partial to the stealth side because I think that [Cindy]
deserves to have just a regular, normal childhood."[1]

This anecdote exemplifies the delicate, and often fraught, maneuverings of these parents to protect their children's privacy, safety, and identity. Meadow observed similar dealings with privacy and nondisclosure
among the parents they studied, especially to evade interventions from

the state. Given how traumatic these interventions can be, Meadow aptly describes families' experiences as "a persistent sense of always being watched, forever at risk."[2] In a separate vein, Meadow also encountered biological explanations among parents for gender nonconformity.[3] In this chapter, however, my focus concerns the *connections between* parents' privacy concerns and their biomedical frameworks for transgender bodies—namely, their use of "birth defect" analogies. These analogies were a noticeable pattern in interviews, and marked another key area where parents' perspectives did not immediately hearken to LGBTQ paradigms.[4] Not all biological understandings of gender bear the same meaning; "born this way" has a very different valence from "something went wrong," and I analyze these accordingly in the sections that follow. Moreover, I argue that these individualized, medicalized accounts intersect with matters of socioeconomics—that is, with living an otherwise "regular, normal" life in the cultural mainstream.

Parents' discussions about maintaining their children's privacy— about keeping their children's "privates private"—frequently confronted the terrain of the body and, in turn, normative logics for sex and gender. As many parents put it, "What my child has between their legs is nobody's business," or as Meredith said, "I don't go around telling everyone I have a vulva." This perspective well supports the position that transgender identity is not a psychiatric disorder or a mental illness, but a physical, bodily matter, most appropriately addressed in the biomedical realm, if treatment is desired at all.[5] In turn, few if any persons should know about it, lest they invade or exploit their child's "medical privacy" or "medical confidentiality." Lorraine, for example, cited "HIPPA violations" in her confrontations with school personnel about Jamie's use of bathrooms. Glenn and Jayne told school directors that should other parents ask about Amy using the girls' restroom, they can say, "It's not their business . . . this is a medical confidentiality issue."

In fact, amid these privacy concerns, a few parents mentioned coaching their children in certain bodily comportments that would help maintain their categorization as male/female in the eyes of others, in ways that recall sociologist Harold Garfinkel's notion of "practical methodology."[6] Nancy, for example, told Mickey how to comport himself if he is hit in the crotch while playing ball with his friends (i.e., he needs to act like it really hurts). Similarly, in response to questions from peers about why he always uses the stall (versus the urinal) in the bathroom, Tory told Connor, "Well, you tell them you're having a number two, or just say, 'My mum doesn't like me making a mess.'" Several parents of transgender girls mentioned searching for bathing suits and leotards that don't reveal "the bulge," and they explain it to their children in terms such as, "We don't want your 'privates' showing," as in, all people's "privates" are personal.

The wellspring of much sociological theorizing on gender arises from just this issue—one woman's (Agnes's) management of her status as female while keeping her "male" genitalia private and undisclosed, save from the few doctors and family members who were privy to it.[7] Indeed, one's ability to live accountably to a self-identified sex category—and not necessarily to an assigned sex—is the basis of sociocultural, versus biological, renderings of "gender." It is the revelation of one's sexed "criteria," or their *body*, that can bring a person's status as male or female under serious scrutiny, *not* necessarily their failure to conform to stereotypical displays of masculinity or femininity.[8] In terms of trans visibility, then, to be "out" is to effectively reveal that you were not "born with the body," or may not currently have the kind of body, that is presumed of the sex category with which you identify. Sociologist and gender theorist Raewyn Connell refers to this as "contradictory embodiment."[9] The parents I studied duly subscribed to this understanding of gender: their children can live as boys and girls, regardless of their sexed insignia, which has little relevance to daily interaction anyway. This is especially the case for prepubescent children whose secondary sex characteristics have not yet developed.

Altogether, parents' privacy negotiations had a great deal to do with managing and protecting their children's transgender embodiment— that is, being "born with one body," but living and presenting as the "other." As I learned, however, parents frequently compared this private embodied status to a "birth defect" or "disability"—that is, something that "went wrong" during fetal development, resulting in a "mismatch" between their child's sexual anatomy and their gender identity. Such biological, bodily matters, they argued, should be nobody's business, save relevant medical professionals, and rightfully so. As one advocate put it, nobody expects a child to openly discuss their "colostomy bag" with others; we shouldn't expect this kind of disclosure from trans kids either.

But on these terms, advocacy in the name of "medical privacy" was often tinged with biopathologizing perspectives of transgender bodies. To be sure, these analogies were issued by parents to support and protect their child and to normalize their transgender status, but they effectively reiterated cisgender bodies as natural, normal, and right.

Critical disability scholars, as well as intersex rights scholars and activists, have long decried "birth defect" frameworks.[10] Rather than seeing disability as an individual, medical abnormality that is the purview of the biomedical clinic, they target the wider sociocultural domain, which *constructs* and enables certain kinds of bodies as "normal" and others as "abnormal" and "disabled." Theirs is a *structural* critique of wider discourses, institutions, and ideologies, not of the private, individual realm. Eli Clare, for example, a queer, trans-identified scholar and disability rights activist, has explicitly challenged "birth defect" frameworks for both disability and transgender identity:

> It's an intense word ["defect"], loaded in this culture with pity and hatred. . . . [S]o when folks name their transness a birth defect, invoking some horrible bodily wrongness and appealing to cure as a means to end that wrongness, I find myself asking . . . what leads us to the belief that our bodies are defective in the first place . . . ?[11]

Of course, Clare does not object to medical treatment, but he argues that medicalized understandings will not address wider social prejudice toward embodied difference. As Clare says:

> I'm not dismissing medical transition. . . . [H]ormones and surgery can be powerful tools along the way for those of us who have money and health insurance. . . . And just as powerful are the choices to live in all kinds of gendered and sexed bodies. . . . All I mean is that medical technology will never be the whole answer for any of us.[12]

The ability to conceal certain nonnormative embodiments, or to be invisibly different—to be "nobody's business"—often intersects with raced and classed capital as well, including the ability to access affordable, patient-centered, trans-aware health care.[13] In terms of transgender identity, this is sometimes called "passing privilege": one's ability to move through the world without people perceiving them as trans many prefer not to use "pass/ing" terminology to avoid connotations of being "deceptive". Depending on one's location within the wider "matrix of domination,"[14] gender and gender nonconformity can intersect with a host of other vulnerabilities, including homelessness, joblessness, poverty, and racialized violence and profiling.[15] Indeed, as noted in the introduction of this book, various scholars have shown that gender, race, class, sexuality, and ability are not separate, additive parts of identity, but are interlocking, co-constructing, mutually dependent systems of disadvantage and inequality.[16] As such, gender nonconformity may be one of several intersecting factors that sets someone outside a "regular, normal" life—especially outside a life where one's embodied difference is protected within the realm of biomedical privacy. Queer politics have worked to address these issues, and all LGBTQ platforms have sought to resist pathologizing accounts of these identities.

Moreover, there are many gender-nonconforming persons whose identities have little to do with traditional schemas for sex and gender "alignment," and some would argue these schemas are as raced and classed as they are gendered.[17] Alok Vaid-Menon, for example, a nonbinary, trans-feminine, Indian American performance artist and queer activist, has decried mainstream LGBT rights for being white-centered, binary-oriented, and overly medicalized. As Vaid-Menon explains, their experience with transphobia and gender-based harassment has as much do with their ethnoracial identity in a "post-9/11 queer body" as it does with their visible gender nonconformity. As they said in an interview, "[I exist] outside of your colonial white-supremacist heteronormative gender binary. . . . I wasn't born in the wrong body, I was born in the wrong world."[18]

I explore the intersection of these themes—privacy, disability, and body logics, along with their connections to race and class—to cautiously and critically consider the ways parents, professionals, advocates, and scholars alike newly attempt to conceptualize and normalize "transgender" in the twenty-first century, particularly in the context of early childhood development and middle-class modes of child-rearing. Which perspectives on trans embodiment might cultivate a context that is safer and more supportive of trans realities, bodies, and experience, *should* these be revealed, disclosed, or "outed," or if they represent particularly visible forms of gender nonconformity? How might we normalize gender nonconformity in the culture at large, beyond the safety of the biomedical clinic and the privacy of the families who support it? Moreover, how might we achieve such gender-expansive understandings while honoring *everyone's* deeply felt sense of self, whether it be having the "wrong body," a "birth defect," or other?

Privacy and Power

One of the most salient, dense themes that arose across interviews concerned parents' management of their child's *privacy*—that is, how public they made their child's transgender status, if at all. Indeed, as I learned, this was a major topic of debate and contention among parents and forums. "There's two camps on the issue," as Janice put it: those who feel their child's transgender status is "nobody's business" and should be kept totally private, and those who entertain more openness with others, in the hopes of promoting more awareness and support of transgender persons. Both "camps" seek to normalize the experience for children, but from very different perspectives. This debate concerns more public advocacy efforts as well. While many parents understand the ethos of public advocacy, they felt they had to check their impulses to do so against their children's own privacy concerns, even as they appreciate, if not feel guilty over, the efforts of other families who do this work. Jeanette and Jazz Jennings, for example, are high-profile, mother-daughter advocates and the veritable poster family for transgender children. In addition to numerous TV specials and interviews, Jazz now has her own reality show on the Learning Channel, *I Am Jazz*. But some parents, I learned, have criticized this choice for compromising Jazz's privacy, which she could never get back if she wanted. Karen spelled out the dialectics of these debates:

> I think that's a struggle for everybody, how public versus how private you want to be. . . . Some people would say that I absolutely have no right sharing this information with you because it's my child's information, and some people are like—like Jazz and Jeanette, they're out there, and I think, how can you criticize Jazz and Jeanette when probably every single one of us, when they were trying to get their mind around this for

our own children, stumbled upon [them]. . . . Jazz is a face on transgender, and . . . I found it was *very* important for me to stumble on them, so how can . . . you criticize them for going public? [But] it's kind of scary to think that, at some point in that kid's life, if she wanted to be private, she couldn't . . . that decision is made. I mean I'm grateful to them for making it, but I sure get how hard it is.

All parents, of course, have to make decisions about whom to tell and when, and some circumstances require frank discussion, such as with old neighbors, close friends, and family, who effectively witness the transition. Outside of these circumstances, however, the majority of parents in the sample erred on the side of nondisclosure, per their children's own wishes, particularly when it came to new persons in the child's life. This meant that the majority of children at the time of the interviews were enrolled in school "privately" (or what parents often referred to as "stealth"). Other than a few key staff persons (e.g., the superintendent, principal, school nurse, school counselor, and/or the child's immediate teachers), nobody was aware that the child is transgender. This includes peers, other staff and teachers, extracurricular instructors or coaches, and/or new friends and neighbors.

For many parents, keeping their child's status private offers the child a "regular" life as a "normal" boy or girl, versus being the token "transgender" child among their peers. As Madalyn said, "If your child wants to present that way, as a female, then they want to be known as a female, they don't want to be known as a *trans* female." Tellingly, several parents started out with a more open position, and their children socially transitioned relatively publicly among their peers, but then they felt more inclined toward privacy, as their children's affirmed identity felt more familiar and as problems surfaced in their social milieu. As Janice said, "I initially felt strongly that people know. . . . I felt like it was important for people to understand that, hey, this is just a normal variation in society, we're not crazy people. . . . [But Eileen] was not invited to a single birthday party last year . . . so since [then], I've really [tried to] fly under the radar."

Heather had similar experiences, wherein negative events with her child's peers made her reconsider a more open approach. The school Samantha was attending—a progressive, explicitly gender-inclusive institution—was highly supportive of Samantha's transition, which was handled relatively publicly. But near the time of our follow-up interview, a classmate had kicked Samantha in the pelvic region on the playground, exclaiming, "You're not really a girl, I *know* where you're not a girl." Heather elaborated:

> I think my thinking's evolving on that. I have and I continue to feel that it's not the right message to give your kids that you need to hide who you are, and so it will be hard for me to let go of that. However, like this situation that happened just recently with Samantha, [it] wouldn't have happened, probably, if everyone didn't know who she was. And I can see having increasing safety concerns as she gets older, and I can see her having a desire to not have to navigate constantly [a public trans identity]. . . . I think she's going to have some decisions to make and she's going to have to figure that part out, and I could see supporting the stealth track if it felt safer for her.

Becca and Nathaniel's case exhibits this as well, where tensions with peers, not to mention with the administration over bathrooms, prompted them to enroll Bo privately in a whole different school district. In these examples, parents are moved to be more private as their child ages through the school system and experiences increased scrutiny from others, in more and more social settings.

Nicole, in contrast, feels very forthright about being open about her daughter, Sadie, who at the time of our interview, was entering the domain of dating, flirtation, and romance. Nicole does not want Sadie pursuing any crushes or love interests who do not know that she is transgender. She is adamant that disclosure is the safer, more ethical route to take, for all children involved. As Nicole said, "I could debate this all day." In fact, Nicole argued that it could be "social suicide" for a young boy if he pursued Sadie not knowing that she is transgender. She also cited the real physical dangers of dating without disclosing, even though she hates having to warn Sadie in these ways:

> I don't want a little boy to be teased in school because he likes the—they call her sometimes the "chick with the dick," that's what she's called behind her back [by a few peers]. . . . Because that's where they get mur-

dered, is if they go on a date and they don't disclose, they can be harmed, greatly harmed or even killed. [. . .] At this point, she's not interested in boys, she knows it's just too complicated . . . but I've told her, I said, "I know it's wrong, but if you have a crush on a guy and it gets out, people will be mean to him," and it's really difficult to have to tell your kid that. . . . That could cause that kid to question their own sexuality. . . . *I know that it doesn't mean anything, it doesn't mean that that person is gay or whatever, but they wouldn't understand it enough, you know what I mean? It could be very harmful to another child. And other people don't feel this way, like other parents of transgender kids, they'll be like, It's nobody's business when my kid goes on a date, it's nobody's business what's between their legs.*

Here, it is the anticipated risks of shielding her child's transgender status, especially in the context of dating, that motivates Nicole's desire to be open. Nicole's position, however, was rare among my sample.

Sutured to parents' anxieties about privacy was the recurring notion of "power"—that is, the power, of unknown severity, that another person might hold over their family and their child if they became privy to their transgender status. If it did get out, what would happen? Moreover, how does a parent manage to instill pride about being transgender, versus shame and secrecy, while navigating such vulnerable terrain? These tensions were exemplified in my interview with Karen. As a tool for managing Izzy's anxiety disorder (with which he was diagnosed), Karen uses a diagram of "big circle worries and little circle worries" and asks Izzy to put his "big" and "little" worries in their respective circles. While Izzy is more comfortable at his new school where everyone knows him as a "regular boy," he had recently described his fear over someone "finding out" as an "*infinity* circle worry." Karen elaborated: "In an instant, without giving it any thought, [the kid who knows] has the power to change the world, so that whole scenario makes me very nervous. . . . What are they going to do with that information? . . . That's what scares me more than anything." Karen had wanted to keep Izzy in his original parochial school for the transition, which was familiar ground for both of them. But his other behavioral needs forced them to transfer to a different school, where she and the staff decided it would be easier to keep the gender aspect of his enrollment private.

Notions of "power" also surfaced starkly in my interview with Theresa and Bill, a white, middle-class, heterosexual-identified married couple in their fifties. Theresa and Bill cited several fraught incidents regarding their daughter Lisa, a twelve-year-old transgender girl. One time, a peer from Lisa's past (before she transitioned) threatened to "out" her on social media. Specifically, Lisa had posted a photo of herself on her Instagram account, remarking how "pretty" it was. The peer responded, "Don't you mean handsome? Because Lisa is a man." Lisa immediately deleted the photo and was incredibly distraught, but nothing further came of the incident. In another story, a friend had heard from some "crossover" people from the past that "Lisa used to be a boy." Upon hearing this, Lisa immediately dismissed it. As Theresa explained:

> The way she handles it is, I mean, she'll use bad language, she'll get very sophisticated about it, she'll go, "*What the fuck?!*" She turns it on its head. Or she'll say, "Who told you that lie? They're lying, you shouldn't be friends with them because they lie. . . ." And I remember thinking, *Oh, this is like gaslighting this poor friend of hers.*

These moments were exemplary for Theresa and Bill of the ways Lisa has learned to manage her privacy adroitly among her peers. But they noted the stress involved in preserving this level of privacy, too, nodding to the notion of "power." As Bill explained:

> I think that is her fear, if someone were out to get her, how would she stop that? Someone who says something by accident, she'd figure out a way to throw up a smoke screen and then things will die down. . . . But if there were an entity, an older kid, or an adult that had some kind of agenda to whom this was important, to really make her miserable, then make our lives miserable, that person would have an incredible amount of power to do exactly that, because if we couldn't embarrass them out of it or . . . straighten them out . . . we are really at their mercy.

Bill and Theresa are determined to honor Lisa's wishes for privacy, as well as her identity (which is a *girl*, not necessarily a *transgender girl*), but they mourn the sense of well-being she might have if she could be more open with her friends and if her gender weren't such a source of "stigma management."[19] While parents do not want their children thinking that being transgender is a "shameful secret" that must be kept hidden, these stories testify to the threats of stigma, vulnerability, and/or disempowerment that managing a child's confidentiality often entails. Indeed, the phrase "it's private, not secret" resounded as a child-rearing mantra across conference spaces to counteract these feelings.

A story from Kari further pinpoints the minefield of privacy and power that families must navigate. Kari's family had recently moved to a new state and, per Emma's wishes, had enrolled Emma in a new school privately, where only the principal knew she was transgender. However, near the time of our interview, a child had peered under the stall when Emma was using the restroom, leaving Emma feeling anxious about staying private among her peers (nothing came of this encounter). Emma proposed to Kari that she just tell everyone she is transgender, so that she could, in her words, "feel free." Kari, however, was unsure if this was the wisest decision, explaining, "Freedom is a state of mind, maybe it's not getting picked on and feeling like a normal little girl like everybody else, there's freedom there too." Kari fears the consequences of going public, but she also wishes Emma could be more open, without worry: "I'd rather her be out . . . scream at the top of her lungs, *God made me perfect! I am who I am and I love exactly how I am!*"

Beyond social ostracism and bullying from peers, parents fear legal interventions, including from the state and CPS—legitimate concerns that at least four families in my sample experienced. These are terrifying, traumatic experiences that have lasting effects on families.[20] Claire and Rick's family experienced one such encounter, wherein all the members of the household were interviewed by CPS after an anonymous member of the community called them in about Andy, their transgender daughter. Claire and Rick immediately contacted a lawyer friend several states away, whom they were prepared to fly in directly at whatever cost as their legal defense. Thankfully, the case was dropped, and Andy was never removed from the family (though this is not always the outcome). But the whole ordeal spooked them deeply about being more open, and resulted in their moving out of state to protect their family's privacy. Claire is a successful writer and has written for several major media outlets, but this run-in with CPS has muzzled her from more public advocacy of trans kids: "I've become very protective. For example, I like that we're now renting; it gives us more freedom [to vacate]."

These stories highlight the extreme sense of vulnerability, and disempowerment, that many parents and children feel in these privacy negotiations. If it does get out, will the child be mocked, ostracized, or excluded? Could the child be physically harmed, as Nicole warned firmly about? Would the family encounter aggression from other families, the school, or the state? Would the child be removed from custody? In the words of Kari and Emma, what personal freedoms are clipped in a world that relies on cisgender presumptions for bodies and gender? How might that power be challenged? In the following sections, I turn to parents' discussions of the body and embodiment.

"Sadie Does Not Hate Her Body, She Just Desires the Body of a Female": Body Talk

As noted in chapter 1, parents and I specifically discussed the conversations they had with their children about their bodies, including their interests in medical options down the line, if any. I use the term "body dysphoria" to note a child's perceived dislike of, or distress over, their sexual anatomy and/or their desire to have anatomical characteristics of the "other sex." But when coding for "body dysphoria" in the interview data, it was difficult to ascribe a definitive "yes" or "no," considering the various ways one might define, measure, or interpret "dysphoria" in the first place, either positively (present) or negatively (absent) in parents' reports. While most parents reported some interest in body modification on the part of their children, few of these scenarios could be described as "feeling trapped in the wrong body" or as dysphoric. Instead, parents perceived their children's embodiment issues with varying levels of intensity or urgency, sometimes with none at all, and they were quite candid about the influence of life course developments on a child's relationship to their body as well.

Nicole's interview, for example, included moments that could be variously coded as negative (absent) and positive (present) for "body dysphoria," even while her daughter Sadie was actively and eagerly pursuing hormone treatments. In several instances, Nicole cited Sadie's dislike of her genital anatomy as a young child; indeed, this was one of the major factors that prompted Nicole to seek professional help: "[The doctor] said this is not normal behavior, wanting to remove her penis at that age [three years old] . . . she said take her to a specialist." However, at other moments, Nicole's description of Sadie's embodied sensibilities was more nuanced:

> Sadie does not hate her body, she's never hated her body, she just desires to have the body of a female. . . . When she was little she was sort of like, *It's not so bad*, but now that's she's older, she knows that she really wants to be a full woman . . . but she's not like, *Ew, I hate this thing*.

Tory delivered a similarly layered and nuanced discussion of her son's relationship to his body:

> Connor'll say, "I'm part girl because my body is female, but I'm a boy," that's how Connor describes himself . . . and you know what, he doesn't seem to have an aversion to his body, he would really like a penis, but he's not [extreme]. . . . Connor has said that she doesn't want boobs and [has asked], "Can we cut them off?"[21] So I guess that's [something], but with having like a preadolescent body, Connor doesn't have an aversion to it.

While interests in body modification certainly surfaced here, Tory intimated that Connor's day-to-day embodied experience is fairly uneventful and nondistressed. In another account, during my follow-up interview with Becca, Becca said that only "recently" had Bo started inquiring about body change options (Bo was nine years old at the time). Her interests especially picked up after attending summer camp, where other transgender children were discussing body modification. Before this, though, Becca said "the body was not even a piece of the picture":

> In the context of like, *How do you see yourself*, the body piece of it doesn't really come into it, as far as I can tell . . . the body is a secondary piece of it. . . . I think different kids have different feelings about this, but I think some kids are really . . . dysphoric . . . and that's not the case for Bo. However, now she is starting to recognize—she's starting to put the two things together, I think, and now she's starting to see that body features and identity, she's starting to put those together, and I can see

that. They're still not totally married, for lack of a better word, but . . . I'm starting to see that. Whereas before, the body was not even a piece of the picture. . . . But recently . . . she has talked about wanting to go on blockers, and wanting to have The Surgery, capital T, capital S, and wanting to have boobs, and we're like, *Wow! OK! So let's talk about that when the time comes.*

In this example, Becca is attributing her child's emerging interests in body change to life course developments, as Bo grows older with the rest of her peers/cohort and becomes more body-conscious, not necessarily to body-related distress. Becca also attributes Bo's awareness of specific medical interventions (i.e., hormone blockers, "The Surgery") to peer socialization among other transgender children, whom Bo has befriended through conferences and summer camp. In these ways, Bo's growing desires for body change are understood more in terms of her age, development, and social context versus as a result of feeling intrinsically "born in the wrong body."

To be sure, some children did express significant discomfort about their bodies or about the biological puberty they would experience in the future (e.g., developing breasts and menstruating, growing facial hair), but these concerns did not present to parents as persistent or ongoing. There were far more examples that would be characterized as less "severe" or "extreme" by parents but that nevertheless signaled to them that their child was interested in body modification in the future. Marie, for example, said that Milo never explicitly said that he "wants a penis," but she did recall Milo stuffing his underwear when he was three years old. Nor did he try to pee standing up (which Marie attributed to the fact that his father does not do this either). Overall, Marie said that the real "game changer" for her was Milo's apparent aversion to pregnancy, childbirth, and having his own babies: "I got a book from the library [that said], 'Mommies have the ability to have babies in their belly,' and I asked him, 'Do you think you would ever be interested in having babies in your belly?' And he was like 'No way!'" Overall, children's interest in having their own babies or not was a common factor parents attempted to discern, in the most age-appropriate ways possible.

According to some parents, there were children who did not seem to express any embodied discomfort or interest in body change. This characterized approximately five cases. Bruce, for example, sensed that Holden was very comfortable with her body, and wondered if this is because her body "didn't keep her from expressing her gender for very long." Bruce's "cheap theory," as he called it, recalls fraught arguments about whether there would be a "need" for body change if gender was not so heavily linked to anatomical sex in the first place:[22]

> Yeah, this is actually fascinating . . . because I don't often think about that [body dysphoria] until I talk to other parents. My child, she doesn't really seem to be dysphoric, and I realize that that's the term that makes people feel like, you know, *Then we are certain we're trans!* or something like that . . . but I think my child is not dysphoric because . . . we didn't withhold the things that she wanted very long and very stridently, we didn't keep her from expressing her gender very long or very hard or very directly. . . . So this is a cheap theory, but I'm thinking maybe she's not showing signs of hating her penis because we haven't taught her that that's the thing that's keeping her from having a dress. . . . I don't know, I talk to parents who have very young kids who [seem very dysphoric], and I'm shocked.

In these scenarios, parents' encounters with an absence of body dysphoria prompted them to think concertedly about alternative embodied understandings for their children, in ways that resisted traditional cisgender body logics.

All told, children's interests in body modification were indeed present in the data, but these manifested in a range of ways, some more fluid, nuanced, and complex than others, and were not quite comparable to "feeling trapped in the wrong body," at least not in early childhood. Of course, all of these accounts refer to the *parents'* assessments of their children's embodied sentiments, however much they were revealed to them and in whichever ways parents interpreted those comments. Yet, it is precisely the *parents'* perceptions that facilitated these transitional processes, especially regarding biomedical interventions—the children weren't the ones consulting doctors or pediatric endocrinologists. In this way, "the body" aspect well captures the child-driven but intensively parent-facilitated nature of the trans-affirmative paradigm. With these factors in mind, I turn more fully to parents' biomedical models for transgender embodiment.

"Birth Defects" and Body Logics

Throughout interviews, I frequently encountered the notion of a "birth defect" or "disability," to which some parents compared their child's transgender status. And these responses were related to parents' privacy approaches. As Karen reported, the "birth defect" analogy was often invoked among the "stealth" camp in parents' online discussions, in terms of why a parent would keep their child's status private: "People with like a six-year-old [say], *It's just a birth defect, I don't need to tell anybody, it's nobody's business that my child doesn't have a penis or has a penis or whatever, I don't walk around telling people that I do or don't have certain body parts.*" Karen also noted, however, that this concept might be easier to embrace with a younger child than an older child, whose body is less visibly sexed to others. This indicates the age-inflected dynamics of *parents'* perspectives on embodiment, as much as the children's. There was not necessarily a one-to-one correlation between parents who espoused birth defect analogies and those who preferred to be private about their child. Some parents drew on these for explaining their ethic of nondisclosure, whereas others, who may have been more open about their child's status, drew on these apart from privacy negotiations (Nicole was one example of this latter type). Nevertheless, themes of both privacy and transgender embodiment often intersected in interviews by way of notions of "disability" and "birth defects." In turn, parents' privacy concerns frequently confronted cisgender logics for sex and gender.

When I probed Karen more personally about the "birth defect" analogy, she defended it: "Well you know what, I think something went wrong. I mean I know a lot of people don't feel that way . . . but I think something went wrong, your brain and your body don't match, it's not right, and it's not easy." Trish subscribed to "wrong body" logics, too, though she also acknowledged the fraught reputation of such logics:

> I bring it back to the simplicity of, his brain is a boy and unfortunately he was born with girl parts. . . . [T]he simplicity for him is that that's how a boy is and that's how a girl is . . . a vagina is a vagina and it does belong to a girl, and a penis is a penis and it does typically belong to a boy, and if you happen to be born with the wrong part—I believe more that it's

you're born with incorrect parts, and I know there's this whole big discussion going on. . . . I don't know if you saw the "Born in the Wrong Body" Katie Couric special, and that was the title of it, and there was this huge debate going on with parents about telling their children they were born in the wrong body . . . it's huge right now on the [listserv]. . . . I've never used that phrase for him. We stick to, *"Your brain's a boy, your body's [a girl's]."* We'd put him in denial if we didn't acknowledge that to him. The reality is his body is a girl's, girls have breasts, you know what I mean?

Similarly, Monica reasoned, "The way that I think of it is, my body didn't make a penis while Hayden was in my belly, my body kind of screwed up and didn't make a penis . . . because truly that's what happened, Hayden's penis didn't come out."

Many parents argued that a biological explanation would be liberating from stigma, not unlike "born-this-way" notions of a "gay gene" or the "transsexual/transgender brain." I often encountered these kinds of claims when asking parents if they had ever thought about potential "causes" of gender nonconformity. Given the question, I arguably primed parents for the kinds of biomedical frameworks, and disability analogies, that I received; the term "causes" in our culture almost always has a biological connotation, not a structural or social-scientific one. However, several parents responded quite specifically and thoroughly to the question, having already ruminated extensively about, if not researched, various biological factors, processes, and/or "comorbidities" that might have resulted in a transgender child. See, for example, Harmony's response to the question, in which she immediately referred to two "traumatic experiences" that potentially influenced her son's gender-nonconforming development:

E: Do you ever think about causes of gender variance?
H: *Oh, all the time!* Oh my God, I think about it all the time because I had two really traumatic experiences with Baldwin [being in a bad storm when she was pregnant with him and his taking a bad fall at the age of two years]. I wonder all the time if there's some sort of like correlation and relationship between a traumatic experience in utero or a traumatic experience in early childhood. It would be interesting, you know, if some research revealed that there's a direct relationship

between physical trauma for a child and trans and we would all have this kind of like, *Oh*, that's *why this is happening*. It wouldn't change who the child is, it wouldn't change anything, it wouldn't make me want to tell him that he needs to go back to being a girl, I mean it's who he is, I mean maybe it would be more of a relief like, *Oh that's why*, and maybe it would help society be more accepting of kids that are like this . . . like it's completely beyond the control of the child.

Similarly, Karen elaborated on specific biomedical causes that she had researched and theorized about, including the use of drugs, alcohol, and a certain anticonvulsant during pregnancy (she found a paper on this), which she suspects of Izzy's birth mother. When I again probed her on this, she was candid about feeling that trans is a birth outcome that is ideally "avoided":

> E: You're making me think . . . how would you respond to someone who says, "Well, then you're saying let's do all these things to prevent gender variance from being caused in the womb?"
> K: Well, I don't look at it as, *Rah-rah transgender, it's all good!* . . . I see it as something to be avoided. I mean I know people would disagree with me, but I consider it like a disability or a disorder, because it's a huge problem, so if you have a choice and if we know what caused it, I would see it as something to be avoided.

Wendy also mused about a range of potential biological correlations, including artificial insemination, alcoholism, drug use, and autism. She had heard about these potential "comorbidities," as she termed them throughout our interview, through other parent forums and practitioners:

> We do know from the conferences that we've gone to and through our time with [a therapist] that there's a strong correlation between adoptive kids, foster kids, and[/or] kids that are artificially inseminated or in vitro and they don't exactly know why that correlation is but . . . that population has higher drug exposure, alcohol exposure, [such] that something might be happening hormonally during the prenatal period. They're talking about some of the synapses being off-balance . . . but we

definitely are under the belief that that is something organic in the brain and it definitely must have something to do with the sensory processing symptoms because that's why [the therapists] will say nearly one-third to higher of all of the kids that come through their clinic either have sensory processing disorder or have autism. Anyway, whatever it is in the brain [that's] causing some gender issues is also causing sensory issues in kids and that's why the autism thing is so high. They just don't know why, or with the adoption or artificial insemination or in vitro people . . . they just haven't had enough studies to factor all that stuff out.[23]

As noted in chapter 3, the "comorbidities" concept surfaced in my most recent follow-up call with Becca, too. I used this as an opportunity to ask her how she felt about the "birth defect discourse" specifically—including the notion that transgender is something that should not occur during "normal" gestational development. She replied, "Well, I can't disagree with that." She then compared it to those who are born with "one brown eye, one blue eye," hedging around framing gender nonconformity as something that "went wrong" per se.

Notably, Karen, Trish, Monica, Wendy, and Becca all have parented around a range of other biomedical, behavioral, and/or disability issues with their children (this includes severe anxiety, reactive attachment disorder, fetal alcohol syndrome, delayed cognitive development, ADHD, and obsessive-compulsive disorder, which they described to me in interviews). Just like transgender identity and gender nonconformity, these circumstances require keen institutional maneuverings from parents to get their children the supports they need, including from schools, teachers, psychologists, doctors, insurance companies, and other specialists. As such, biomedical or psychiatric frameworks, including the disability analogies these conjure up, would strongly resonate with parents' experiences in the transgender context—"disability" is a familiar and meaningful framework. In *The Trans Generation*, for example, Travers uses an overarching "critical disability" framework to analyze the dis-abling effects of binary institutions on trans students, who must push for better accommodations and recognition. Indeed, the literature on parents with children with disabilities resounds with resonant themes and patterns when compared to those of parents with gender-nonconforming kids.[24]

Parents' "disability" analogies, however, did not quite depict critical structural analyses; instead, their focus was on the individual realm and the "abnormalities" perceived there. Monica echoed this logic when she said she believed something "screwed up" in her womb. She then compared her position to the politics of persons who are deaf, with which she didn't fully align: "It kind of reminds me of the deaf thing, like a lot of deaf people don't think that they're handicapped, they don't think there's anything wrong with them . . . they're like proud of being deaf, that's why they don't like [people who get implants to hear]." Monica's husband Dan chimed in, corroborating her position:

> I look at it as something that went wrong . . . the typical human development is to have a brain that matches your body . . . but I really hope one day they identify exactly what it is because it would just make this so much easier . . . [so] you can say, look my child's this way because of this, you know? My child has autism because of this, my child is deaf because of this, and people go, *OK*, they don't question it. If my child is transgender because they've identified this . . . then that is the same in all of that.

In line with this mode of thinking, several other parents compared their children's transgender status to specific medical conditions. In my interview with Nicole, for example, I asked her about an infamous 20/20 interview with Jazz Jennings and her family, in which her sister described transgender as a "disorder" or a "birth defect." Nicole concurred with this analogy, comparing transgender to other congenital "abnormalities":

> You know, part of me agrees with her [Jazz's sister], I hate the word "defect," but she looked at it like, a girl with a penis could be considered a person with a cleft palette or born with one arm or born deaf or blind, you know? Like it's not supposed to be that way, you're not supposed to have a penis if you're a girl, so to me it is a birth *abnormality*, let's say. I mean I don't like the word "defect," but it is certainly not what was *supposed* to happen.

When discussing her legal battles with her ex-husband (who does not support raising their child as transgender), Madalyn compared being able to pursue hormone options to chemotherapy: "To me, it's just like if she had cancer and he wasn't willing to get treatment for her or something like that, like I just can't deal with that." In this vein, embracing the medical model is a matter of giving their children something that they need, like insulin, helping their children to achieve a kind of able-bodiedness. And for many trans children and youth, medical intervention indeed feels necessary.

I encountered similar biomedical frameworks and analogies with some of the professionals I interviewed as well. For example, when discussing the implications of having a gender dysphoria diagnosis in the *DSM*, Lina (a therapist) refuted the notion that transgender is a "mental disorder," framing it instead as a "medical condition that creates a mismatch of the brain and body": "I mean, you can have a lot of mental distress from having a brain tumor or something else that's ailing you, but that doesn't give you a mental disorder." Similarly, when discussing issues of privacy versus advocacy, Gail (an educator) turned to biomedical analogies:

> Some people feel that by not being out, you are keeping a secret. We prefer to say, his body is private. You know, if you have a kid with a colostomy bag, are you going to school and telling everybody, "Hey, I want to train you, I want to let you know my child has a colostomy"? Would we be asking that about [a child] who has a mild case of cerebral palsy?

In all of these instances, parents and professionals invoked biomedical understandings, and arguably biopathologizing understandings, to frame transgender embodiment and experience.

Alternative Discourses

Not all parents subscribed to these biomedical frameworks. Several parents, albeit a minority in the sample, explicitly gestured to alternative notions instead, such as "natural biological variation," countering the "biological mishap" line of thinking. Linda exemplified this position: "I call her an evolutionary inevitability, there's just no way that human beings aren't going to get to the point where gender gets revealed as being a complete and total mental construct and it's reached its limits in her, she is a manifestation of that. . . . I think she has a lot to teach many of us about human existence." Linda went on to say, "Gender is completely an utter construct that we have been force-fed for generations, and it's starting to get revealed and that's part of what makes people so fucking terrified."

Kari said that she used the metaphor of X-Men and "genetic mutations" to explain transgender to her other child, but she clarified her *nondefect* meanings behind this terminology:

> I said, "These are special kids with genetic mutations, and mutations in the gene pool are important because they sustain life, they're how the species carries on." . . . I hate to use the words "genetic mutations" because the connotation is pretty negative, but as a science major, it doesn't feel that way to me . . . because [trans people have] been around forever . . . we are evolving as a species . . . and I think it's an important step in humanity because [it gets] us out of our binary thinking. . . . I think that you should be allowed to be born a male and transition to a female and have male parts and still be a female.

Even when referring to "genetic mutations" and evolution—interesting claims in their own right—these parents describe transgender not as something that "went wrong," but more as a matter of natural human variation, as part of our inevitable, biodiverse potential. This kind of normalizing perspective is quite different from the framework of "defective," "mismatched" bodies. The parents in this alternative "camp" represent a mind-set that gender is a social category that social actors coproduce, and while this category has vast implications for children's happiness and safety, the realities of transgender children signal that the category itself is no longer working, *not* that these children's development went awry. This is not so much a political rallying cry as a call to recognize that these children are perhaps the inevitable "social evolution" beyond cisgender assumptions and ideals. Of course, as Kari notes, children like this have always existed, but in these parents' eyes, society has lacked the capacity to really confront or consider what this means for normative gender ideology until now.

Notably, Linda and Kari were two of four mixed-race-identified parents in the study, and both noted that their experiences with race and ethnicity informed their viewpoints on gender nonconformity. As Linda said:

> One thing I should clarify, though, is that . . . I'm biracial, my father was Black and my mother was white. . . . I grew up "passing" quote-unquote as a white girl living a Black experience. . . . I've lived a lifetime of seeming to be one thing and perceived as another in the world of race, so I have a lot of history with this world, in a totally different context.

Similarly, Kari, who identifies as half Arab, half white, said, "I've always questioned everything, I question society, I question society's rules. . . . [I was] always living in between worlds anyway, never quite fitting in." In short, both of these women drew on their experiences with mixed-race identity in a racialized society as an analogue for making sense of their children's gender, leaning toward a more critical, social-structural, and deconstructionist approach and understanding.

Bruce was also fervently resistant to "wrong body" logics and related "birth defect" discourses, challenging specifically some of the psychologists who employ a "body of a [boy/girl], brain of a [boy/girl]" framework for children. He feels this unnecessarily forces a "misalignment" perspective, especially since his own daughter exhibits no conflict around her embodiment. As he said in one e-mail:

> I hate the idea of a body that is "boy" or "girl" as distinctive from the heart and mind, I would tell these psychologists to stop implying to children that these things are distinct. They are invested in a misalignment, and I am invested in a notion that my child's body is a girl's body because she is a girl. If she ever tells me it is not, I will listen, but until she states a misalignment, it is not [that]. This is part of the medicalization of trans identities. Don't provide a template for the trans person to fit themselves into. Let them define freely.

Bruce also noted that the language they have adopted in their family is that his daughter is "like her friends from the [trans conference]," *not* that she is "different from other kids." Bruce prefers this language because it emphasizes community, not difference. For Bruce, "transgender embodiment" is a concept that is culturally imposed on children, rather than flowing from some logic of the body. As his "cheap theory" goes, as he referred to it earlier, the feeling of dysphoria may only develop as children are made aware of such embodied "difference" in the first place. Of course, for many other parents, whose children have articulated "wrong body" logics and queries since very early on (e.g., *"Why don't I have a penis?"*), these alternative positions don't answer to their experiences. Karen and Grace, for example, were keen to emphasize their children's desires for different anatomy in their accounts.

Interestingly, regardless of what they said in interviews, parents intimated that they tried to avoid explicit "wrong body" or "birth defect" narratives with their children, sayings things instead like, "You're a girl who has a penis," "Some girls have pee-pees on the inside, some girls have pee-pees on the outside," or "You're perfect the way you are." As Linda said, "I want her to get that her privates are private . . . and that there's nothing wrong with them, that she's whole, perfect, and complete and beautiful, and she is a girl who has a penis, which is very, very unusual and very unique, and then I always say that every human has their own strengths, gifts, and talents." Similarly, Kari advised, "I started changing the way that I talk to Emma and telling her . . . 'You're not a transgender . . . you are a little girl who happens to have a penis.'" And Glenn said, "That comment of, *God made a mistake with my body*, my response is, *No, God doesn't make mistakes, your body is perfect, your body is beautiful.* . . . I try so hard to convey to Amy that she's perfect just the way she is, there's no mistake, there's nothing wrong." Jazz Jennings's response in the *20/20* interview bears noting as well. When Barbara Walters turned to Jazz to ask how she feels about the term "disorder," Jazz resisted: "Personally, I don't like that word that much, I prefer 'special' or 'unique' 'cause that's what I think transgender is." While I cannot know for sure what Jazz meant, her response at least implicitly resists pathologizing or medicalizing frames for transgender experience.[25]

In many ways, the transgender child's body is where the social and the natural collide, and parents become the necessary interpreters and mediators of this complex merger. Parents must negotiate the received knowledge of what sex and gender are vis-à-vis the child's experience of their own body. Parents are thus in the very difficult role of wanting to avoid imposing cisgender, pathologizing language and beliefs onto children's bodies while at the same time trying to give credence to their very real embodied sensibilities. This delicate discursive labor among these parents, however, helps to produce the alternative affirmative rhetorics they practiced with their children (i.e., "*You don't have a 'boy's body,' you have your body*"). Parents' attempts with these alternative discourses with their children motivate my evaluation of the more biopathologizing frameworks and analogies they marshaled in our interviews.

I encountered additional critiques of biomedical frameworks from one of the major advocacy voices in this terrain, Meryl, who founded one of the largest advocacy organizations for parents of trans youth:

I think sometimes [a biological theory] would make people feel better. . . . It gives *me* discomfort in a lot of ways, because then does that open the door to aborting fetuses who have this particular gene, what does it give rise to? Is this now a defect that we should get rid of? . . . [These kids] can teach us how to jump gender roles and stereotypes.

Admittedly, I was surprised to hear this critique from Meryl, as her group was occasionally characterized as the more normative, or normativizing, binary-oriented outpost for parental support. Perhaps I was not expecting such a candid rejection of the "birth defect" analogy that so many of the parents within her network had apparently espoused. Nevertheless, later in our interview, Meryl mused about the otherwise normative status of these children, many of whom have been raised in culturally normative families and contexts, who are living otherwise "regular, normal" lives in the middle-class mainstream. In turn, she wondered if these kids may not identify with, or perhaps "lose out" on cultivating, a more politicized and radicalized trans consciousness:

Kids who transitioned early . . . are our parents trying to fit our kids into a heteronormative sort of mold, you know? . . . It just sort of dawned on some of us one day that, do our children live a transgender experience, or is their experience becoming something we've never seen before, and are we consciously thinking about that and what that looks like? . . . Are we *de-transgendering* them, in a way, are we putting them in the position of being ashamed of having a transgender identity, and I do think that's a risk. . . . Have we created such a protective bubble for them to live in? I think that we're at that point where . . . have we done such a good job of [early transitioning] that we somehow have made them feel that being transgender is a bad thing?

This perspective resonated with Meadow's observations of the "transgender activism, cisgender logic" of the parent-advocacy movement.[26] It also recalled an essay by gender and sexuality studies scholar Jason Jacobs, "Raising Gays," in which he writes about the *Glee* phenomenon and parents' normalizing approaches with LGBTQ youth: "The emergent fantasy of lovingly parented, 'accepted' gay kids . . . assumes that unpersecuted gayness will fall easily into the structures and rhythms of straight life rather than charting out new ways of living—other forms of care, friendship, community, and political alliance."[27]

Meryl's comments echoed those of a physician I interviewed as well, Dr. Molio, who directs one of the largest gender clinics for gender-nonconforming youth in the United States. In Dr. Molio's view, many of the transgender children she sees at her clinic are living in a "cisgender world," which their parents have helped to create and protect. There is nothing really "transgender" about their lives, she claimed, other than an early "contradictory embodiment" that will be addressed through hormone blockers and, eventually, cross-sex hormones and/or surgery. As she told me, "We're [hormone-]blocking all the white, upper-class kids." Dr. Molio wondered if trans identity will become an increasingly racialized experience, especially for low-income, trans-feminine persons of color, who cannot easily access the kinds of biomedical management, and related privacy protections, that these children do. This view recalled Becca's experiences, too, when she said she has to "drag" Bo to the trans marches because she is so uninterested in them. As these comments indicate, what becomes of trans experience, identity, community, and politics in the wake of this new trans-affirmative parenting paradigm, and following this first generation of trans-affirmed kids, is a pressing question.[28]

Conclusion

A substantial component of parents' privacy efforts concerned keeping their children's "contradictory embodiment" private and concealed, as a matter of "medical confidentiality." As Linda said, "I don't walk up to you and say, 'Hi Elizabeth, it's nice to meet you, and by the way, I have a vagina.'" In the world of gender displays, these parents well understand that while sexual anatomy may be presumed in social interaction, it is rarely explicitly revealed or referenced, and nor should their children's be. Their children are boys and girls, they should be seen as boys and girls, and their bodies should have nothing to do with it. In these ways, these parents afford their children the lives and identities of "regular, normal" boys and girls, just as the children fervently express that they are. From a sociological point of view, this reveals both the otherwise invisible and practical scaffolding that makes gender and sex intelligible and natural to others. And it provides the detail that portends a great deal about how practices and presumptions can change.

However, as part of their medical perspectives, parents often invoked analogies of "birth defects" or medical impairment, such as cleft palates, cancer, Down syndrome, cerebral palsy, brain tumors, and deafness. Of course, these analogies do not necessarily pathologize gender nonconformity. Disability rights activists and scholars, as well as intersex rights scholars, have challenged that logic for decades. Parents' disability analogies could well harbor *challenges* to normative logics for sex and gender: boys *shouldn't* necessarily have penises, and girls *shouldn't* necessarily have vaginas. That is, normative expectations about the relationships between bodies and gender identities are interrogated, not the embodiments themselves. And as observed among several parents who have advocated around other disabilities for their children, "disability" seems like an analogous framework indeed. But parents' analogies did not quite exhibit the tenor of such critical "crip" interrogation, or of queer or social-structural deconstruction.[29] These kinds of body logics did not challenge or disrupt normative expectations, but effectively reinstated them, upholding cisgender embodiment as healthy, normal, and "right."

To be clear, these parents do not expect or require body modification for their kids down the line, hormonally, surgically, or otherwise. Like so many things, that is regarded as a child-centered, child-directed decision, determined via the most age-appropriate dialogues parents can manage along the way. Parents were cognizant of a range of embodied options for the future, and they hoped that their child would feel comfortable to choose whatever felt best for them. Many parents intimated that, on some level, they wished their child didn't have to change their body at all, indicating an awareness that bodies and gender do not necessarily have to "match." But most children indicated some interest in body change, at varying degrees and points in their development. As such, parents' biomedical frameworks worked to normalize and validate those interests and the medical options that would assist.

Parents' biomedical frameworks offer children an empowering explanatory narrative, one that holds much cultural sway and intelligibility, especially when a child asks, "Why did God make a mistake?" Indeed, that was not an uncommon question from the children. Moreover, parents were not necessarily invoking their children's bodies as "wrong," but sometimes their own bodies, in terms of a failure to properly gestate. As Monica said, "My body didn't make a penis." Similarly, Becca couldn't help but wonder about her diet during her pregnancies. Other mothers wondered about the habits of their children's birth mothers during pregnancy.

In *Whipping Girl*, Julia Serano tackles the "wrong body" issue head-on. While she resists that terminology, she explains that her trans experience, like many people's, had less to do with her "gender" and more to do with her physical body. She sensed a strong, intrinsic dissonance between the "subconscious sex" she knew herself to be (female) and the physical sex she was assigned (male). Once she finally embarked on medical modifications, including hormones, things just felt "right."[30] This is why she gives credence to theories of the "hard-wiring" of gender identity in the brain.[31] Seeber would refer to this as Serano's "sex identity," not to be confused with matters of gender or gendered behaviors.[32] These perspectives are also affirmed in the biography *Becoming Nicole* by journalist Amy Ellis Nutt, which summarizes the data on the "transgender brain."[33] A parent specifically referred me to this source, which she found helpful.

Gender theorist Talia Bettcher actually claims that "wrong body" narratives hold powerful resistant potential, since transphobia is most often experienced when trans people are *wrongly* held accountable to their physically perceived sex (assigned sex) and not to the sex category with which they actually identify.[34] On these terms, to assert that one is in the "wrong body" is to resist being held wrongly accountable. For a child who actively expresses interest in having the "other parts," or wonders why they weren't born with certain parts, these frameworks are an affirmative, validating response to the kind of embodiment that can feel so "wrong" to them.

Regardless this analysis does not question gender-affirming medical interventions or a child's interests in these. As these parents understand, every person has a right to privacy, safety, and self-determination about their own embodied experiences, especially young children. Nor do these families' experiences with privacy beg for more visibility or advocacy work—that is not their job, let alone the children's. Neil, the educator, was firm about this in our interview: "It's not the job of the oppressed to explain and fix their oppression." As far as these kids' relationship to trans culture and community, it is hard to mourn the loss of a more politicized trans consciousness when it was born out of undue prejudice and oppression in the first place.

But parents' negotiations with privacy and confidentiality, and the anxieties wrapped up in them, do underscore the grave vulnerabilities that exist in a world still grounded in cisgender assumptions. They also signal the kinds of rhetorics and frameworks that might sooner emerge from less precarious positions within structural hierarchies, where broader forms of resistance and critique may be less salient within the fabric of "regular, normal" everyday life. As Meryl's and Dr. Molio's comments suggest, these perspectives raise questions about the state of gender nonconformity at large, for a diverse range of gender-nonconforming bodies and demographics, beyond the clinic's walls and the families who protect them. What happens to wider cultural ideologies that make gender nonconformity—especially more visible forms of gender nonconformity and "contradictory embodiment"—a "problem" in the first place? How will such powerful presumptions about bodies and gender be challenged? These are important questions to consider in the new trans-affirmative era. As several of these parents attest, we face a critical opportunity to challenge old presumptions, craft new logics, and speak new truths to power.

Conclusion

You raise the child standing before you.
—Claire, parent

During our interview, Glenn—the father whose family's story opened this book—proudly displayed his pink T-shirt to me. As he told me, "I purposely wore this today just to get the visual that I wanted to show Amy that as a man, you can wear pink. . . . I'd never worn pink, I wasn't drawn to that personally, so I started wearing flare and I got four pink shirts and purple shirts and pink board shorts, and ever since then I wear them all the time . . . it's really added to my wardrobe." While Glenn has embraced Amy as the transgender girl she is, his trans-affirmative parenting journey clearly shifted his own perspectives on gender. Toward the end of the interview, he reflected, "I've evolved so much in the last four years." Indeed, both Jayne and Glenn repeated the resounding refrain of the parent-advocacy community I studied: "This was *our* transition, not hers." In this conclusion, I summarize the major themes and findings of the book and synthesize its contributions for understanding this new model of trans-affirmative parenting. I aim to highlight the potential limits, as well as the great liberating implications, of the phenomenon.

To borrow a phrase from Valentine, this book represents "a snapshot of a moment in a rapidly changing field of meanings," both within these families' lives and in society at large.[1] Transgender identity as we know it today is not new, but the category is increasingly central to popular media, discourse, and politics. This is reflected in proliferating trans-inclusive policies in health care, schools, and identity documentation; popular TV programs (*Transparent*, *I Am Jazz*, *My House*, *Pose*, *RuPaul's Drag Race*); and vocal public figures, including Janet Mock, Laverne Cox, Caitlyn Jenner, Jazz Jennings, and Jacob Tobia. Within this cultural context, some parents are deciding to raise their young children as transgender, facilitating relatively unprecedented early childhood transitions from one sex-categorical "box" to the "other" in ways that were unavailable, if not inconceivable, to prior generations, just as Leigh reflected on in our interview. These decisions extend gender-neutral or feminist parenting principles beyond their original conceptions and practices, rupturing the fundamental link between sex and gender that had been flexed, but ultimately maintained, in parents' early approaches.[2]

In many ways, the LGBT rights movement, as well as queer deconstructionist theorizing and politics, set the stage for this phenomenon. Thanks to these historical scaffolds, contemporary parents are increasingly aware of LGBTQ possibilities for their children, even if they are only vaguely familiar with, or connected to, the more specific events, schisms, and intersections within that history. In the face of a persistently gender-nonconforming child, parents come to understand the flaws of traditional expectations for sex, gender, and sexuality, and a wider cultural stage of LGBTQ advancements helped to validate that realization. But parents' experiences, perspectives, and decisions did not always hearken to LGBTQ tenets, and were driven instead by intensive, child-centered parenting processes. There is important research on families of LGBTQ youth that addresses how parents support, or do not support, these kids, including the "biopsychosocial" risk factors involved here.[3] But this book shows that the intensive parent-child relationship of the twenty-first century is also where new possibilities for sex, gender, and sexuality are realized, (re)imagined, and brought to life, especially when parents have the time, energy, resources, and support networks to explore them. These dynamics were observed in three main conceptual areas: gender and sexuality, the gender binary, and the body.

Gender and Sexuality at a Crossroads

A critical part of parents' conceptual work is establishing firm distinctions between "gender" and "sexuality"—*gender identity* is one thing, *sexual orientation* is another. Their children's gender nonconformity is a matter of *(trans)gender*, not *(homo)sexuality* or being "gay." Today, many parents and advocates would all but dismiss sexual orientation as an irrelevant interpretive grid, if not as a preposterous suggestion, for young gender-nonconforming children. Here, parents' understandings are well aligned with those of mainstream LGBT rights. But parents' "trans" interpretations of their children's behaviors depart from the "insights" of decades of longitudinal data, as well as from a deeper cultural legacy that links gender nonconformity with homosexuality. Indeed, much of the controversy over early childhood transitions concerns the purported legacy of "just gay," not trans, statistical outcomes for childhood gender nonconformity. Parents' trans-affirming decisions, then, are no small juncture in history.

Parents engaged in several discursive and deliberative practices to tease apart these different types of gender nonconformity, and different grids of understanding, to distinguish their child as "truly trans." They evaluated previous research as immaterial and flawed, dismissing "just gay" outcomes as irrelevant to their child. They also compared gay-identified adults to their children and noted key differences, including the different ways they identified their sex and gender and their (lack of) interest in body modification. However, in other moments, parents entertained something more fluid and open to reinterpretation between these separate grids of understanding. Statistics previously assessed as a matter of "just gay" were occasionally reexamined as something about "truly trans" after all. The myriad ways transgender identity might present in a child were increasingly cataloged and cited, troubling the likelihood of a "just gay" outcome. And "homosexual" examples of gender nonconformity in parents' midst were reconsidered as potentially *(trans) gendered* as well. Here, "gender" and "sexuality" reappeared on slightly more fungible terms.

In these ways, parents' deliberative processes were not solely a matter of identifying distinct types of gender nonconformity, but a matter of reinterpreting them, too, of allowing room, opportunity, and liberty for reassessment and reconsideration, over and against the "research" and reigning cultural associations. This is where, actually, firm distinctions between "gender" and "sexuality" were shaken in parents' testimonials—to gender-expansive ends. And this is *how* nonnormative expressions and sensibilities are becoming increasingly available to *(trans) gendered* understandings in our current cultural moment. As Vanessa said, "My eyes are more open. That boy wants to be pretty today and have fun? Is it a sexual thing, or a gender thing? That's what I feel has changed for me." No official "biological" designation or marker determined this approach for these parents. Rather, a new set of discourses, modes of advocacy, and shifting professional opinions, matched with *child-driven* parenting processes, helped to bring these possibilities about. This is not just descriptive work, but *productive* work, helping to bring broadening *(trans)gendered* possibilities into being.

At base, this conceptual labor legitimizes transgender possibilities for those who express them and for whom they resonate. However, it signals something even more expansive, and up for grabs, than the idea of distinct, unalterable, preordained parts of the self. In *Imagining Transgender*, Valentine theorized shifts in meaning for "gender" and "sexuality" across ethnoracial, cultural, and class boundaries, where one category may "leak" into the other.[4] Similarly, parents' approaches signal the potential for shifts in meaning across broad historical and cultural junctures, as well as across "boundaries" of the life course, and maybe within "boundaries" of the self. Indeed, parents' deliberative practices applied not just in the present moment of early childhood, but also down the line, if new expressions and sensibilities came to pass. It was being "open to change," and allowing room for the uncertainty of developmental changes, where parents most clearly articulated the potential for fluidity between these otherwise distinct realms of self. In the face of skeptics and naysayers who caution these parents against getting childhood gender transitions "wrong," I believe this is an important, empowering, counterdiscursive premise to call out. For on these more fluid terms, what is there to get "wrong"?

For many of the kids represented here, firm categories and assessments capture unequivocally who they are—transgender boys and girls. For other kids, their gender nonconformity may well be understood as part of their sexuality and sexual orientation, with no interests in gender-related identity transitions or changes. But for some kids, firm distinctions between "just gay" and "truly trans" may not answer to their experiences. Alternative understandings, if not entirely alternative schemas, might make more sense. Becca reflected on this our first interview:

> One of the things I've really had to struggle with is the labeling, because like everybody wants to understand their child. . . . *Are you gay, are you queer, are you transgender, are you a boy, are you a girl?* I mean, we're just trying to put our own experiences around it, and the more we're in this, the more I realize I need to step back from that . . . so in terms of like

labels and language . . . I want him to define himself. . . . It's really his job to [come up] with a definition that works for him.

Sociological theory has long exposed the limits and fallacies of the "male-female" binary. This construct is recognized as overly rigid and simplistic, and cannot possibly account for the complexity and overlap in human social experiences. The same has been said about the "straight-gay" binary.[5] But some of this material troubles the "gender-sexuality" binary, too, as another limiting and potentially inhibitory discursive apparatus. The pressures of parsing out what is a matter of "gender," and what is a matter of "sexuality" and sexual orientation, and what may be none of these, might actually complicate more self-determined possibilities and vocabularies for some kids—including possibilities that resist such tidy classifications of being. Indeed, "nonbinary" identities may be perforating those boundaries a bit, as they erode current terms and conceptions for sexuality that rely on a gender binary (i.e., gay, straight, bi, etc.).

Parents' deliberations between these two separate realms of "outcomes"—and their slippages across a whole "spectrum" of possibilities—gestured as much to fluidity and ambiguity as they did to finite, opposing grids of interpretation. On such gender-expansive terms, there are no risks in socially transitioning a young child "too soon" or fundamental truths to try to capture as accurately as possible. Rather, these parents are accommodating their child's most authentic sense of self, as this comes to be known, expressed, and guided by the child, within a particular field of meanings and at each phase of the life course their parents nurture. This honors a range of possible self-understandings, some no less "true" than others. This also beckons to the potential for alternative understandings of "gender" and "sexuality," which may be more resonant for some. Indeed, one of the key insights of sociocultural analyses is that there is no "right" way to understand one's expression in any given cultural context, or at any given point in the life course.[6] This describes the emancipatory potential of parents' *child-rooted, child-driven* decision-making and meaning-making, too, where there is no "right answer" other than the one that makes most sense to the child here and now, even if it comes to contradict cherished LGBT distinctions and discourses.

Male Femininity and the Gender (Non)Binary

Deliberations between different kinds of gender nonconformity also surfaced regarding *binary* and *nonbinary* possibilities. In their journeys, parents realize that there is a whole range of gendered possibilities that fall "somewhere in the middle," including some that resist any relationship to the gender binary at all. Skylar, who identified as two-spirit, and Vic, who identified as agender, offer critical examples of these possibilities, as do several children from the follow-up sample. For several families, however, nonbinary possibilities seemed nearly impossible to realize and protect, especially in the long term. It would be remiss to characterize nonbinary possibilities as the "messy" or "murky middle," or transgender transitions as definitively "easier." But given the relentless binary ordering of our social world—especially for children's clothes, toys, and school enrollments—it is not surprising that such descriptions surfaced among parents. In fact, parents almost always couched nonbinary possibilities in terms of how much "harder" they found these to navigate, either based on firsthand experience or from the experiences of other parents in their networks. As Wendy said, "It's nice to have your kid fit in a box, even if it's the 'other box.'" There were very few examples of nonbinary identities within my own sample beyond the age of seven. This space was marked by retreat, in either transgender or cisgender directions, especially for children assigned male.

Moreover, the difficulties of nonbinary options were not experienced gender-neutrally, but were compounded by the constrictions of hegemonic masculinity. For a child assigned male, the borderlands of gender nonconformity seemed so narrow, and it seemed so hard to live as both, or as neither, or more fluidly. As Ally said, Raya's peers "weren't going to let you be a blend, they were going to insist that you had to be one or the other." These complications arose among the transgender boys, too, whose seeming "effeminate" interests and preferences troubled affirmed "male" designations for some parents. Whenever parents spoke of the challenges of nonbinary possibilities, and of their own admitted discomfort with them, the example they conjured up was almost always the "boy in a dress." Lorraine, for example, the one queer-identified parent in the sample, joked about her own discomfort when her transgender son started playing with dresses at home: "It's getting to be too Victor-Victoria for me."

Many scholars would argue that positing blanket differentials between "male" and "female" gender nonconformity is overly simplistic and not nearly attentive enough to the specificities of masculinities and femininities, as they are variously expressed and interpreted in different contexts.[7] Moreover, scholars increasingly attest to proliferating options in masculinity and maleness, which depart from more stereotypical and hegemonic forms.[8] In other words, there may be more room in the "male box" than conventional expectations and performances would suggest. Female masculinity does not experience unbridled self-expression throughout our culture either, or throughout age-groups. Indeed, all parents of transgender boys testified to the eventual limits of the "tomboy" epithet for explaining their child's pronounced masculinity. But these scholars also caution against fixating on the pluralities and specificities, lest we lose sight of what they *all* aim to signify—an acceptably masculine, male self.[9] I observed quite intimately the anxieties that so often surfaced around the feminine "male" child, especially when that male child wanted to don girls' clothes and accoutrements, including in the cases of transitioned transgender boys. While parents worked hard to exercise feminist, gender-neutral, and/or more fluid principles, these efforts always shrank back in the case of boys, cisgender *or* transgender, in a way they did not with girls. In short, "male femininity" was not just a problem at the beginning of parents' journeys, but complicated the capacity for living out *nonbinary* possibilities, too, farther down the trans-affirmative line. Public figures like Jacob Tobia and Alok Vaid-Menon, who are trans-feminine and nonbinary-identified, challenge these limitations, and might serve as important examples for those families and kids experiencing these obstacles.[10]

While the majority of parents' kids were identified as transgender, parents' experiences no doubt implicate the cisgender "boys who just like girl things"—the "pink and purple boys" for whom Laurie has long advocated. This space is still so confined, if unintelligible, before more earnest contemplations about gay, transgender, and/or nonbinary possibilities take hold. As Laurie insinuated in our interview, this may impact the range of available options for these children's own self-understandings. In a "post-trans kid," "post-binary" era, there may be rich research terrain among parents like Laurie, who strive to realize long-term "tomgirl" possibilities for their cisgender sons, and who work to widen the "male box," without retreating or moving toward other gender-nonconforming signifiers.

Notwithstanding, the majority of children did not identify in nonbinary capacities. Despite increasing sociopolitical emphasis on nonbinary, genderqueer, and/or gender-fluid identities—including a growing number of youth who identify in these ways—most parents described their children as firmly binary-identified, as well as stereotypically masculine and feminine. Indeed, for many of these parents, exploring nonbinary potentials proved more of a crutch against "going all the way" than reflective of their child's authentic sense of self. In fact, several parents of transgender girls intimated that their Barbie-loving, princess-obsessed "girly girls" were flexing their "feminist" principles—they did not want to restrict their child's most authentic self-expressions, but they also did not want to succumb to hyperfeminine ideals for young girls.[11] As Bruce said, "I was just thinking a gender rebel! . . . [B]ut instead I have this child who is *so* conformist, just against her own birth sex."

This marked another key instance in which parents' decisions and understandings shifted from LGBTQ-inclusive paradigms in the service of child-rooted directions. Of course, LGBTQ platforms have never denied binary identities and transitions; indeed, many would argue these have been unduly privileged and valorized within the movement. Moreover, all advocates recognize that even a very binary, gender-normative kind of self-determination is self-determination nonetheless, and they would reject concerns about "reifying the binary" as archaic and trans-exclusionary. As such, honoring a firmly binary-identifying transgender child was not a rejection of LGBTQ paradigms for these parents. But LGBTQ politics have become increasingly attuned to gender-expansive options "beyond the binary." Parents readily encountered these perspectives in their journeys, and felt compelled to explore them, especially in the name of freeing their young child from the limiting boxes that adult culture has set for them. Indeed, many of the parents I originally interviewed were *determined* to explore these options for their kids, seemingly hailed and consumed by a heady deconstructionist call to unpack the gender binary, if not abandon it. This was reflected in these parents' embrace of new gendered terms that resisted binary thinking, including ones their children had derived themselves—such as "boygir," Bo's coinage, or "boygirl," Jackie's preferred lingo as a child.

Nevertheless, the majority of children had "picked a box," and as many parents saw it, their child had been in that box "all along." Indeed, the "other box" was often far more meaningful to these children than anything "LGBTQ." This contrasts with research on older LGBTQ youth, who are found to engage in more fluid and complex processes toward identity claims.[12] In making sense of these statuses, parents engaged in queer, deconstructionist debates about the gender binary, and sometimes felt they had to defend their decisions to transition "to the other box." None of these parents would ever deny the realities of identities "somewhere in the middle." But they eventually had to recognize, in both concrete and conceptual ways, that these simply did not apply to their child and to let their child lead. In short, for the majority of these parents, their gender-expansive parenting journey ultimately looked quite stereotypically male and female, perhaps more than they ever anticipated once they became immersed in gender-inclusive advocacy communities and discourses. As Bruce said, "We're raising the most normal girl in the world."

Tellingly, many of these young children did not really identify with "transgender"—although some did after their parents explained it to them—but, plainly, as "regular, normal" boys and girls. Jayne articulated this: "Amy's [told us], 'I've *always* been a girl, I never *realized* I was a girl, I just always *am* a girl, you just didn't know.'" This was echoed in some parents' comments that their children did not seem interested in, or connected to, a wider transgender community or politics. Theresa, for example, mentioned that Lisa adamantly resisted the label, as well as the need to attend family support groups and conferences. She frequently grilled Theresa on why she would need to go, intimating that she's just a "regular" mother of a regular girl. These experiences indicate that these children may not operate with the same logics and schemas that have produced the "transgender" conceptions their parents hold. As Bruce advised, "Don't provide a template for the trans person to fit themselves into. Let them define freely." While these examples speak to children's self-determination, they also raise questions about the future of trans identity and politics. Indeed, several interviewees intimated that these children are not really living a "transgender" life, but a "de-transgendered" one, and wonder if this new parenting paradigm will compromise a more politicized trans consciousness for transgender youth.[13]

I cite these perspectives cautiously, though, as it is hard to argue that these children are not living a "transgender life" when they intuit quite early that revealing that status to others could risk social sanction, rejection, or worse. In fact, one time, when overhearing Claire prepare to tell a close fellow parent that Andy is transgender, Andy intervened and said, "My Mommy's going to tell you [something], but you have to still like me after she tells you." Moreover, it is hard to mourn the loss of an identity or politics that was a bridge away from a faulty formula in the first place. These children's fervent articulations of who they are—and it is often not "transgender"—are a powerful reminder of the flaws of assigned sex designations. If these families work to erode the import of the flesh you were born with for how you can identify, "transgender" indeed presents as a disappearing category. And with the help of rapidly evolving biomedical technologies, these children will evade the puberty that might otherwise complicate these normative sensibilities later in life.

Body Logics

In making meaningful sense of their child's gender identity, especially in more binary cases, many parents glommed on to biomedical understandings of transgender embodiment. Their children really are typical boys and girls, especially in the brain, but something went "wrong," and they were born with the "wrong parts." Trans experience is often felt at the level of the physical body, and as a matter of *sex* identity, which many seek to address through hormone therapy and other medical interventions.[14] As such, placing it squarely within the biological realm makes sense, and parents' claims duly honor the body modification interests that any person has a right to pursue. They also challenge the stigma of trans as a "mental disorder" or "mental illness." As Lorraine said of her husband, Cory, "I'm not in a relationship with somebody who's queer, I am not in a relationship with somebody who is trans, I am in a relationship with *a man* whose maleness was sustained with medical intervention." For a boy or a girl for whom being transgender has been a "normal" part of growing up, save visits to the clinic, "wrong body" frames might well resonate with their sense of self. Indeed, many of the children reiterated just these sentiments, and their parents' biomedical frameworks validated these. At the current point in their journeys, the biomedical clinic is the one arena where "transgender" may be most immediately felt by these children.

These individualized, medicalized understandings, however, mark a strong departure from LGBTQ advocacy discourses in ways that may be more limiting than expansive for the trans-affirmative parenting paradigm. Nor do these understandings reverberate with critical queer or "crip" deconstructionist principles, which would sooner question *cisgender, cissexual* experience as natural, normal, or right, not trans bodies. For decades, LGBTQ politics have challenged pathologizing takes on gender and sexual diversity, even while affirming biomedical options. But biomedical frameworks that gesture to "birth defects" implicate the same cisgender logics and assumptions that are exacted every day outside the clinical domain—certain bodies "should" pair with certain gender identities and displays. These rhetorics also collide with material conditions and disparities, which impact access to biomedical options in the first place, including the bodily privacy and "normalcy" this might afford. Nor do these perspectives speak for visibly "queer-er" bodies and expressions, which have no interest in conformity and congruence, binary-identified or not.

These parents are well aware of the implications of "birth defect" analogies, and they have debated them online. They are also aware of a range of embodied possibilities, which may or may not entail biomedicine, and they practice articulating as much to their children (i.e., "You're a girl with a penis," "You don't have a boy's body, you have *your* body," and "You're perfect the way you are"). As such, while these parents often situated their understandings of sex and gender in medicalized frameworks, they also indicated practicing alternative discursive strategies with their children. These alternative body logics would make equally meaningful sense in a world in which a child born with a penis is not presumed to be a boy, or a boy at the grocery store is not presumed to have one.

These frameworks would also make room for genderqueer, gender-fluid, or nonbinary possibilities and embodiments, which are tougher to graft to "hard-wiring in the brain." Ultimately, of course, the relevant explanatory model is for the trans person to decide, not anyone else, but parents' strategies signal the opportunity for crafting a wider range of discourses. Many of my own college students are quick to reject "birth defect" frames and "wrong body" logics when these rhetorics surface in class discussions. If parents risk reiterating traditional body logics for sex and gender, their fully affirmed kids may well be the agents to bust past them anyway. As Linda said, "The term 'transgender' is indicative to me of how primitive we still are as a culture, as a literal societal frame-work." Parenting according to her child's earnest proclamations of who she was brought Linda to that perspective.

Trans-Affirmative Parenting Here and Now

In the twenty-first century, child-rearing is not only a matter of cultivating unique skills and talents, actively nurturing educational pursuits and career interests, preparing kids for adulthood, consulting extracurricular coaches or resources, or molding personal values; it is also a matter of realizing, and facilitating, the (trans)gendered self a child can become. Advancements in LGBTQ rights helped bring this about, but they did not do it alone—indeed, parents often challenged LGBTQ discourses and tenets as much as they harnessed them, in both subtle and explicit ways. This required a particularly *child-driven, child-rooted, intensive* approach to parenting, in which a host of resources, specialists, and support networks are rallied around a child to interpret, understand, and ultimately affirm who that child says they are. Contemporary parents already had a model for such active parenting, coupled with a legacy of feminist child-rearing principles. Childhood gender nonconformity was an issue onto which to graft and apply that model. Through this approach, a child's gender-nonconforming expressions are heard and logged in earnest by their parents, versus corrected or quieted, from very early on in the life course. As sociologist Annette Lareau said, children under this paradigm "have a sense that they are special, that their opinions matter, and that adults should, as a matter of routine, adjust situations to meet children's wishes."[15]

Studies have shown that parenting and childhood socialization can be a site of social reproduction, especially with regard to traditional gender norms and expectations, among other social inequalities.[16] Indeed, the parents in my study were not immune from traditionally gendered patterns in family life—including women-dominated child care labor, in light of how many of the mothers were researching the issue and found me in the process. But parenting is also a site of radical social change, where agentic children lead their parents into the new identities, norms, and understandings they embody. Here, intensive, child-driven, bidirectional parenting helped to bring childhood transgender possibilities into being. As childhood sociologist William Corsaro asserts, "Children are not simply internalizing society and culture but are actively contributing to cultural production and change."[17] In this context, "follow the child's lead" well makes sense, even if that means following the child out of one of the most fundamental social designations in our lives. In their efforts, parents often troubled LGBTQ premises and discourses, but all in ways that honored their children's self-understandings, both for today and what may come after.

As of the writing of this book, I was not aware of any child who had been formally socially transitioned by their parents at the time of the study and then "switched back." Per the parents I stayed in touch with, it was quite the opposite—their children's identities were ever cemented and embraced. These children were described as happy, healthy, and thriving in those identities—the ideals of what childhood should look like. As Jayne said, "Amy now is this dancing, happy, pierced ears, short little edgy haircut, likes the color blue—[she's] her own self, she's just happy and dancing and thriving, goofy and funny and silly, and my friend said, '*Oh my god, what a difference to see this happy little girl!*'" Many scholars in this burgeoning research terrain are interested in tracking these families in a much more longitudinal capacity, over longer stretches of time (following up after ten, twenty, or thirty years).[18] Given how "new" the phenomenon is, many wonder what the long-term future will look like—will there be any changes, will some children "switch back," are these children "really" going to be transgender as adults, what "problems" might arise with the current approach? I am not interested in tracking more long-term "outcomes" or experiences, and I understand these can be important questions, as far as capturing the best practices for supporting gender-nonconforming and transgender youth. But I believe focusing on long-term prospects risks eclipsing the exceptional work occurring in the present for these kids— ideological, practical, and otherwise. These approaches in the here and now of twenty-first-century parenting may be as close to cutting the cord of presumption, from the start, as we've seen yet. That is a story worth sharing.

ACKNOWLEDGMENTS

First and foremost, I am grateful to the parents I interviewed, some of whom I first met a decade ago and whose children may now be entering college (this is hard to wrap my head around). These parents gave me incredible amounts of time, candor, and insights, and connected me to other parents, without which this book would not have been possible. They entrusted me with their stories, and that has been the greatest honor of my own life's story to date. I am grateful for their endless patience, too, which they offered both during the interviews, when I frequently probed for more detail and clarification, and in the many years following, as I prepared and revised this manuscript, multiple times over. Several parents who read earlier versions of this book offered excellent and detailed feedback and comments, to which I am indebted. I am forever humbled and inspired by these parents' passion, bravery, advocacy, and initiative on behalf of their children. You rock my world, which is a better place because of you.

I am also grateful to the professionals and advocates I interviewed along the way, who offered spirited insights and dialogue about gender, identity, trans kids, and parenting. Their perspectives, experience, and commitment to advocacy greatly enriched this text.

Since this project's inception, I was deeply fortunate to be mentored by two powerhouse scholars and thinkers in the fields of gender and sexualities, Sarah Fenstermaker and Beth Schneider. I benefited greatly from their insights, intellects, and guidance, and I am grateful for their long-term support.

Research and writing for this project were conducted in part with the help of several generous grants and fellowships from the University of California, including a UC Regents Fellowship, a UCSB Dean's Fellowship, and a UCSB Affiliates Graduate Fellowship. Portions of this book's material previously appeared in "Re-interpreting Gender and Sexuality: Parents of Gender-Nonconforming Children," *Sexuality & Culture*

22, no. 4 (2018): 1391–411, and "The Gender Binary Meets the Gender-Variant Child: Parents' Negotiations with Childhood Gender Variance," *Gender & Society* 29, no. 3 (2015): 338–61.

I am grateful to my editor at NYU Press, Ilene Kalish, who has been enthusiastic about this book since I first proposed it and whose keen eye pushed the manuscript forward at several key junctures. Thank you also to the wonderful assistant editor, production editor, and copyeditor of the project, Sonia Tsuruoka, Alexia Traganas, and Susan Ecklund, respectively, who were always at the ready with answers, guidance, and formatting expertise, as well as with excellent attention to detail. In addition, I am extremely grateful to the four anonymous reviewers of the manuscript, whose rigorous feedback and comments were essential to reworking and refining the book.

There were many scholars whose works and writing were deeply informative and inspiring of my own, and I take pleasure in acknowledging them here: David Valentine, one of my my greatest intellectual muses; Karl Bryant; Julia Serano; Dean Spade; Sarah Lamble; Andrew Seeber; Jack Halberstam; Judith Butler; CJ Pascoe; Cathy Cohen; Siobhan Somerville; Emily Kane; Karin Martin; Jane Ward; Susan Stryker; Pat Califia; Anne Fausto-Sterling; and the "Doing Gender/Doing Difference" framework, including Candance West, Don Zimmerman, and Sarah Fenstermaker.

Thank you to my wonderful colleagues at Trinity University for their support and encouragement during critical phases of the writing and revising, as well as for their exceptional feedback during a related research talk, including Amy Stone, Sarah Beth Kaufman, David Spener, and Jennifer Mathews. My time was short but extraordinary with you all. Thank you also to Jade Aguilar and Annamaria Muraco for their kind mentoring and support as I made my way after grad school and for our important conversations about LGBTQ youth. In addition, many thanks to the Disability and the Body panel at the 2018 annual meeting of the American Sociological Association for the opportunity to present on a portion of the book, comments from which were instrumental in advancing my ideas, including from the discussant, Elroi Windsor. Thank you also to my newfound colleagues and friends at Georgia Southern University, who believed in the importance of this scholarship and offered excellent comments and questions during my presentation of the work. I look forward to many years of collaboration with you, and feel incredibly lucky to find a new collegiate home among you.

I am deeply grateful for fierce friends and colleagues in the post-college and post-grad diaspora, who cheered me on at all times, fueled me with humor and laughter from afar, and proved that non-bio blood is just as thick. This includes Andrew Seeber, whose book *Trans* Lives in the United States* informed several key parts of my analysis. Thank you for hours of heady dialogue about gender, identity, the body, and the theoretical canon, and for your generosity of spirit, which has been a model for me for academic discourse. I look forward to many more guest lectures with you and many more conversations. I am very thankful for Maryam "Mimo" Griffin, the sweetest friend, most generous listener, and greatest intellectual comrade. I am also grateful for the kindness, support, and friendships of Heather Hurwitz, Vanessa Witenko, Greg Prieto, Jennifer Geizhals, and of course Lina Assad-Cates, who graciously put me up several times during several rounds of interviewing.

Thank you to my sisters, Catherine Rahilly-Tierney and Louisa Rahilly-Montoure, who were tough acts to follow, but who managed to be proud of my efforts and help fund cross-country flights along the way. Thank you also to my Saffy, my ride or die, who kept me company in the most arduous moments of writing and revising.

Finally, at my roots, I am grateful to my mother, Anne Rahilly, the original feminist in my life, who was a huge source of support and encouragement as I brought this book to the finish line, year after year, job after job, move after move. In honor of you and a book on parenting: thank you, from the bottom of my heart. I could not have done this without you. This book reminds me that you are at the foundation of my growth and accomplishments.

APPENDIX I

Table AI.1. Participant Reference Chart (Parents and Children)

Parent(s)[a]	Child	Child ID	Child Age	Parent Age	Parent Race	Parent Class[b]	Sexual Identity and Marital Status
Ally, Elias[c]	Raya	Trans girl	7, 11	52, —	W, Latino	UM	Bi, none; married
Annie	Noa	Trans boy	16	48	W	UM	Het, single
Becca, Nathaniel	Bo	Trans girl	7, 9	44, —	W, W	UM	Het, het; married
Beth, Barry	Tim	GNC boy	5, 8	41, 42	W, W	UM	Het, het; married
Bruce	Holden	Trans girl	5	60	W	UM	Gay, married
Carolyn	Vic	Agender	12	44	W	MC	Bi, married
Christine	Eli	GNC boy	7, 12	53	W	WC	Het, single
Claire, Rick	Andy	Trans girl	6	44, 47	W, W	UM	Het, het; married
Dana	Skylar	Two-spirit	9	35	W	WC	Het, married
Grace	Nick	Trans boy	7	35	W	UM	Het, married
Harmony	Baldwin	Trans boy	8	40	W	UM	Het, married
Heather	Samantha	Trans girl	7, 11	56	W	UM	Lesbian, married
Janice	Eileen	Trans girl	7	38	W	WC	Gay, single
Jonie	Mabel	GNC girl	7	36	W	UM	None, married
Julie	Macy	Trans girl	5	39	W	WC	Het, single
Karen	Izzy	Trans boy	10	50	W	MC	Het, single
Kari	Emma	Trans girl	5	40	W/Middle Eastern	MC	Het, married
Jayne, Glenn	Amy, Jared	Trans girl, Trans boy	6, 9	36, 37	W	UM	Het, het; married
Laurie	Phillip	GNC boy	7, 11	43	W/Jewish	UM	Het, married

[a] All names are pseudonyms.
[b] Determining socioeconomic class is not straightforward. I used several key variables to assign class designations based on biographical questionnaires, including educational background, occupational status, and household income. MC = middle class; UM = upper middle class; WC = working class.
[c] Grayscale indicates at least one of these parents was interviewed twice, as part of the follow-up cohort. Children's ages at each interview are noted. Parents' ages refer to the most recent age at interview.

Table AI.1. Participant Reference Chart (Parents and Children) (*cont.*)

Linda	Violet	Trans girl	6	41	W/African American	MC	Bi, married
Lorraine, Cory	Jamie	Trans boy	7, 11	46, 46	W, W	MC	Queer, het; married
Louise	Dawn	Trans girl	16	44	W	MC	Het, single
Madalyn	Talia	Trans girl	5	29	W/Latina	WC	Het, single
Marie	Milo	Trans boy	7	38	W	UM	Het, married
Martsy, Emilio	Cindy	Trans girl	5	36, 38	W, Latino	UM	Het, het; married
Meredith	Martin	Trans boy	7	39	W/Latina	UM	Het, married
Mia	Billy	Trans boy	18	36	Latina	MC	Het, married
Michelle	Rian	Trans girl	5	42	W	MC	Het, single
Monica, Dan	Hayden	Trans boy	5	31, 35	W, W	UM	Het, het; married
Nancy	Mickey	Trans boy	8	43	W	MC	Het, single
Nicole	Sadie	Trans girl	12	46	W/Jewish	UM	Het, married
Nina	Mikey	GNC boy	5, 7	43	W	UM	Het, married
Patrice	Casey	Trans girl	9	50	W	UM	Bi, single
Sara	Jackie	GNC girl	11, 13	56	W	MC	Lesbian, married
Shella	Tegan	Trans girl	7, 10	43	W	WC	Het, single
Sheryl, Richard	Gil	Trans boy	8, 11	51, 55	W, W	UM	Het, het; married
Theresa, Bill	Lisa	Trans girl	9, 12	55, 58	W	MC	Het, het; married
Tina	Isa	Trans girl	14	32	Latina	MC	Het, married
Tory	Connor	Trans boy	7	43	W	UM	Het, married
Tracy, Kat	Dave	GNC boy	5, 8	38, 35	W	MC	Lesbian, bi; married
Trish, Mark, Vanessa (sibling)	Joe	Trans boy	11	51, 58, 18	W	MC	Het, het; married
Wendy, Rita	Hazel	Trans girl	5	51, 52	W, Latina	UM	Bi, lesbian; married

APPENDIX II

Methods, Ethics, Politics

This appendix supplements the key methodological descriptions given in the introduction. The sample and recruitment for the project reflect two different waves and cohorts between 2009 and 2015, with 13 "follow-up" cases and 30 more "additive" cases. Because of the layered nature of the sample and the interviewing schedule, giving simple figures for the number of parents I spoke with is complicated, since each juncture represented a different assortment of parents: some interviews included couples, (step)parents, and/or family members who were present at the first interview but not at the second, and vice versa. In total, I spoke with 59 parents, or 45 families, during that time frame, but this book concerns 55 of those parents and their 43 childhood cases. There were 2 original cases from 2009 regarding teenagers who were in or approaching young adulthood (aged 16 and 19); these parents indicated then that they felt their parental role in the child's transition was largely complete. As such, I decided not to request a follow-up interview with them.

The Parents

Demographically, I will refer to the 55 parents I interviewed between 2012 and 2015, either as follow-up or in a single interview, who represent all 43 childhood cases and 42 households. More than half of the families (23) were from California, while the rest come from various regions of the United States and Canada, including 5 in the Midwest, 4 in the Southeast, 4 in the Northeast, 3 in the Northwest, 1 in the Southwest, and 2 from eastern Canada. The majority of the sample is white, with 9 parents who are mixed-race or persons of color, including 1 white/African American, 1 white/Middle Eastern, 2 white/Latinx, and 5 Latinx parents.[1] The majority of children are white as well, although several white parents I interviewed have mixed-race or adopted children of color, so there were more children of color than adults of color represented in the sample. (There were 13 mixed-race or children of color total, which includes American Indian, African American, Asian American, Latinx, and Middle Eastern backgrounds; 7 of these children have one white or biracial parent.)

The households represented a range of incomes, with most firmly in the middle class to upper middle class: 4 had an annual income below $30,000; 6 between $30,000 and $50,000; 11 between $60,000 and $100,000; 14 between $100,000 and $150,000; and 5 greater than $150,000.[2] Educationally, the majority of the sample is college-educated, with at least a bachelor's degree (approximately 75 percent), and nearly half of the parents hold graduate or advanced degrees (25 parents; these include 6 doctoral degrees and a plethora of master's degrees). Of the remaining portion, approximately 15 percent have associate degrees or some college education (8), and 2 are high school educated.

All told, the sample is predominantly college-educated, middle-class to upper-middle-class, and white. These demographics do not represent the only kinds of parents engaging in trans-affirmative or gender-expansive parenting. They do reflect potential sampling biases in my approaches, since the forums I approached evidently yielded a less diverse sample (these include annual conferences, online networks, and support group networks).[3] Other forums and avenues, such as local LGBT resource centers or school programs and initiatives, might recruit more diverse kinds of parents. Diversifying the families represented will be an important undertaking in future research efforts, and will allow for more robust intersectional analyses of the socioeconomic and racialized dimensions of the trans-affirmative parenting paradigm.[4] Notwithstanding, my participants' demographics do exhibit the kinds of parental capital—literal, cultural, linguistic, and otherwise—that would assist such intensive advocacy labor on behalf of gender-nonconforming kids, vis-à-vis schools, the medical establishment, and the state. Indeed, during the interviews, several of the parents acknowledged, unprompted, their relative socioeconomic privilege and how that benefited the supports they could secure for their child.

In terms of gender, the sample is heavily skewed toward women: I spoke with 11 men/fathers total (approximately 20 percent of the parents). This includes 1 stepfather, who was the one transgender parent in the study, and 1 cisgender gay man. Throughout recruitment, only 2 fathers ever contacted me directly to participate; the rest were women/ mothers. The sample does include various sexual identities, although the parents are predominantly heterosexual-identified (40) and/or heterosexually married. Fifteen participants identify as nonheterosexual, including gay (2), lesbian (4), bisexual (6), queer (1), and "none" (2). Among the households were represented 26 heterosexual marriages (within these, 3 women identify as bisexual, 1 woman and 1 man selected "none" as their sexual identity, and 1 of the partnerships consists of a queer-identified woman and a heterosexual-identified transgender man); 5 same-sex marriages (1 male/gay relationship and 4 female/lesbian relationships; of the 6 women I interviewed from these, there are 4 lesbian- and 2 bisexual-identified members); and 11 single mothers (1 identifies as bisexual whose co-parent is a woman, 1 identifies as gay whose co-parent is a man, and the rest are heterosexual-identified).

Other demographics that might impact parents' responses include their political and religious affiliations. Over half of parents identify politically as Democrat (39 parents), 12 identified as Independent or "none," 3 identified as Republican (including 1 as "Independent/Conservative"), and 1 as Moderate. The most popular response under religious affiliation was "none" (24), while 10 listed Christian, 7 listed Catholic, 5 listed "UU" (Universal Unitarian), 4 listed Jewish, 3 listed Buddhist (including "Quaker/Buddhist"), and 2 listed Spiritual. Thus, on both political and religious indices, the majority of parents are associated with more "liberal" or "progressive" groups on LGBTQ issues.

The Children of the Parents

Among the 43 childhood cases, 26 children were assigned male at birth and 17 children were assigned female. This disparity could well reflect more stringent standards for children assigned male over females (i.e., "boys" who like dresses vs. "girls" who like cars). However, the male-to-female ratio represented here (1.5:1) echoes other trends in psychiatry where both male and female referrals are increasingly on par, if not inverted.[5] Specifically, the sample includes 20 transgender girls, 14 transgender boys, 1 agender child, 1 two-spirit child, 2 gender-nonconforming girls, and 5 gender-nonconforming boys. Of these last 5 children, parents once considered them some degree of gender-nonconforming but less significantly than before, though the children would not be described as stereotypically masculine or gender-normative. The majority of the sample (37 cases) represents children who are twelve years of age and under, with only 6 teenagers (aged thirteen to eighteen). Four of the 6 teenagers, as well as one twelve-year-old, "came out" to their parents as transgender or gender-nonconforming, whereas the other 2 were identified and transitioned "by" their parents in preadolescence, consistent with the rest of the children represented.

As discussed in the introduction, these descriptors cannot necessarily denote objective, authentic identifications for the children. The children assigned male, for example, who were still presenting as such to their parents and using male pronouns at the time of the follow-up interviews, may well personally identify in more transgender or gender-nonconforming capacities. The gender-nonconforming "girls," as I've listed them here, may not actually identify with "girl" or "female." At every turn, I refer to *parents'* descriptions and assessments, as best they understood their children at the time (and they took pains to do so). To be sure, relying on the parents' reports, and not the children's, is a methodological limitation of the study. However, the project was a sociology of *parents'* decisions and understandings about their children's gender, and thus inevitably entailed such a tension.

Methods

Because the research participants are located throughout the United States, as well as 2 cases in Canada, approximately half of the interviews were conducted via telephone, while the rest were conducted in person at parents' homes when they were within reasonable driving distance (namely, in California). Telephone interviews forfeited a level of insight and rapport that only body language, nonverbal communication, and face-to-face interaction can capture, but they also allowed for access and participation in a way that finances and geography might have prevented. Interviews conducted in parents' homes did tend to run longer (although several phone interviews were broken into two or three sessions). Ultimately, however, the kinds of stories and perspectives I could glean on the phone versus those in person were not noticeably limited or bereft of insight; indeed, some of the richest accounts featured in this book are from telephone interviews.

In the semistructured interviews with the parents, I asked about a range of themes, including how they first came to observe and identify their child as gender-nonconforming or transgender; which terminology they preferred and/or used with their child; the means of support and resources they sought, including professionals, online forums, and advocacy organizations; their child's school life and parents' negotiations with school administration; siblings' reactions; specific dialogues they had with their children about gender, sexuality, and/or their bodies; thoughts about medical options; debates or sources of contention they encountered among other parents; explanations they had for gender nonconformity; and new understandings about sex, gender, and/or sexuality they had developed. Parents' responses produced a wealth of anecdotes and perspectives. Questions in the follow-up interviews prioritized events and moments that had transpired in the family's journey since our first conversation and how parents made sense of their child's new (or consistent) identification, expression, and transition, where relevant.

During 2013–15, I also interviewed 9 professionals for the project, who represent some of the leading experts in the care, management, and support of transgender and gender-nonconforming children. These professionals include 2 medical doctors (pediatrician and endocrinologist); 4 advocacy professionals and educators from major organizations; and 3 mental health professionals (including clinical counseling and psychology, social work, and psychiatry). All but 2 of these interviews occurred via telephone. Interview guides were tailored to the specific profession, and I asked these individuals about how and why they became involved in this field; their opinions regarding when to socially transition a child; how a "truly transgender" child is identified and/or distinguished from a "just gender-nonconforming" child among professionals, including their opinions about these kinds of distinctions; longitudinal studies on gender-nonconforming children; theories on "causes" of gender nonconformity; medical interventions and their timing; and differential experiences between children assigned male and children assigned female.

The duration of the interviews ranged from approximately 1.5 to 4 hours, with an average of 2.25 hours, all of which were recorded with a digital voice recorder. Approximately half of the interviews were transcribed by transcription assistants (pending informants' approval on consent forms), and I transcribed the rest. Drawing on grounded theory methods, I started drafting memos at several key intervals, before the completion of all transcripts.[6] These charted significant themes and concepts that were surfacing in parents' comments (e.g., "birth defect," "disability analogy," "transgender as easier," "freaked out/freaky," "just gay vs. truly trans"), which helped develop the major codes and categories I used in the data analysis. I also prepared separate detailed memos for each follow-up case, reviewing both transcripts side by side from each interview multiple times for key events and junctures in parents' understandings. Once all transcripts were complete, I engaged in more formal thematic analysis and coding with the help of ATLAS.ti coding software. Within this program, I built on the major themes developed from the memos and identified new ones. I also flagged counteroccurrences in those themes and codes (e.g., no verbal declarations from the child about identity or the body, alternative biological discourses). It is important to note, however, that objective, concrete themes do not "emerge" from the data on their own, but that I played an active part in selecting the themes and issues I found most pertinent to a sociological analysis.[7] Subsequent outlines, memos, and reflections on these themes forged the substantive focus of each chapter of this book.

Ethics and Politics

As noted in the introduction, I considered myself an "outsider" on most fronts of the research process: I am not transgender or gender-nonconforming, and I am not a parent. I felt hyperaware of this outsider status at all times, but I felt it most acutely at the conferences and with conference organizers, who seemed, understandably, very wary of me, unsure of my purpose and my agenda. As moved and inspired as I was by the advocacy work being done at the conferences—and in witnessing the profound positive impact it had on parents—I often felt uncomfortable there, that I risked voyeurism and opportunism, and that I was treading on "sacred ground" in a space that was dedicated to parents and their children. The directors asked me not to use any specific data or comments from the conference settings or to directly approach participants about my research. I was admittedly relieved by this protocol, and I let parents come to me at a vendor table or leave me their contact information there. Some also contacted me directly via blurbs I had posted in the conference brochures. At the second conference, I asked one of the directors if they would be open to sharing aggregate demographic data on the attendants with me (race, gender, age, financial assistance for conference fees, total number of attendants, etc.), but they hesitated, as they had not indicated to conference attendees that this information would be used outside the purposes of their own organization. While I sometimes felt they were overly wary of me, I also understood, fundamentally, that this was a community they fiercely protected, and that they did not owe me anything, of any kind.

This dimension of my outsider status was palpable during an interview with one advocacy director, who started the interview by referring to my first conference attendance and stating, almost anticipatorily, "We didn't offer you much help there, did we?" I tried to graciously counter the notion by saying that no, I had actually secured much of my early sample from their conference (and thus was very much helped). In hindsight, I regret not just clarifying that I never expected any assistance from them, especially in the way of parent connections and contacts. (I also knew that securing research participants for my project might be an unwelcome, opportunistic effect of my attendance in their eyes.) At several points in our interview, I sensed that this person found my questions to be overly "fraught," "provocative," and uselessly "intellectual" to the families they serve, per some of the words they used. For example, at one point, I asked for their thoughts about older statistics that suggest most gender-nonconforming children grow up to be "just gay" and what the rapidly changing face of those statistics might mean for these categories and assessments. They replied:

[That's] super-provocative, and it gets at, I mean, if you really boil it all down, it gets at . . . the people asking that question—I'm not saying [this] about you—but, there's some underlying motives about why that question's getting asked, I think, that are about, *You see, they don't really—trans isn't real, or trans is real.* I mean it is fraught.

At another point, they insinuated that the kind of "conceptual arguments" undergirding some of the topics I raised—for example, "gay versus trans" identities, the difficulties of nonbinary identities that might force a child's hand in "picking a box"—were unhelpful compared with the practical needs of families and children on the ground:

> So these conceptual arguments . . . it's like y'all have that conversation, I'm going to be down here working with some folks who've got real lives to live and choices to make in the moment that have real implications, and yes, all this stuff impacts that, but for them it's about what do I put on tomorrow? . . . I would probably find myself more aligned with . . . trying to understand the world in service of changing it versus trying to understand the world just to understand it in this really esoteric, intellectual way. . . . But, yeah, that's just me because I'm not an academic, I'm just a little old teacher trying to make a small difference.

Overall, the interview was extremely engaging. Despite the limited number of times we conversed, I have always had profound respect and affinity for this person, for the tireless work that they do, and for how they approach the cause (i.e., loosening gender proscriptions for *all* children, not just transgender-identified ones). I also felt a bit schooled and criticized by them as a researcher, in ways I expected and understood.

In many ways, our interview encapsulated the tensions and challenges of conducting qualitative research, which mark a legacy of dialogue, debate, and theorizing among feminist researchers.[8] Namely, I refer to the risks of engaging in "critical" analytic work that does not wholly serve or align with the interests and viewpoints of one's subjects. Many researchers feel that analysis, advocacy, and activism should be one and the same, such as in "social action" or "participatory action" research. This approach is exemplified in Ann Travers's book *The Trans Generation.*[9] Tey Meadow reflected on these issues regarding their own work on parents of trans kids:

> I remain keenly attuned to the sense carried by my research informants (which I share) that the products of the representation have the potential to influence the political and emotional landscape they inhabit. What I've come to believe fundamentally is that the goal of feminist ethnography,

and perhaps for ethnography more generally, is to be "for, not merely about" (Risman 1993) the particular individuals we study.[10]

Of course, these concerns run deep in the field of transgender studies, which has been plagued by a legacy of cisgender, gender-normative researchers fetishizing trans experience as some enthralling social phenomenon or gender-bending theoretical prospect, versus serving and benefiting vulnerable trans communities.[11] Nearly every interview I conducted ended on the note of, *Thank you for doing this research, it's so necessary for helping our kids.* One informant closed her e-mail with, "Thank you again for your work. We rely on it." And with every interview, I felt the weight of balancing my informants' wishes and desires—protecting and validating their children—against my own sociological analyses and observations. How could I *dare* risk being "critical" of parents who do the awe-inspiring, all-important work of nurturing, supporting, and protecting norm-defiant children in a culture that is otherwise ruthless about norm compliance, let alone as a nonparent? In what ways do sociological and social-constructionist perspectives serve these families, and in what ways may they be at odds?

To be clear, when it comes to affirming and advocating for any child's full, authentic self-expression, unfettered and unharmed—including the parents who facilitate that—I am committed, full stop. But some of my research interests extended beyond this fundamental advocacy position, toward parents' shifting understandings of gender, sexuality, the binary, and the body, which felt like separate points of analysis. These included, for example: fraught debates between "just gay" and "truly trans" outcomes, in which I observed something more complex, and expansive, develop in parents' thoughts than necessarily distinct parts of the self; the challenges of living out nonbinary identities in early childhood, especially for children assigned male, in ways that might limit one's development and authentic self-expression; and parents' potentially biopathologizing frameworks for transgender embodiment.

The paradigms and scholarship I draw from—including "social constructionism"—have had a dicey relationship with LGBT identities. For some, these paradigms insinuate that there is something "not real" about people's identities, that these are fashioned or "constructed" from external cultural matter, versus from a core, precultural, essential self.

Some feel social-scientific and/or deconstructionist perspectives risk undermining "born-this-way" narratives for LGBT experience, which have been instrumental to civil rights advancements. In turn, these kinds of analyses feel like risky business relative to more "conservative" or phobic audiences, who might co-opt these approaches and frame children's transgender identities as "fake," "wrong," and "unnatural."[12] Social-constructionist analyses also run counter to a wider societal milieu that valorizes the authority of the "hard sciences" and vies for firmer, presocial, unmediated understandings of who we are, including in the way of genes, brain structure, and hormones. This is especially true for LGBTQ identities, which have long been the object of scrutiny and for which "just born this way" is a powerful explanatory retort.[13] Indeed, these frameworks were important for parents to use so that others would not accuse them of "causing" their children's gender non-conformity, in a way that parents of cis-heteronormative children never have to experience.

But I have come to believe that skirting issues for being overly fraught or provocative, or for being potentially "critical" of one's subjects, is equally flawed and risky, and falsifies a representation of social life, in all its complexity, that defies the purpose of the social-scientific enterprise. As a sociologist, I remain a champion of on-the-ground advocacy work and activism, and I would be the first to champion these parents and their kids. But I am also committed to capturing and telling a story as I encounter it in the field, according to my subjects' complex understandings and experiences. I believe that the "conceptual arguments" the data dredge up do impact more practical concerns of everyday life on the ground—of what is intelligible and possible for living a life in the first place. To strive toward the widest range of self-determination, we must closely observe how some possibilities are engendered, imagined, supported, and affirmed—discursively, politically, practically, ideologically, institutionally—as well as how some might be limited, eclipsed, or compromised. I also feel that to "hold back," and oblige interests that I perceived as solely my participants', would misrepresent the deep critical thinking they practiced, including with me in interviews. I am acutely aware of my participants' adroit ability to wrangle with fraught questions, concepts, and debates—and to reject them, too, if they want, for themselves and for their children. Indeed, several parents responded to earlier versions of this book with alternative sources and suggestions, as well as with specific edits and corrections, which I reviewed intently.

Given my distance and my outsider status, it is surprising how much parents trusted me and invited me in—literally and figuratively—from the get-go. These parents had little to no information about me, other than I was a (young, female) researcher interested in "raising awareness" about transgender children and parents' experiences, per my blurb (which also included a photograph of myself). This is especially true for those who obliged long-distance phone interviews with me, who have never laid eyes on me otherwise. I believe they knew, at a baseline level, that I did not question their decisions in raising and transitioning a young child as transgender, nor did I find honoring childhood gender nonconformity a problem or pathology (if anything, I find the strictly gender-normative contexts the problem). I think that personal referrals via previous participants, online and otherwise, greatly assisted with that. I also think that being a nonparent benefited the research relationship: I brought zero presumptions about child-rearing to the interviews; parents were the experts. Fundamentally, I believe their trust in me speaks to their "therapeutic" need to dialogue with someone, candidly, about all that they had experienced and feared in their journeys, with someone who was "on their side." I believe that our interview space afforded them the freedom and anonymity to do that, in a way that other spaces, and persons, did not.

At times, however, the "therapeutic" aspects of the interviewing context were complicated for me, especially when I raised questions that tapped into parents' fears about their children's safety, or about pursuing medical interventions or not. I also knew I had critical information to share that my participants might be interested in. Indeed, many of my participants indicated that they hoped I could be a resource for them. But at times, this may have entailed sharing unwanted information, and I did not want parents to feel judged or to add to their sources of worry.

A clear example of this surfaced in my first interview with Sara, when the issue of her child's body and puberty blockers came up. Sara was vaguely aware of the role of puberty blockers, but when I asked her if she had looked into "Tanner testing"—indirectly referring to a prepubertal stage in children's development when blockers are usually administered and take effect—she became very distraught and emotional.

Fumbling in the moment, I immediately tried to apologize, backtrack, and change topics, but she was kind and reassuring with me: "No, no, don't be sorry . . . we have to have these conversations, do not be sorry, you just have to see moms having feelings." She admitted she did not want to think too far down that path, that it "scared" her. She also reflected candidly on the burdensome ethical decision this meant for her: Would she be denying her child a critical opportunity that she would regret later, if she evaded the blockers option? As an interviewer, I did not feel it was appropriate for me to weigh in with any kind of guidance or prescription, and I deeply sympathize with the burden these kinds of decisions entail for parents. (Following this interview, I did not ask any other parent directly about Tanner stage testing; I left it to surface naturally in the conversation.) At the same time, however, and as an advocate of trans kids, not relaying the opinions and perspectives I had learned about puberty blockers felt challenging.

Toward the end of another interview, a parent asked me for resources for parents of gender-nonconforming kids. When I started listing some, she immediately bristled at the term "transgender" in some of the titles. Even though she and her husband had contemplated transgender possibilities for their child, she suggested these were too "extreme." I wanted to assist her, and I provided alternative sources, but this felt like I was acquiescing to potentially transphobic sentiments and fears. In the first example, I do not believe Sara's child necessarily wanted medical interventions. Of course, that is not my call to make as a sociologist, and I trust parents' capacities to assess their children's needs and desires. I also strive to be as sensitive as possible to the immense task and charge these parents have in protecting and raising their kids and to meet them where they are in their journeys. But both of these exchanges are emblematic of some of the more conflicting moments I encountered between my different roles in the field, including as a sociological researcher, a compassionate and safe listener for parents, and an advocate of trans and gender-nonconforming youth. These are intersecting roles I feel I am still perfecting and navigating.

Of course, there is one last dimension to my ethical and political considerations, and it is perhaps the weightiest: the children, who do not speak for themselves in this study, but whom are spoken for by the parents. While I studied "the parents," it is their children who informed the testimonials I captured. This book holds their stories, their identities, their truths, if not explicitly, then between the lines that are written on the pages. It is a profound honor, privilege, and responsibility that I carry. Doing justice to their lives and their privacy—access to which I was granted by sole virtue of my role as "researcher"—is what I ultimately hold paramount. One day, the children might speak to me about this work. I cannot presume or predict what they will say. But it is an interview, conducted by them, to which I will ever and always answer.

NOTES

INTRODUCTION

1 All names that appear in this book are pseudonyms. This includes children's birth names, chosen names, and nicknames, as well as names of the parents, professionals, and clinicians I interviewed. For all parents, I include demographic descriptors the first time they appear in the book, according to their biographical forms at the time of the interviews (e.g., age, race, gender, sexual identification, marital status, socioeconomic classification). After this, I defer to the reference chart in appendix I. To protect my participants' anonymity, I do not include their educational, occupational, or geographic backgrounds.

2 I recognize the problems of referencing persons' assigned sex designations, which more and more scholars and advocates seek to resist (see, e.g., Travers, *Trans Generation*, 8; Darwin, "Doing Gender"). In few contexts is this information relevant to someone's identity, nor should it be anyone's business. But, as I address in chapter 1, the birth sex designations of the children greatly impact parents' experiences and reporting; this is a key sociological dimension of the study and the phenomenon.

3 My use of ellipses throughout this book serves two functions: (1) to excise portions of my respondents' comments that are redundant or that contain "filler" words or stuttering (e.g., "you know," "um," "yeah," "like"), or (2) to excise larger portions of our conversations that switch back and forth between me and the interviewee that detract from the point. I am aware of the editorial risks of qualitative analyses, and I aim to best represent my informants' perspectives at any given moment, in the service of exemplifying the theme I am describing.

4 Rahilly, "The Gender Binary."

5 As I will discuss later in the chapter, interviewing parents about, and between, various moments in their trans-affirmative journeys proved tricky, as far as honoring the children's correct identities and pronouns. Here, for instance, Jayne is using female pronouns for a child who was later affirmed as a boy. This is especially true for the "follow-up" families quoted throughout this book, who used different pronouns and markers between the first and second interviews. Some parents acknowledged that they were prone to "slipping up," too, but that they were working on it. This is reflected in instances where parents are switching between male and female pronouns within the same quote. In addition to pronouns, some parents were using terminology that would now be considered outdated or offensive—such

as "transgendered" instead of "transgender." In the interest of focusing on the *parents'* experiences and perspectives—including the longitudinal changes inherent here—I quote them directly and do not indicate "[*sic*]," as would be required in other contexts. Outside of direct quotes, I will only use the markers that the child prefers to the best of my knowledge at the time of this writing.

6 Anthropological records have long documented gender nonconformity in other cultures and time periods, including cases from childhood and young adulthood. See, e.g., Herdt, *Third Sex, Third Gender* and Nanda, *Neither Man nor Woman*. For a critical analysis of these texts, see Towle and Morgan, "Romancing the Transgender Native."

7 Meadow, *Trans Kids*, 224.

8 "Transgendered" is considered an errant term to describe a person; someone is "transgender," not "transgendered." I use the term here *not* to refer to trans individuals, but to refer to a *gender-*based *interpretation, conception, or understanding* of experience, as opposed to a (homo)sexual one, especially by others. I explore this more fully in chapter 2.

9 Robertson, *Growing Up Queer*; Travers, *Trans Generation*.

10 One of the major advocacy organizations for transgender and gender-nonconforming children is called Gender Spectrum. Although the word "spectrum" is included in this book's title, this publication is not affiliated with that group. My use of the term reflects parents' routine references to this concept throughout our conversations.

11 At the time of the interviews, parents were using "gender-variant" as commonly. For simplicity's sake, I will only use "gender-nonconforming."

12 Stryker, *Transgender History*, 19.

13 Califia, *Sex Changes*, 223–25; Stryker, *Transgender History*, 19.

14 Sociologists and gender theorists have long distinguished "sex" and "gender," but I occasionally elide these terms for the sake of persons' self-identifications. A transgender woman, for example, may identify as "female," regardless of her sexual anatomy or birth sex assignment, which may be synonymous for her with "woman." This is reflected in some parents' use of the terms "affirmed female" or "affirmed male" to describe their transgender girls and boys, respectively. I seek to honor the identifications of the parents/children as much as possible, even as I understand critical analytic distinctions between sex, sex category, and gender. For the canonical dissection of these categories, see West and Zimmerman, "Doing Gender." See also Seeber's discussion in *Trans* Lives*, 11–20.

15 Physicians generally wait until Tanner stage 2, a critical stage in the onset of biological maturation, before administering hormonal interventions and treatments to children—namely, puberty blockers, which stave off the "normal" progression of puberty. While this stage varies per child and per assigned sex, it generally occurs anywhere between the ages of ten and fourteen. For a critical race analysis of the limits of the Tanner framework, see Travers, *Trans Generation*, 176; Gill-Peterson, "Technical Capacities."

16 Spade, "Mutilating Gender."
17 Travers, *Trans Generation*, 2. Travers asserts that studying a new generation of trans youth and their families demands interviewing and understanding the youth's perspectives themselves.
18 Meadow articulates similar concerns and decisions in their appendix (*Trans Kids*, 237).
19 The IRB reviews and vets all research proposals for meeting ethical standards for human research subjects. The IRB exercises heightened scrutiny over studies involving minors and vulnerable populations, of which gender-nonconforming children are a part.
20 The term "purposive" refers to recruiting specific research participants who explicitly fit the kind of subject one is interested in studying (e.g., parents attending trans-affirmative conferences, support groups, or forums), versus sampling from a broad, generalizable population (e.g., all parents in the United States or all parents of gender-nonconforming kids, however that might be defined or measured).
21 Indeed, trans youth mark a disproportionate percentage of the US homeless population. See Ray, *Lesbian, Gay*.
22 Gray, Johnson, and Gilley, *Queering the Countryside*; Rogers, "Drag as a Resource." Scholars in this domain, however, also caution against regional stereotypes (e.g., "urban" as necessarily more progressive, the South as necessarily more phobic). See Thomsen, "Post-raciality."
23 I use "Latinx" here as a gender-neutral term to refer to a group of parents or children.
24 See Meadow, *Trans Kids*, for an analysis of different advocacy groups' rhetorical strategies and framings.
25 See Rubin, *Deviations*, 196–98, for a concise explanation of "social constructionism."
26 See Epstein, "Gay Politics, Ethnic Identity"; Namaste, *Invisible Lives*; Serano, *Whipping Girl*; Weber, "What's Wrong."
27 See also Katz, *Invention of Heterosexuality*; Rupp, "Toward a Global History."
28 The term "transgender child" did not appear in mental health literature until the late 1990s. See Meadow, "The Child," 57.
29 See, e.g., Robertson, *Growing Up Queer*; Travers, *Trans Generation*, 25.
30 Bianchi, Robinson, and Milkie, *Changing Rhythms*; Nelson, *Parenting Out of Control*.
31 Coontz, *Social Origins*; Mintz, *Huck's Raft*.
32 Mintz, *Huck's Raft*.
33 Briggs, *How All Politics*; Coontz, *Social Origins*.
34 Senior, *All Joy and No Fun*.
35 Senior.
36 Warner, *Perfect Madness*.
37 Hays, *Cultural Contradictions of Motherhood*, x.
38 Hays, x.
39 Lareau, *Unequal Childhoods*, 111. See also Calarco, *Negotiating Opportunities*.

40 Hagerman, *White Kids*.

41 For references to several different data sources, see Miller, "Relentlessness of Modern Parenting."

42 Crumdy et al., "CUNY Graduate School Student Collective."

43 Collins, *Black Sexual Politics*; Crenshaw, "Mapping the Margins."

44 Collins, *Black Feminist Thought*.

45 See cases of structurally marginalized families in Meadow, *Trans Kids* and Travers, *Trans Generation*.

46 Lamble, "Retelling Racialized Violence," 31.

47 Maccoby, "The Role of Parents."

48 Coltrane and Adams, "Children and Gender"; Denzin, *Childhood Socialization*, 3; Handel, Cahill, and Elkin, *Children and Society*; Peterson and Rollins, "Parent-Child Socialization."

49 Thorne, "Re-visioning Women," 101.

50 Thorne, *Gender Play*, 3.

51 Cahill, "Language Practices."

52 Corsaro, *Sociology of Childhood*, 18.

53 Bem, "Gender Schema Theory"; Bem, *An Unconventional Family*; Statham, *Daughters and Sons*.

54 Bem, "Gender Schema Theory," 611–12.

55 Bem, 611–12.

56 Bem, *Unconventional Family*, 107.

57 See, e.g., Letty Cottin Pogrebin's much-celebrated book, *Growing Up Free*, 295, 300. Pogrebin was one of the founding editors of *Ms.* magazine.

58 Martin, "William Wants a Doll," 475.

59 Martin, 475.

60 Kane, *Gender Trap*, 3.

61 Kane, "'No Way.'"

62 Kane, *Gender Trap*, 150.

63 For overviews of the major schools of thought here—including psychoanalytic, cognitive-developmental, and behaviorist—see Bem, "Gender Schema Theory"; Maccoby, "The Role of Parents"; Risman and Myers, "As the Twig Is Bent."

64 For example, Cahill, "Language Practices"; Thorne, *Gender Play*.

65 The *DSM* is the guidebook of diagnostic criteria that mental health practitioners use. It is published and updated by the APA.

66 Bryant has produced an incisive body of analysis on this longitudinal psychiatric research; see, e.g., "Making Gender," "In Defense," and "Diagnosis and Medicalization." For the development of adult transsexual medicine in the United States, see Meyerowitz, *How Sex Changed*.

67 See Green, *The "Sissy Boy Syndrome,"* for one of the more (in)famous products of this clinical history.

68 See, e.g., Sedgwick, "How to Bring Your Kids Up Gay." Bryant's scholarship, however, including "Making Gender" and "In Defense," complicates the "homophobic" interpretation of the diagnoses.

69 See, e.g., Rekers, *Pathological Sex-Role Development*.

70 Wallien and Cohen-Kettenis, "Psychosexual Outcomes."

71 See, e.g., Drummond et al., "A Follow-Up Study." The majority of the children assigned female in these studies do *not* necessarily identify as homosexual or bisexual as adults. Rather, gender-nonconforming females are potentially *more likely* to identify with LGB categories as adults than their gender-normative counterparts, but *not* as a majority.

72 See, e.g., Ehrensaft, *Gender Born*; Krieger, *Helping Your Transgender Teen*; Lev, *Transgender Emergence*.

73 See also Kuvalanka et al., "Trans and Gender-Nonconforming Children," for this affirmative paradigm.

74 See Meadow, *Trans Kids*, 77, for a graph of these trends.

75 Olson, Key, and Eaton, "Gender Cognition."

76 These are very similar to debates about homosexuality that ultimately removed it from the *DSM* in 1973. The diagnosis of GD aims to emphasize the stress and distress one might experience with one's gender nonconformity, versus the gender nonconformity itself. Under this new diagnosis, not all persons who are transgender or gender-nonconforming are relevant to *DSM* diagnoses, just those who experience the "distress" that may come with it. For a critical analysis of the new GD diagnosis, including how it may cause some patients to feign "distress" when seeking support, see Davy, "The DSM-5."

77 Some of the claims made in the external report that shut down Zucker's clinic have since been rescinded in a settlement agreement (see Hayes, "Doctor Fired"). For further discussion of Zucker and his clinic, see Meadow, *Trans Kids*, 81–93.

78 See, e.g., Delemarre-van de Waal and Cohen-Kettenis, "Clinical Management." Researchers in the Netherlands are largely credited with pioneering the use of hormones and hormone blockers on gender-nonconforming children.

79 This physician told me that the Dutch recommendations were only regarded as a "good jumping-off point," not as firm protocols, because they posed the only real data anyone had at the time.

80 Menvielle, "Transgender Children."

81 Drescher and Byne, "Gender Dysphoric/Gender Variant (GD/GV) Children," 506. Some researchers suggest that children who score "higher" on gender identity assessments at intake are more likely to "persist" in their gender nonconformity for the long term. See Wallien and Cohen-Kettenis, "Psychosexual Outcomes."

82 Friedman, "How Changeable Is Gender?"

83 Singal, "When Children Say," n.p.

84 For additional discussion of "regret narratives," see Meadow, *Trans Kids*, 77–81.

85 The "Don't Ask Don't Tell" policy effectively barred LGB persons from serving openly in the US military. The Defense of Marriage Act (1996), section 3, prevented legally married same-sex couples from receiving the same federal benefits and protections that married heterosexual couples do. In a historic decision on June 26, 2015, the US Supreme Court ruled that bans on same-sex marriage are unconstitutional, legalizing gay marriage across all fifty states and the District of Columbia.

86 Steinmetz, "Transgender Tipping Point."

87 See the Movement Advancement Project (MAP) for up-to-date, color-coded maps detailing a range of trans-related laws and policies state by state; www.lgbtmap.org.

88 Williams, "All Seven Sister Schools."

89 Davis, *Beyond Trans*.

90 For a comprehensive list of the administration's anti-LGBT policy initiatives, see National Center for Transgender Equality (NCTE), "Trump's Record," https://transequality.org.

91 Green, Benner, and Pear, "'Transgender' Could Be Defined." In contrast, the former administration under President Barack Obama issued broad interpretations of sex and gender under Title IX, which helped to expand protections for transgender persons.

92 Valentine, *Imagining Transgender*.

93 Valentine, 100 (emphasis in original). For similar themes, see also Lamble, "Retelling Racialized Violence," and Moore, "Lipstick or Timberlands." For a critical review of Valentine, see Seeber, *Trans* Lives*, 20–24.

94 For further discussion, see Califia, *Sex Changes*, 240–41; Stryker, *Transgender History*, 150–52.

95 Califia, *Sex Changes*, 240–41; Stryker, *Transgender History*, 150–52.

96 Cultural theorist Lisa Duggan famously coined the term "homonormative" to refer to the neoliberal and assimilationist nature of mainstream gay rights politics, which upholds heteronormative institutions and depoliticizes gay identity. See Duggan, "The New Homonormativity," 179.

97 Conrad, *Against Equality*; Spade, *Normal Life*; Stanley and Smith, *Captive Genders*.

98 The Stonewall riots of June 1967 are largely considered the founding moment of the modern-day LGBT rights movement.

99 There is growing recognition of the work of Marsha P. Johnson, Sylvia Rivera, and Miss Major, among other trans women of color, as foundational to the movement. See Gossett, Stanley, and Burton, *Trap Door*.

100 Califia, *Sex Changes*; Cohen, "Punks"; Gamson, "Must Identity Movements"; Yep, Lovaas, and Elia, "Critical Appraisal." The 1990s were not the first time these "queer" principles and positions manifested. The gay rights movement that emerged in the 1960s and 1970s had a strong anticonformist, antiassimilationist arm, as did much of AIDS activism in the 1980s. But many argue these ap-

proaches were eclipsed by more mainstream tactics and positions, especially in terms of "marriage equality." See Engel, "Making a Minority."

101 Conrad, *Against Equality*; Spade, *Normal Life*; Stanley and Smith, *Captive Genders*.

102 Califia, *Sex Changes*; Spade, "Mutilating Gender."

103 Puar, *Terrorist Assemblages*; Snorton and Haritaworn, "Trans Necropolitics."

104 Throughout this book, I will use "LGBT" to refer to "mainstream" discourses, political platforms, and distinctions for gender, sexuality, and LGBT identities, as described here. I will use "LGBTQ" to refer to discourses and platforms that are more inclusive and aware of "queer" politics, identities, and interventions, including nonbinary and nonmedicalizing perspectives.

105 See Gamson, *Freaks Talk Back*, for a critical analysis of LGBT visibility in talk shows.

106 See note 5 earlier in this chapter.

107 Meadow, *Trans Kids*, 116. See also Travers, *Trans Generation*, 155, for similar observations at the family conferences.

108 See, e.g., the memoirs by Pepper, *Transitions of the Heart*; Whittington, *Raising Ryland*; or the documentary films by Skurnick, *I'm Just Anneke* and *The Family Journey*.

109 One of my participants, Claire, used the term "child-rooted" in an e-mail, and I have adopted it; it fits well with the child-centered, child-driven meanings and decisions parents made in their journeys.

CHAPTER 1. "SHE'S JUST WHO SHE IS"

1 Trans politics works to affirm and normalize all trans experiences, including those depicted by parents here. Gamson's *Freaks Talk Back* challenges the notion that such sensationalistic talk show depictions of LGBT persons are necessarily bad or problematic. He argues that this kind of visibility offers important exposure of more phobic understandings in society, which are packaged as tolerant. This exposure enables candid, critical dialogue about the real state of LGBT acceptance in society. Here, parents did come to see their understandings of "transgender" as problematic, but only in the very personal context of affirming their own transgender child.

2 This made for an interesting moment in our interview, when I marveled candidly at how seemingly easily and early they made this pronoun switch, all before embracing a "transgender" conception of their child. Claire and Rick were understandably "defensive" about my reaction, as they felt I was insinuating they had done something "too soon" or, as Claire put it, had "put the cart before the horse." I would never assert that social transition must follow a certain sequence, or that one label is objectively more correct than another. My reaction was based in the fact that, for most parents, formally embracing a transgender designation paves the way for a pronoun switch, which often proves the last major boundary parents cross in accepting their child. Indeed, many parents were still in the throes of

that transition during interviews, as noted by the different pronouns used in the quotes. Regardless, this gut reaction on my part, a bad move in interviewing, resulted in additional dialogue and an e-mail exchange to clarify my position.

3 Serano, *Whipping Girl.*

4 See also Kane, "'No Way'"; Kane, *Gender Trap*; Martin, "William Wants a Doll"; Meadow, *Trans Kids*; Pascoe, *Dude, You're a Fag*; Serano, *Whipping Girl.*

5 See, e.g., Darwin, "Doing Gender"; Travers, *Trans Generation.*

6 Ethnomethodology is the study of how people make sense of their social worlds and, in turn, reproduce those understandings in social interactions, however seemingly arbitrary the rules (e.g., *"Why are you in that shirt? Pink is for girls!"*). See West and Zimmerman, "Doing Gender"; West and Fenstermaker, "Doing Difference."

7 Bem, "Gender Schema Theory"; Green and Friedman, *Chasing Rainbows*; Kane, *Gender Trap*; Martin, "William Wants a Doll."

8 Lareau, *Unequal Childhoods*; Hays, *Cultural Contradictions of Motherhood.* See also Travers, *Trans Generation*, 118.

9 Approximately half of my sample can be credited to this one participant, who, unbeknownst to me, posted my research blurb on a large online forum for other parents, to which I otherwise did not have access.

10 Martsy gave me unrestricted access to her journal entries and an online blog site, which she mainly updated for extended family and friends. I was grateful for this material, but admittedly struggled with the level of voyeurism that reading it might entail. That Martsy offered up such personal and sensitive material is a testament to how eager she was to contribute to my project and to raise awareness about transgender children and their families.

11 Other factors may have played a role, too, including a neoliberal, consumerist economy, which encourages and commodifies individual choice and preference, including at the toy store. See Orenstein, *Cinderella.* But these trends fit within a child-driven approach to parenting as well.

12 For additional writings on such strategic boundary work, including inside versus outside the home, see Kane, "'No Way'"; Rahilly, "The Gender Binary."

13 Seeber, *Trans* Lives.*

14 This case also includes behavioral health factors that the family feels influenced their readings of the child's behaviors, including fetal alcohol syndrome, which has delayed his psychosocial development. For these reasons, the mother Trish, introduced later in the chapter, feels that Joe's seeming "tomboy" preferences as a kid are just one more part of him that are "outside the [normative childhood] box." The family feels that since Joe's social transition, his maturity and psychosocial development have advanced exponentially. As such, Trish feels that in some ways his early development may have been hampered by not being able to grow into his true gendered self. I return to the intersections of gender and disability for parents in chapter 4.

15 See, e.g., Kane, *Gender Trap*; Meadow, *Trans Kids.*

16 Halberstam raised similar questions about "tomboys" in *Female Masculinity*, 142, before transgender childhoods had truly appeared on the cultural scene.

17 When I probed Wendy in the interview about these specific kinds of indicators, she clarified that the therapist does not necessarily require any or all of these markers to make a firm identification either way (especially in terms of "I am" versus "I want to be" identity statements. In other instances, I heard both forms of the phrase characterized as significant and indicative).

18 See also the theme of "playing along" in Rahilly, "The Gender Binary."

19 Meadow, "'Deep Down,'" 728.

20 Seeber, *Trans* Lives*. See also the documentary film *Diagnosing Difference* (2009), directed by Annalise Ophelian.

21 These arguments do not just interrogate or antagonize parents' decisions, but can criminalize them in the eyes of the court. See, for example, the Arizona case of a woman who lost custody of her six-year-old child to her ex on grounds that she was "forcing" the child's transgender transition (Polletta, "Why Parents Are Losing Custody").

22 Califia, *Sex Changes*; Meyerowitz, *How Sex Changed*; Serano, *Whipping Girl*; Spade, "Mutilating Gender."

23 Clarise was part of an early round of interviewees whose child was a grown teenager at the time, here nineteen years old. She indicated at the time that she felt her role in his transition was largely over, so I did not include her as part of the cumulative sample for the book. She is thus not reflected in the participant chart or the demographic statistics of the sample (see appendix I).

24 Bem, "Gender Schema Theory"; Bem, *An Unconventional Family*.

25 See, e.g., Jeffreys, "The Transgendering of Children"; Raymond, *The Transsexual Empire*; see also Serano's critique of these perspectives in *Whipping Girl*.

CHAPTER 2. "OUR WORLD HAS BEEN ROCKED"

1 The term "ontology," or "ontological," refers to the nature or essence of being. Here, "gender" is taken to be a different part of one's core self from "sexual orientation." That is, they are considered "ontologically" distinct parts of who someone is, developing separately. See Valentine, *Imagining Transgender*. These understandings also reverberate throughout LGBT advocacy websites and resource pages.

2 See also Meadow, *Trans Kids*.

3 See, e.g., Halberstam's interrogation of this linear "spectrum" conception in *Female Masculinity*.

4 Some scholars have argued that Western culture is "sex-negative" and "sex-panicked," and with that, frames children as asexual beings, at least through puberty. See Gayle Rubin's canonical essay, "Thinking Sex." Evidently, like Heather here, parents often invoked this line of thinking when rejecting sexuality-based explanations for childhood nonconformity.

5 Valentine, *Imagining Transgender*, 15.

 6 Valentine, 40–42.

 7 Chauncey, *Gay New York*; Taylor, Kaminski, and Dugan, "From the Bowery to the Castro."

 8 Katz, *Invention of Heterosexuality*; Rupp, "Toward a Global History." This has resulted in contentions among contemporary LGBT scholars and activists regarding which gender-nonconforming figures from the past can be reclaimed as "gay" or "trans" in the present. See Halberstam, *Female Masculinity*, 45–73; Valentine, *Imagining Transgender*, 29–31.

 9 Valentine, *Imagining Transgender*, 100.

10 Rubin, *Deviations*, 197–98.

11 Bryant, "In Defense," 464. See also Spade, "Mutilating Gender."

12 Bryant, "Diagnosis and Medicalization."

13 Butler, *Gender Trouble*; Butler, "Performative Acts." See also Bettcher's discussion of "gendered desire" and "erotic structuralism" in "When Selves Have Sex."

14 Pascoe, *Dude, You're a Fag*.

15 Salamon, *Life and Death*; Schilt and Westbrook, "Doing Gender, Doing Heteronormativity." Increasing numbers of US states are banning the "gay panic" defense in hate crimes cases.

16 Kane, "'No Way'"; Martin, "William Wants a Doll"; Sedgwick, "How to Bring Your Kids Up Gay."

17 See, e.g., Soh, "The Unspoken Homophobia."

18 Wallien and Cohen-Kettenis, "Psychosexual Outcomes," 1414–17, provides an overview of these studies. The protocols and assessment tools used in these studies found a significant degree of gender dysphoria for the majority of participating children.

19 See, e.g., Brill and Pepper, *Transgender Child*; Menvielle, "Comprehensive Program." Some argue there are risks to promulgating the suicide-risk narrative for trans youth. See Meadow, *Trans Kids*, 124–25; Robertson, *Growing Up Queer*.

20 Some advocates are concerned that the new diagnosis will result in patients having to feign "distress" to access the care they need, and that it too limits accurate portrayals of trans experience. See Davy, "The DSM-5."

21 Meadow, *Trans Kids*, 116–22.

22 See, e.g., the *New York Times* op-eds of psychiatrists Jack Drescher, "Our Notions of Gender," and Richard Friedman, "How Changeable Is Gender?" For more critical interrogations of "regret narratives," see Hines and Sanger, *Transgender Identities*; Meadow, *Trans Kids*, 77–81.

23 The "older brother effect" posits that a (male) child is more likely to be gay the more older brothers he has because the mother's womb starts to "reject" the male fetus as a foreign body (see Blanchard, "Birth Order"). My discussion with Claire and Rick about this theory proved a memorable, and tense, methodological moment. As we discussed on the phone, and later over e-mail, Claire said she "could hear [my] wheels turning on any kind of sociological reasons as opposed to scientific, biological reasons" for homosexuality. She wanted to impress upon me

that this was "not hokey fanokey science." The problems of research participants sensing disagreement from interviewers are duly noted. I return to biological frameworks in chapter 4.

24 Bollinger, "Transgender Kids' Brains"; LeVay, "A Difference in Hypothalamic Structure"; Smith et al., "The Transsexual Brain." For critical analyses of these kinds of biological models, see Birke, "Unusual Fingers"; Fausto-Sterling, *Sexing the Body*; Fine, *Delusions of Gender*.

25 See, e.g., Nutt, *Becoming Nicole*, 159–64. The 2015 interview with Caitlyn Jenner on *20/20* also featured the neurological model for transgender identity.

CHAPTER 3. "PICKING THE 'OTHER BOX'"

1 Brinlee, "12 States."

2 Travers, *Trans Generation*. See also Robertson, *Growing Up Queer*.

3 See the 2017 annual survey, "Accelerating Acceptance," conducted by the LGBTQ advocacy organization GLAAD (fka Gay & Lesbian Alliance Against Defamation).

4 Butler, *Gender Trouble*.

5 See, e.g., the gender-expansive parenting perspectives in the anthology *Chasing Rainbows* by Green and Friedman, including Jane Ward's chapter, "Get Your Gender Binary Off My Childhood!"

6 Meadow, *Trans Kids*, 5.

7 Califia, *Sex Changes*, 223–25; Halberstam, *Female Masculinity*, 141–73; Roen, "'Either/Or' and 'Both/Neither.'"

8 Serano, *Whipping Girl*, 346.

9 Seeber, *Trans* Lives*, 57–84.

10 One of the many criticisms of this line of thought (i.e., "more/less progressive genders") is its neglect of the roles of race and class in gender transitions. For some people and locations, being more visibly nonconforming is simply too risky, whether they feel that way or not. On the other hand, many people cannot afford the costs of medical transitions, leaving them more visibly nonconforming or "transgressive" of the gender binary in a way that has nothing to do with their personal identities or their politics.

11 Butler, "Performative Acts"; Butler, "Doing Justice"; Lorber, *Paradoxes of Gender*; Lucal, "What It Means."

12 Acker, "Hierarchies, Jobs, Bodies"; Martin, "Gender as Social Institution"; Risman, "Gender as a Social Structure."

13 Schilt and Connell, "Do Workplace"; West and Zimmerman, "Doing Gender."

14 West and Zimmerman; West and Fenstermaker, "Doing Difference."

15 Travers, *Trans Generation*; Darwin, "Doing Gender."

16 Kane, *Gender Trap*; Pascoe, *Dude*.

17 Serano, *Whipping Girl*, 14.

18 Serano, 18.

19 Not everyone would agree with this scale. Visibly butch-masculine or gender-nonconforming persons assigned female might well experience as much cultural

scrutiny, prejudice, and danger as feminine persons assigned male (see Halberstam, *Female Masculinity*; Lucal, "What It Means"). I am mindful of this, particularly with regard to the limits of the "tomboy" category for young female masculinity. At the same time, parents' conundrums with less binary possibilities seemed to hinge on the "boy in the dress," not the "boyish girl."

20 See, e.g., Lucal, "What It Means."

21 This book included traditional indigenous and Native American gender terminology, which Dana thought Skylar might appreciate.

22 Several other parents of trans boys specifically indicated that they think their child might be gay or bisexual, based on conversations they had with their children, although they were not sure if this was part of the child's own sorting out of their gender and sexuality (recalling themes from chapter 2). This pertains to at least five of the fourteen transgender boys.

23 Virulent strains of this position—that sex-categorical binary transitions, inclusive of "sex change," dangerously uphold the gender binary and the patriarchy—are now largely rejected as "TERF" mentality (see chapter 1) and were perhaps best exemplified by Janice Raymond's infamous book *The Transsexual Empire*. Nevertheless, this notion is a subtext that has run throughout much of gender scholarship (e.g., Gagné, Tewksbury, and McGaughey, "Coming Out"; Lorber, *Paradoxes of Gender* and "Paradoxes of Gender Redux") and that others have long challenged. See Serano, *Whipping Girl*.

24 See, e.g., Bornstein, *Gender Outlaw*; Travers, *Trans Generation*, 30, 34.

25 Both Claire and Rick were candid in acknowledging their white racial privilege in supporting a transgender child, unprompted by me in the interview. The raced and classed dimensions of this mode of trans-affirmative parenting, especially relative to binary and medicalized understandings and discourses, are discussed in chapter 4.

26 I was unable to reach Sam for a follow-up interview.

27 For similar usages of vignettes, see Thai, *For Better or for Worse*, 19, 163.

28 Unfortunately, I was not proficient enough in Spanish to allow for more extensive interviewing with Elias, who was less fluent in English than Ally. This resulted in more limited conversation between the two of us, though he was equally candid about his feelings along their journey. Like many instances in this book, the quotes marshaled here are mom-centric. Elias did not list his age on the biographical paperwork.

CHAPTER 4. "A REGULAR, NORMAL CHILDHOOD"

1 "Stealth" is a fraught, unpopular term, which many have abandoned for its connotations of secrecy. The director of one of the first conferences I ever attended specifically addressed the problems of this term with parents. Nevertheless, it was used frequently in my interviews.

2 Meadow, *Trans Kids*, 152.

3 Meadow, 191–95.

4 Interestingly, Travers did not heavily encounter these kinds of medicalized discourses among their sample. See Travers, *Trans Generation*, 153.

5 See Wilchins, "Gender Identity Disorder Diagnosis," for a discussion of this position. Wilchins compares trans identity to pregnancy, as in a "normal" medical condition warranting medical, not psychiatric, care.

6 Garfinkel, "Passing."

7 West and Zimmerman, "Doing Gender."

8 West and Zimmerman, 132; Schilt and Westbrook, "Doing Gender, Doing Heteronormativity."

9 Connell, "Transsexual Women." See also Jenness and Fenstermaker, "Agnes Goes to Prison."

10 Clare, *Exile and Pride*; Colligan, "Why the Intersexed Shouldn't Be Fixed"; Davis, *Contesting Intersex*; Kafer, *Feminist, Crip, Queer*; McRuer, *Crip Theory*.

11 Clare, "Body Shame," 263.

12 Clare, 263.

13 See Seeber, *Trans* Lives*; Travers, *Trans Generation*.

14 Collins, *Black Feminist Thought*.

15 Spade, *Normal Life*; Stanley and Smith, *Captive Genders*. See also Enke, "Education of Little Cis," 236.

16 Collins, *Black Feminist Thought*; Collins, *Black Sexual Politics*; Crenshaw, "Mapping the Margins."

17 Lamble, "Retelling Racialized Violence"; Somerville, *Queering the Color Line*.

18 Vaid-Menon, "The Pain and Empowerment."

19 Goffman, *Stigma*.

20 See, e.g., Meadow, *Trans Kids*.

21 At the time of our interview, Tory was still using both male and female pronouns to refer to Connor, a transgender boy, as observed here. However, when we reconnected in 2015, I noticed that Tory was using male pronouns exclusively during our call. I cite this to emphasize the dynamic, transitional aspects of parents' journeys with their children.

22 See, e.g., Lorber, *Paradoxes of Gender*; Serano, *Whipping Girl*, 26–27, 345–62.

23 Potential correlations between autism and gender dysphoria have been explored by researchers; see, e.g., De Vries et al., "Autism Spectrum Disorders."

24 Blum, *Raising Generation Rx*; Landsman, *Reconstructing Motherhood*; Litt, "Women's Carework"; Panitch, *Disability, Mothers, and Organization*. See also Karkazis, *Fixing Sex*, for parents' experiences with intersex children.

25 Similarly, Stephen Beatty (Warren Beatty and Annette Benning's adult child), who identifies as a trans man, has publicly criticized Chaz Bono for analogizing trans identity to a "birth defect" or "cleft palate" in interviews, stating on his blog that Bono "does not represent us."

26 Meadow, *Trans Kids*, 116.

27 Jacobs, "Raising Gays," 319–20.

28 See also Meadow, *Trans Kids*, 141, and Travers's call for anti-oppression, coalitional politics in *Trans Generation*, 201.

29 McRuer, *Crip Theory*.

30 Serano, *Whipping Girl*, 86.

31 Serano, 81.

32 Seeber, *Trans* Lives*.

33 Nutt, *Becoming Nicole*, 159–64.

34 Bettcher, "Trapped in the Wrong Theory."

CONCLUSION

1 Valentine, *Imagining Transgender*, 253.

2 Bem, "Gender Schema Theory"; Martin, "William Wants a Doll."

3 Burgess, "Internal and External Stress Factors"; D'Augelli, Hershberger, and Pilkington, "Lesbian, Gay, and Bisexual Youth"; Grossman et al., "Parents' Reactions"; Herman, Haas, and Rodgers, "Suicide Attempts"; Ray, *Lesbian, Gay*; Ryan, "Engaging Families"; Rodgers, "Transgendered Youth Fact Sheet"; Savin-Williams, "Verbal and Physical Abuse."

4 Valentine, *Imagining Transgender*, 100.

5 See, e.g., Diamond, *Sexual Fluidity*; Ward, *Not Gay*.

6 Diamond, *Sexual Fluidity*; Halberstam, *Female Masculinity*; Rupp, "Toward a Global History"; Towle and Morgan, "Romancing the Transgender Native"; Valentine, *Imagining Transgender*.

7 For a review of this literature, see Schrock and Schwalbe, "Masculinities."

8 Adams, "Josh Wears Pink Cleats."

9 Schrock and Schwalbe, "Masculinities," 280–81; Serano, *Whipping Girl*.

10 Tobia, *Sissy*.

11 As Julia Serano discusses in *Whipping Girl*, concerns about "idealized femininity" largely animate trans and feminist political conflicts.

12 Robertson, *Growing Up Queer*; Travers, *Trans Generation*.

13 See Meadow, *Trans Kids*, 140–41, for similar observations.

14 Bettcher, "Trapped in the Wrong Theory"; Seeber, *Trans* Lives*; Serano, *Whipping Girl*.

15 Lareau, *Unequal Childhoods*, 111.

16 Bem, "Gender Schema Theory"; Kane, *Gender Trap*; Hagerman, *White Kids*; Lareau, *Unequal Childhoods*; Maccoby, "The Role of Parents."

17 Corsaro, *Sociology of Childhood*, 18.

18 See, e.g., the work of Olson, Key, and Eaton, "Gender Cognition."

APPENDIX II

1 Two of the parents I identify as white in this book identified as "White/Jewish" or "Russian Jew" on biographical forms.

2 Two parents did not list an income.

3 For a discussion of selection biases, see Sprague, *Feminist Methodologies*, 127–30.

4   For a discussion of diversifying LGBTQ samples, see Sheff and Hammers, "Privilege of Perversities."

5   Aitken et al., "Evidence for an Altered Sex Ratio."

6   Charmaz, *Constructing Grounded Theory*; Glaser and Strauss, *Discovery of Grounded Theory*.

7   See Aguilar, "Pegging," 282; Clarke, Braun, and Hayfield, "Thematic Analysis."

8   Fonow and Cook, "Feminist Methodology"; Haraway, "Situated Knowledges"; Harding, "Is There a Feminist Method?"; Naples, *Feminism and Method*; Oakley, "Interviewing Women"; Smith, *Everyday World*; Sprague, *Feminist Methodologies*; Stacey, "Can There Be a Feminist Ethnography?"

9   Travers, *Trans Generation*, 9.

10 Meadow, "Studying Each Other," 478.

11 For important discussions of this, see Hale, "Suggested Rules"; Namaste, *Invisible Lives*, 32–33; Schilt and Connell, "Do Workplace," 6–7; Serano, *Whipping Girl*, 116–60.

12 This was actually seen in the Proposition 8 marriage equality trials, where the "antigay" side of the litigation marshaled social-constructionist theory and scholarship to refute the reality of gay identity. See Weber, "What's Wrong."

13 Weber.

REFERENCES

Acker, Joan. "Hierarchies, Jobs, Bodies: A Theory of Gendered Organizations." *Gender & Society* 4, no. 2 (1990): 139–58.

Adams, Adi. "'Josh Wears Pink Cleats': Inclusive Masculinity on the Soccer Field." *Journal of Homosexuality* 58, no. 5 (2011): 579–96.

Aguilar, Jade. "Pegging and the Heterosexualization of Anal Sex: An Analysis of Savage Love Advice." *Queer Studies in Media and Popular Culture* 2, no. 3 (2017): 275–92.

Aitken, Madison, Thomas D. Steensma, Ray Blanchard, Doug P. VanderLaan, Hayley Wood, Amanda Fuentes, and Cathy Spegg. "Evidence for an Altered Sex Ratio in Clinic-Referred Adolescents with Gender Dysphoria." *Journal of Sexual Medicine* 12, no. 3 (2015): 756–63.

Aveline, David. "'Did I Have Blinders on or What?': Retrospective Sense Making by Parents of Gay Sons Recalling Their Sons' Earlier Years." *Journal of Family Issues* 27, no. 6 (2006): 777–802.

Bem, Sandra. "Gender Schema Theory and Its Implications for Child Development: Raising Gender-Aschematic Children in a Gender-Schematic Society." *Signs* 8, no. 4 (1983): 611–62.

———. *An Unconventional Family*. New Haven, CT: Yale University Press, 1998.

Bettcher, Talia Mae. "Trapped in the Wrong Theory: Rethinking Trans Oppression and Resistance." *Signs* 39, no. 2 (2014): 383–406.

———. "When Selves Have Sex: What the Phenomenology of Trans Sexuality Can Teach about Sexual Orientation." *Journal of Homosexuality* 61, no. 5 (2014): 605–20.

Bianchi, Suzanne M., John P. Robinson, and Melissa A. Milke. *The Changing Rhythms of American Family Life*. New York: Russell Sage, 2006.

Birke, Lynda. "Unusual Fingers: Scientific Studies of Sexual Orientation." In *Handbook of Lesbian and Gay Studies*, edited by Diane Richardson and Steven Seidman, 55–57. Thousand Oaks, CA: Sage, 2002.

Blanchard, Ray. "Birth Order and Sibling Sex Ratio in Homosexual versus Heterosexual Males and Females." *Annual Review of Sex Research* 8 (1997): 27–67.

Blum, Linda. *Raising Generation Rx: Mothering Kids with Invisible Disabilities in an Age of Inequality*. New York: NYU Press, 2015.

Bollinger, Alex. "Transgender Kids' Brains Resemble Their Gender Identity, Not Their Biological Sex." *LGBTQ Nation*, May 22, 2018. https://www.lgbtqnation.com/2018/05/transgender-kids-brains-resemble-gender-identity-not-biological-sex/.

Bornstein, Kate. *Gender Outlaw: On Men, Women, and the Rest of Us*. New York: Vintage Books, 2016.

Bridges, Tristan, and C. J. Pascoe. "Hybrid Masculinities: New Directions in the Sociology of Men and Masculinities." *Sociology Compass* 8, no. 3 (2014): 246–58.

Briggs, Laura. *How All Politics became Reproductive Politics: From Welfare Reform to Foreclosure to Trump*. Vol. 2. Berkeley: University of California Press, 2018.

Brill, S., and Rachel Pepper. *The Transgender Child: A Handbook for Families and Professionals*. New York: Simon and Schuster, 2008.

Brinlee, Morgan. "12 States with a Third Gender Option on IDs Pave the Way for Non-binary Recognition." *Bustle*, June 20, 2019. https://www.bustle.com/p/12-states-with-a-third-gender-option-on-ids-pave-the-way-for-non-binary-recognition-17988940.

Bryant, Karl. "Diagnosis and Medicalization." In *Sociology of Diagnosis*, edited by P. J. McGann and David J. Hutson, 33–58. Bingley, UK: Emerald Group Publishing, 2011.

———. "In Defense of Gay Children? 'Progay' Homophobia and the Production of Homonormativity." *Sexualities* 11, no. 4 (2008): 455–75.

———. "Making Gender Identity Disorder of Childhood: Historical Lessons for Contemporary Debates." *Sexuality Research and Social Policy* 3, no. 3 (2006): 23–39.

Burgess, Christian. "Internal and External Stress Factors Associated with the Identity Development of Transgendered Youth." *Journal of Gay and Lesbian Social Services* 10, nos. 3–4 (2008): 35–47.

Butler, Judith. "Doing Justice to Someone: Sex Reassignment and Allegories of Transsexuality." *GLQ: A Journal of Lesbian and Gay Studies* 7, no. 4 (2001): 621–36.

———. *Gender Trouble: Feminism and the Subversion of Identity*. New York: Routledge, 2011.

———. "Performative Acts and Gender Constitution: An Essay in Phenomenology and Feminist Theory." *Theatre Journal* 40, no. 4 (1988): 519–31.

Cahill, Spencer. "Language Practices and Self-Definition: The Case of Gender Identity Acquisition." *Sociological Quarterly* 27, no. 3 (1986): 295–311.

Calarco, Jessica McCrory. *Negotiating Opportunities: How the Middle Class Secures Advantages in School*. New York: Oxford University Press, 2018.

Califia, Patrick. *Sex Changes: Transgender Politics*. San Francisco: Cleis Press, 2003.

Cohen, Cathy. "Punks, Bull Daggers, and Welfare Queens: The Radical Potential of Queer Politics?" *GLQ: A Journal of Lesbian and Gay Studies* 3, no. 4 (1997): 437–65.

Charmaz, Kathy. *Constructing Grounded Theory*. Los Angeles: Sage, 2014.

Chauncey, George. *Gay New York: Gender, Urban Culture, and the Making of the Gay Male World, 1890–1940*. New York: Basic Books, 1994.

Chodorow, Nancy. *The Reproduction of Mothering*. Berkeley: University of California Press, 1978.

Clare, Eli. "Body Shame, Body Pride." In *Transgender Studies Reader 2, edited by Susan Stryker and Aren Aizura*, 261–65. New York: Routledge, 2013.

———. *Exile and Pride: Disability, Queerness, and Liberation*. Boston: South End Press, 1999.

Clarke, Victoria, Virginia Braun, and Nikki Hayfield. "Thematic Analysis." In *Qualitative Psychology: A Practical Guide to Research Methods*, 3rd ed., edited by J. A. Smith, 222–48. Thousand Oaks, CA: Sage, 2015.

Colligan, Sumi. "Why the Intersexed Shouldn't Be Fixed: Insights from Queer Theory and Disability Studies." In *Gendering Disability*, edited by Bonnie G. Smith and Beth Hutchinson, 45–60. New Brunswick, NJ: Rutgers University Press, 2004.

Collins, Patricia Hill. *Black Sexual Politics: African Americans, Gender, and the New Racism*. New York: Routledge, 2004.

———. "Learning from the Outsider Within: The Sociological Significance of Black Feminist Thought." *Social Problems* 33, no. 6 (1986), S14–S32.

Coltrane, Scott, and Michele Adams. "Children and Gender." In *Contemporary Parenting*, edited by Terry Arendell, 219–53. Thousand Oaks, CA: Sage, 1997.

Connell, Raewyn. "Transsexual Women and Feminist Thought." *Signs* 37 (2012): 857–81.

Conrad, Ryan. *Against Equality: Queer Revolution, Not Mere Inclusion*. Oakland, CA: AK Press, 2014.

Coontz, Stephanie. *The Social Origins of Private Life: A History of American Families, 1600–1900*. Brooklyn, NY: Verso Books, 2016.

Corsaro, William A. *The Sociology of Childhood*. 4th ed. Thousand Oaks, CA: Sage, 2015.

Crenshaw, Kimberlé. "Mapping the Margins." *Stanford Law Review* 43, no. 6 (1991): 1241–99.

Crumdy, Angela, Nadja Eisenberg-Guyot, Zoltán Glück, Samuel Novacich, Sarah Molinari, Helen Panagiotopoulos, Cecilia María Salvi, and Daniel Schneider. "CUNY Graduate School Student Collective: Bodies and Violence." *Anthropology Now* 8, no. 1 (2016): 67–77.

D'Augelli, A. R., Scott L. Hershberger, and Neil W. Pilkington. "Lesbian, Gay, and Bisexual Youth and Their Families: Disclosure of Sexual Orientation and Its Consequences." *American Journal of Orthopsychiatry* 68, no. 3 (1998): 361–71.

Darwin, Helana. "Doing Gender beyond the Binary: A Virtual Ethnography." *Symbolic Interaction* 40, no. 3 (2017): 317–34.

Davis, Georgiann. *Contesting Intersex: The Dubious Diagnosis*. New York: NYU Press, 2015.

Davis, Heath Bogg. *Beyond Trans: Does Gender Matter?* New York: NYU Press, 2018.

Davy, Z. "The DSM-5 and the Politics of Diagnosing Transpeople." *Archives of Sexual Behavior* 44, no. 5 (2015): 1165–76.

Delemarre-van de Waal, H. A., and P. T. Cohen-Kettenis. "Clinical Management of Gender Identity Disorder in Adolescents: A Protocol on Psychological and Pediatric Endocrinology Aspects." *European Journal of Endocrinology* 155 (2006): S131–S137.

Denzin, Norman K. *Childhood Socialization*. New Brunswick, NJ: Transaction Publishers, 1977.

De Vries, A. L., L. J. Noens, P. T. Cohen-Kettenis, I. A. van Berckelaer-Onnes, and T. A. Doreleijers. "Autism Spectrum Disorders in Gender Dysphoric Children and Adolescents." *Journal of Autism and Developmental Disorders* 40, no. 8 (2010): 930–36.

Diamond, Lisa M. *Sexual Fluidity: Understanding Women's Love and Desire*. Cambridge, MA: Harvard University Press, 2009.

Drescher, Jack. "Our Notions of Gender." *New York Times*, June 29, 2013. https://www.nytimes.com/2013/06/30/opinion/sunday/sunday-dialogue-our-notions-of-gender.html

Drescher, Jack, and William Byne. "Gender Dysphoric/Gender Variant (GD/GV) Children and Adolescents: Summarizing What We Know and What We Have Yet to Learn." *Journal of Homosexuality* 59, no. 3 (2012): 501–10.

Drummond, K. D., S. J. Bradley, M. Peterson-Badali, and K. J. Zucker. "A Follow-Up Study of Girls with Gender Identity Disorder." *Developmental Psychology* 44 (2008): 34–45.

Duggan, Lisa. "The New Homonormativity: The Sexual Politics of Neoliberalism." In *Materializing Democracy: Toward a Revitalized Cultural Politics*, edited by Russ Castronovo and Dana D. Nelson, 175–94. Durham, NC: Duke University Press, 2002.

Ehrensaft, Diane. *Gender Born, Gender Made: Raising Healthy Gender-Nonconforming Children*. New York: The Experiment, 2011.

Engel, Stephen. "Making a Minority: Understanding the Formation of the Gay and Lesbian Movement in the United States." In *Handbook of Lesbian and Gay Studies*, edited by Diane Richardson and Steven Seidman, 377–402. Thousand Oaks, CA: Sage, 2002.

Enke, Finn A. "The Education of Little Cis." In *Transgender Studies Reader 2*, edited by Susan Stryker and Aren Aizura. 234–47. New York: Routledge, 2013.

Epstein, Steven. "Gay Politics, Ethnic Identity: The Limits of Social Constructionism." In *Social Perspectives in Lesbian and Gay Studies: A Reader*, edited by Peter M. Nardi and Beth E. Schneider, 134–59. New York: Routledge, 1998 [1993].

Fausto-Sterling, Anne. *Sexing the Body: Gender Politics and the Construction of Sexuality*. New York: Basic Books, 2000.

Fine, Cordelia. *Delusions of Gender: How Our Minds, Society, and Neurosexism Create Difference*. New York: WW Norton & Company, 2010.

Fonow, Mary Margaret, and Judith A. Cook. "Feminist Methodology: New Applications in the Academy and Public Policy." *Signs* 30, no. 4 (2005): 2211–36.

Friedman, Richard. "How Changeable Is Gender?" *New York Times*, August 22, 2015. https://www.nytimes.com/2015/08/23/opinion/sunday/richard-a-friedman-how-changeable-is-gender.html

Gagné, Patricia, Richard Tewksbury, and Deanna McGaughey. "Coming Out and Crossing Over: Identity Formation and Proclamation in a Transgender Community." *Gender & Society* 11, no. 4 (1997): 478–508.

Gamson, Joshua. *Freaks Talk Back: Tabloid Talk Shows and Sexual Nonconformity*. Chicago: University of Chicago Press, 1998.

———. "Must Identity Movements Self-Destruct? A Queer Dilemma." *Social Problems* 42, no. 3 (1995): 390–407.

Garfinkel, Harold. "Passing and the Managed Achievement of Sex Status in an 'Intersexed' Person." *Studies in Ethnomethodology*, 116–85. Malden, MA: Prentice-Hall, 1967.

GLAAD. "Accelerating Acceptance." Survey. 2017. https://www.glaad.org/files/aa/2017_
GLAAD_Accelerating_Acceptance.pdf.

Glaser, Barney G., and Anselm L. Strauss. *Discovery of Grounded Theory: Strategies for Qualitative Research.* New York: Routledge, 2017.

Gill-Peterson, Julian. "The Technical Capacities of the Body: Assembling Race, Technology, and Transgender." *Transgender Studies Quarterly* 1, no. 3 (2014): 402–18.

Goffman, Erving. *Stigma: Notes on the Management of Spoiled Identity.* Englewood Cliffs, NJ: Prentice-Hall, 1963.

Gossett, Reina, Eric A. Stanley, and Johanna Burton. *Trap Door: Trans Cultural Production and the Politics of Visibility.* New York: New Museum, 2017.

Gray, Mary L., Colin R. Johnson, and Brian J. Gilley, eds. *Queering the Countryside: New Frontiers in Rural Queer Studies.* New York: NYU Press, 2016.

Green, Erica, Katie Benner, and Robert Pear. "'Transgender' Could Be Defined Out of Existence under Trump Administration." *New York Times,* October 21, 2018. https://www.nytimes.com/2018/10/21/us/politics/transgender-trump-administration-sex-definition.html.

Green, Fiona J., and May Friedman, eds. *Chasing Rainbows: Exploring Gender Fluid Parenting Practices.* Bradford, ON: Demeter Press, 2013.

Green, Richard. *The "Sissy Boy Syndrome" and the Development of Homosexuality.* New Haven, CT: Yale University Press, 1987.

Grossman, A. H., A. R. D'Augelli, T. J. Howell, and S. Hubbard. "Parents' Reactions to Transgender Youths' Gender Nonconforming Expression and Identity." *Journal of Gay and Lesbian Social Services* 18, no. 1 (2006): 3–16.

Hagerman, Margaret. *White Kids: Growing Up with Privilege in a Racially Divided America.* New York: NYU Press, 2018.

Halberstam, Judith. *Female Masculinity.* Durham, NC: Duke University Press, 1998.

Hale, Jacob. "Suggested Rules for Non-transsexuals Writing about Transsexuals, Transsexuality, Transsexualism, or Trans." 2010. https://hivdatf.files.wordpress.com/2010/09/suggested-rules-for-non-modified.pdf.

Handel, Gerald, Spencer. E. Cahill, and Frederick Elkin. *Children and Society: The Sociology of Children and Childhood Socialization.* New York: Oxford University Press, 2006.

Haraway, Donna. "Situated Knowledges: The Science Question in Feminism and the Privilege of Partial Perspective." *Feminist Studies* 14, no. 3 (1998): 575–99.

Harding, Sandra. "Is There a Feminist Method?" In *Feminism and Methodology,* edited by Sandra Harding, 1–14. Bloomington: Indiana University Press, 1987.

Hayes, Molley. "Doctor Fired from Gender Identity Clinic Says He Feels 'Vindicated' after CAMH Apology, Settlement." *Globe and Mail,* October 7, 2018. https://www.theglobeandmail.com/canada/toronto/article-doctor-fired-from-gender-identity-clinic-says-he-feels-vindicated/.

Hays, Sharon. *The Cultural Contradictions of Motherhood.* New Haven, CT: Yale University Press, 1996.

Herdt, Gilbert. *Third Sex, Third Gender: Beyond Sexual Dimorphism in Culture and History.* New York: Zone Books, 2012.

Herman, J., A. Haas, and P. Rodgers. "Suicide Attempts among Transgender and Gender Non-conforming Adults." *UCLA: The Williams Institute*, 2014. https://escholarship.org/uc/item/8xg8061f.

Hines, Sally, and Tam Sanger. *Transgender Identities: Towards a Social Analysis of Gender Diversity*. New York: Routledge, 2010.

Jacobs, Jason. "Raising Gays: On *Glee*, Queer Kids, and the Limits of the Family." *GLQ: A Journal of Lesbian and Gay Studies* 20, no. 3 (2014): 319–52.

Jeffreys, Sheila. "The Transgendering of Children: Gender Eugenics." *Women's Studies International Forum* 35, no. 5 (September-October 2012): 384–93.

Jenness, Valerie, and Sarah Fenstermaker. "Agnes Goes to Prison: Gender Authenticity, Transgender Inmates in Prisons for Men, and Pursuit of 'The Real Deal.'" *Gender & Society* 28, no. 1 (2014): 5–31.

Kafer, Alison. *Feminist, Queer, Crip*. Bloomington: Indiana University Press, 2013.

Kane, Emily. *The Gender Trap: Parents and the Pitfalls of Raising Boys and Girls*. New York: NYU Press, 2012.

———. "'No Way My Boys Are Going to Be Like That!': Parents' Responses to Children's Gender Nonconformity." *Gender & Society* 20, no. 2 (2006): 149–76.

Karkazis, Katrina. *Fixing Sex: Intersex, Medical Authority, and Lived Experience*. Durham, NC: Duke University Press, 2008.

Katz, Jonathan. *The Invention of Heterosexuality*. Chicago: University of Chicago Press, 2007.

Krieger, Irwin. *Helping Your Transgender Teen: A Guide for Parents*. 2nd ed. Philadelphia: Jessica Kingsley, 2018.

Kuvalanka, Katherine A., Judith L. Weiner, Cat Munroe, Abbie E. Goldberg, and Molly Gardner. "Trans and Gender-Nonconforming Children and Their Caregivers: Gender Presentations, Peer Relations, and Well-Being at Baseline." *Journal of Family Psychology* 31, no. 7 (2017): 889–99.

Lamble, Sarah. "Retelling Racialized Violence, Remaking White Innocence: The Politics of Interlocking Oppressions in Transgender Day of Remembrance." *Sexuality Research and Social Policy* 5, no. 1 (2008): 24–42.

Landsman, Gail. *Reconstructing Motherhood and Disability in the Age of Perfect Babies*. New York: Routledge, 2008.

Lareau, Annette. *Unequal Childhoods: Class, Race, and Family Life*. Berkeley: University of California Press, 2003.

LeVay, S. "A Difference in Hypothalamic Structure between Heterosexual and Homosexual Men." *Science* 253, no. 5023 (1991): 1034–37.

Lev, Arlene I. *Transgender Emergence: Therapeutic Guidelines for Working with Gender-Variant People and Their Families*. Binghamton, NY: Haworth Press, 2004.

Litt, Jacquelyn. "Women's Carework in Low-Income Households: The Special Case of Children with Attention Deficit Hyperactivity Disorder." *Gender & Society* 18, no. 5 (2004): 625–44.

Lorber, Judith. *Paradoxes of Gender*. New Haven, CT: Yale University Press, 1994.

———. "Paradoxes of Gender Redux: Multiple Genders and the Persistence of the Binary." In *Gender Reckonings*, edited by James W. Messerschmidt, Michael A. Messner, Raewyn Connell, and Patricia Yancey Martin, 297–313. New York: NYU Press, 2018.

Lucal, Betsy. "What It Means to Be Gendered Me: Life on the Boundaries of a Dichotomous Gender System." *Gender & Society* 13 (1999): 781–97.

Maccoby, Eleanor E. "The Role of Parents in the Socialization of Children: An Historical Overview." *Developmental Psychology* 28, no. 6 (1992): 1006–17.

Martin, Karin. "William Wants a Doll. Can He Have One? Feminists, Child Care Advisors, and Gender-Neutral Child Rearing." *Gender & Society* 19, no. 4 (2005): 456–79.

Martin, Patricia Yancey. "Gender as Social Institution." *Social Forces* 82, no. 4 (2004): 1249–73.

McGuire, Jenifer K., Katherine A. Kuvalanka, Jory M. Catalpa, and Russell B. Toomey. "Transfamily Theory: How the Presence of Trans* Family Members Informs Gender Development in Families." *Journal of Family Theory and Review* 8, no. 1 (2016): 60–73.

McRuer, Robert. *Crip Theory: Cultural Signs of Queerness and Disability.* New York: NYU Press, 2006.

Meadow, Tey. "The Child." *Transgender Studies Quarterly* 1, no. 1 (2014): 57–59.

———. "'Deep Down Where the Music Plays': How Parents Account for Childhood Gender Variance." *Sexualities* 14, no. 6 (2011): 725–47.

———. "Studying Each Other: On Agency, Constraint, and Positionality in the Field." *Journal of Contemporary Ethnography* 42, no. 4 (2013): 466–81.

———. *Trans Kids: Being Gendered in the Twenty-First Century.* Berkeley: University of California Press, 2018.

Menvielle, E. "A Comprehensive Program for Children with Gender Variant Behaviors and Gender Identity Disorders." *Journal of Homosexuality* 59, no. 3 (2012): 357–68.

———. "Transgender Children: Clinical and Ethical Issues in Prepubertal Presentations." *Journal of Gay and Lesbian Mental Health* 13, no. 4 (2009): 292–97.

Meyerowitz, Joanne. *How Sex Changed: A History of Transsexuality in the United States.* Cambridge, MA: Harvard University Press, 2004.

Miller, Claire Cain. "The Relentlessness of Modern Parenting." *New York Times*, December 25, 2018. https://www.nytimes.com/2018/12/25/upshot/the-relentlessness-of-modern-parenting.html.

Mintz, Steven. *Huck's Raft: A History of American Childhood.* Cambridge, MA: Harvard University Press, 2004.

Namaste, Viviane K. *Invisible Lives: The Erasure of Transsexual and Transgendered People.* Chicago: University of Chicago Press, 2000.

Nanda, Serena. *Neither Man nor Woman: The Hijras of India.* Boston: Cengage Learning, 1999.

Naples, Nancy A. *Feminism and Method: Ethnography, Discourse Analysis, and Activist Research.* New York: Routledge, 2013.

Nelson, Margaret K. *Parenting Out of Control: Anxious Parents in Uncertain Times.* New York: NYU Press, 2010.

Nutt, Amy Ellis. *Becoming Nicole: The Transformation of an American Family.* New York: Random House, 2016.

Oakley, Ann. "Interviewing Women: A Contradiction in Terms." In *Turning Points in Qualitative Research*, edited by Y. Lincoln and N. Denzin, 243–64. Walnut Creek, CA: Timtamira Press, 2003.

Olson, K. R., A. C. Key, and N. R. Eaton. "Gender Cognition in Transgender Children." *Psychology Science* 26, no. 4 (2015): 1–8.

Ophelian, Annalise. Dir. *Diagnosing Difference.* Floating Ophelia Productions, 2009.

Orenstein, Peggy. *Cinderella Ate My Daughter.* New York: Harper Collins, 2012.

Panitch, Melanie. *Disability, Mothers, and Organization: Accidental Activists.* New York: Routledge, 2008.

Pascoe, C. J. *Dude, You're a Fag.* Berkeley: University of California Press, 2007.

Pepper, Rachel. *Transitions of the Heart: Stories of Love, Struggle and Acceptance by Mothers of Transgender and Gender Variant Children.* Berkeley, CA: Cleis Press, 2012.

Peterson, Gary W., and Boyd C. Rollins. "Parent-Child Socialization: A Review of Research and Applications of Symbolic Interaction Concepts." In *Handbook of Marriage and the Family*, edited by Marvin B. Sussman and Suzanne K. Steinmetz, 471–507. New York: Plenum Press, 1987.

Pogrebin, Letty Cottin. *Growing Up Free.* New York: Bantam, 1981.

Polletta, Maria. "Why Parents Are Losing Custody of Trans and Gender-Nonconforming Kids." *The Republic/AZ Central*, April 10, 2018. https://www.azcentral.com/story/news/local/arizona/2018/04/10/why-parents-losing-custody-trans-and-gender-non-conforming-kids/485928002/.

Puar, Jasbir K. *Terrorist Assemblages: Homonationalism in Queer Times.* Durham, NC: Duke University Press, 2007.

Rahilly, Elizabeth. "The Gender Binary Meets the Gender-Variant Child: Parents' Negotiations with Childhood Gender Variance." *Gender & Society* 29, no. 3 (2015): 349–61.

Ray, Nicholas. *Lesbian, Gay, Bisexual and Transgender Youth: An Epidemic of Homelessness.* New York: National Gay and Lesbian Task Force Policy Institute and the National Coalition for the Homeless, 2006.

Raymond, Janice G. *The Transsexual Empire: The Making of the She-Male.* Boston: Beacon Press, 1979.

Rekers, G. A. "Pathological Sex-Role Development in Boys: Behavioral Treatment and Assessment." PhD diss., University of California, Los Angeles, 1972.

Risman, Barbara J. "Gender as a Social Structure: Theory Wrestling with Activism." *Gender & Society* 18, no. 4 (2004): 429–50.

Risman, Barbara J., and Kristen Myers. "As the Twig Is Bent: Children Reared in Feminist Households." *Qualitative Sociology* 20 (1997): 229–52.

Robertson, Mary. *Growing Up Queer: Kids and the Remaking of LGBTQ Identity.* New York: NYU Press, 2018.

Rodgers, L. L. "Transgendered Youth Fact Sheet: Treatment Services Guidelines for Substance Abuse Treatment Providers." Edited by the Transgender Protocol Team, 7–8. San Francisco: Lesbian, Gay, Bisexual, Transgender Substance Abuse Task Force, 1995.

Roen, Katrina. "'Either/Or' and 'Both/Neither': Discursive Tensions in Transgender Politics—TEST." *Signs* 27, no. 2 (2002): 501–22.

Rogers, Baker A. "Drag as a Resource: Trans* and Nonbinary Individuals in the Southeastern United States." *Gender & Society* 32, no. 6 (2018): 889–910.

Rubin, Gayle. *Deviations: A Gayle Rubin Reader.* Durham, NC: Duke University Press, 2011.

———. "Thinking Sex: Notes for a Radical Theory of the Politics of Sexuality." In *Social Perspectives in Lesbian and Gay Studies: A Reader,* edited by Peter M. Nardi and Beth E. Schneider, 100–133. New York: Routledge, 1998 [1984].

Rupp, Leila. "Toward a Global History of Same-Sex Sexuality." *Journal of the History of Sexuality* 10, no. 2 (2001): 287–302.

Ryan, Caitlin. "Engaging Families to Support Lesbian, Gay, Bisexual, and Transgender Youth: The Family Acceptance Project." *Prevention Researcher* 17, no. 4 (2010): 11–13.

Salamon, Gayle. *The Life and Death of Latisha King: A Critical Phenomenology of Transphobia.* New York: NYU Press, 2018.

Savin-Williams, Ritch C. "Verbal and Physical Abuse as Stressors in the Lives of Lesbian, Gay Male, and Bisexual Youths: Associations with School Problems, Running Away, Substance Abuse, Prostitution, and Suicide." *Journal of Consulting and Clinical Psychology* 62, no. 2 (1994): 261–69.

Schilt, Kristen, and Catherine Connell. "Do Workplace Gender Transitions Make Gender Trouble?" *Gender, Work and Organization* 14, no. 6 (2007): 596–618.

Schilt, Kristen, and Laurel Westbrook. "Doing Gender, Doing Heteronormativity: 'Gender Normals,' Transgender People, and the Social Maintenance of Heterosexuality." *Gender & Society* 23, no. 4 (2009): 440–64.

Schrock, Douglas, and Michael Schwalbe. "Masculinities." *Annual Review of Sociology* 35 (2009): 277–95.

Sedgwick, Eve. "How to Bring Your Kids Up Gay: The War on Effeminate Boys." In *Tendencies,* edited by E. Sedgwick, 154–64. Durham, NC: Duke University Press, 1993.

Seeber, Andrew. *Trans* Lives in the United States: Challenges of Transition and Beyond.* New York: Routledge, 2018.

Senior, Jennifer. *All Joy and No Fun: The Paradox of Modern Parenthood.* New York: Ecco Press, 2015.

Serano, Julia. *Whipping Girl: A Transsexual Woman on Sexism and the Scapegoating of Femininity.* Emeryville, CA: Seal Press, 2007.

Sheff, Elizabeth, and Corrie J. Hammers. "The Privilege of Perversities: Race, Class and Education among Polyamorists and Kinksters." *Psychology & Sexuality* 2, no. 3 (2011): 198–223.

Singal, Jesse. "When Children Say They're Transgender." *The Atlantic,* July/August 2018. https://www.theatlantic.com/magazine/archive/2018/07/when-a-child-says-shes-trans/561749/.

Smith, Dorothy, E. *The Everyday World as Problematic: A Feminist Sociology*. Boston: Northeastern University Press, 1987.

Smith, E. S., J. Junger, B. Derntl, and U. Habel. "The Transsexual Brain: A Review of Findings on the Neural Basis of Transsexualism." *Neuroscience and Biobehavioral Reviews* 59 (2015): 251–66.

Snorton, C. Riley, and Jin Haritaworn. "Trans Necropolitics: A Transnational Reflection on Violence, Death, and the Trans of Color Afterlife." In *The Transgender Studies Reader 2*, edited by Susan Stryker and Aren Aizura, 66–76. New York: Routledge, 2013.

Soh, Debra. "The Unspoken Homophobia Propelling the Transgender Movement in Children." *Quillette*, October 23, 2018. https://quillette.com/2018/10/23/the-unspoken-homophobia-propelling-the-transgender-movement-in-children/.

Somerville, Siobhan. *Queering the Color Line: Race and the Invention of Homosexuality in American Culture*. Durham, NC: Duke University Press, 2018.

Spade, Dean. "Mutilating Gender." In *The Transgender Studies Reader*, edited by Susan Stryker and Stephen Whittle, 315–32. New York: Routledge, 2006.

———. *Normal Life: Administrative Violence, Critical Trans Politics, and the Limits of Law*. Durham, NC: Duke University Press, 2015.

Sprague, Joey. *Feminist Methodologies for Critical Researchers*. Walnut Creek, CA: Altamira Press, 2005.

Stacey, Judith. "Can There Be a Feminist Ethnography?" *Women's Studies International Forum* 11, no. 1 (1988): 21–27.

Stanley, Eric A., and Nat Smith, eds. *Captive Genders: Trans Embodiment and the Prison Industrial Complex*. Oakland, CA: AK Press, 2011.

Statham, June. *Daughters and Sons: Experiences of Non-sexist Childraising*. New York: Basil Blackwell, 1986.

Steinmetz, Katy. "Gender and Sexuality: Beyond 'He' or 'She.'" *Time*, March 16, 2017. https://time.com/4703309/gender-sexuality-changing/.

———. "The Transgender Tipping Point." *Time*, May 29, 2014. https://time.com/135480/transgender-tipping-point/.

Stryker, Susan. *Transgender History*. Berkeley, CA: Seal Press, 2008.

Taylor, Verta, Elizabeth Kaminski, and Kimberly Dugan. "From the Bowery to the Castro: Communities, Identities, and Movements." In *Handbook of Lesbian and Gay Studies*, edited by Diane Richardson and Steven Seidman, 99–114. Thousand Oaks, CA: Sage, 2002.

Thai, Hung Cam. *For Better or for Worse: Vietnamese International Marriages in the New Global Economy*. New Brunswick, NJ: Rutgers University Press, 2008.

Thomsen, Carly. "The Post-raciality and Post-spatiality of Calls for LGBTQ and Disability Visibility." *Hypatia* 30, no. 1 (2015): 149–66.

Thorne, Barrie. *Gender Play: Girls and Boys in School*. New Brunswick, NJ: Rutgers University Press, 1993.

———. "Re-visioning Women and Social Change: Where Are the Children?" *Gender & Society* 1, no. 1 (1987): 85–109.

Tobia, Jacob. *Sissy: A Coming-of-Gender Story.* New York: G. P. Putnam's Sons, 2019.

Towle, Evan B., and Lynn Marie Morgan. "Romancing the Transgender Native: Rethinking the Use of the 'Third Gender' Concept." *GLQ: A Journal of Lesbian and Gay Studies* 8, no. 4 (2002): 469–97.

Travers, Ann. *The Trans Generation: How Trans Kids (and Their Parents) Are Creating a Gender Revolution.* New York: NYU Press, 2018.

Vaid-Menon, Alok. "The Pain and Empowerment." Interview by Elisa Goodkind and Lily Mandelbaum, for StyleLikeU's What's Underneath Project. New York, June 22, 2015. https://www.youtube.com/watch?v=j7Gh2n9kPuA.

Valentine, David. *Imagining Transgender: An Ethnography of Category.* Durham, NC: Duke University Press, 2007.

Wallien, M., and P. T. Cohen-Kettenis. "Psychosexual Outcomes of Gender-Dysphoric Children." *Journal of the American Academy of Child and Adolescent Psychiatry* 47, no. 12 (2008): 1413–23.

Ward, Jane. "Get Your Gender Binary Off My Childhood!" In *Chasing Rainbows: Exploring Gender Fluid Parenting Practices,* edited by Fiona J. Green and May Friedman, 43–51. Bradford, ON: Demeter Press, 2013.

———. *Not Gay: Sex between Straight White Men.* New York: NYU Press, 2015.

Warner, Judith Ann. *Perfect Madness: Motherhood in the Age of Anxiety.* New York: Penguin Group, 2006.

Weber, Shannon. "What's Wrong with Be(Com)ing Queer? Biological Determinism as Discursive Queer Hegemony." *Sexualities* 15, nos. 5–6 (2012): 679–701.

West, Candace, and Sarah Fenstermaker. "Doing Difference." In *Doing Gender, Doing Difference,* edited by Sarah Fenstermaker and Candace West, 55–80. New York: Routledge, 2002.

West, Candace, and Don H. Zimmerman. "Doing Gender." *Gender & Society* 1, no. 2 (1987): 125–51.

Whittington, Hillary. *Raising Ryland: Our Story of Parenting a Transgender Child with No Strings Attached.* New York: HarperCollins, 2016.

Wilchins, Riki. "Gender Identity Disorder Diagnosis Harms Transsexuals." *Transgender Tapestry* 79 (1997): 26, 46.

Williams, Michele. "All Seven Sister Schools Now Admit Transgender Students, Including Mount Holyoke and Smith." *MassLive,* June 5, 2015. https://www.masslive.com/news/2015/06/all_seven_sister_schools_now_a.html.

Yep, Gust A., Karen E. Lovaas, and John P. Elia. "A Critical Appraisal of Assimilationist and Radical Ideologies Underlying Same-Sex Marriage in LGBT Communities in the United States." *Journal of Homosexuality* 4, no. 1 (2003): 45–64.

ABOUT THE AUTHOR

Elizabeth Rahilly is Assistant Professor of Sociology at Georgia Southern University. Her research and teaching interests include gender, sexualities, LGBTQ issues, and qualitative research methods.